32.—

Sept. 17 '85
Chicago

DESIGN AND ANALYSIS OF DISTRIBUTED REAL-TIME SYSTEMS

PAUL J. FORTIER

Intertext Publications, Inc.
McGraw-Hill, Inc. New York, NY

Library of Congress Catalog Card Number 85-60356

10 9 8 7 6 5 4 3 2 1

ISBN 0-07-021619-3

Intertext Publications, Inc.
McGraw-Hill Book Company
1221 Avenue of the Americas
New York, NY 10020

Table of Contents

Acknowledgments

The realization of this book is due to more than just the efforts of the author. In order to put the record straight I wish to express my appreciation to the following individuals. First, I wish to thank all my instructors throughout my formative and present period of instruction for instilling in me the zest for knowledge and the seeds of thought. They truly made this effort possible. Additionally, I wish to give special thanks to Robert Charette of Softec for his many enlightening discussions on various portions of this text, to Thomas Conrad for his inputs in the area of software engineering, and to Daniel Juttelstad for his blue-sky discussions and constant prodding. A very special level of gratitude is due to Lloyd Watts for putting my handwritten notes into usable form, and to William Giallo for the artwork which appears throughout the book. Finally, I want to thank my wife, Kathleen, for her crucial efforts at clarifying and organizing my original illustrations, and for her undying support during the preparation of this manuscript. Finally, I want to thank my children, Daniel, Brian, and Nicole, for their patience with me while I constantly neglected them during the writing of this book.

Paul J. Fortier
Newport, Rhode Island
April, 1985

CHAPTER ONE
Introduction

The design of computer systems, whether distributed or otherwise, is made up of the selection and design of the basic building blocks which comprise the system (such as memories, CPUs, I/O devices, networks, software, etc.), the combination of these elements into a system architecture, and the evaluation of whether the collection of components constitutes a successful computer system. This evaluation can be done before the computer is built via analytical simulation models, during design time via modeling and testing to verify that the initial specification or expectations are being met or through user acceptance via rigorous use and feedback once the system has been delivered.

Each one of these evaluation techniques has merit from a designer's viewpoint. At one extreme they allow total flexibility to build anything wanted and see what happens afterwards (the architect's Heaven). That is, one can wait until the system is delivered and used to see if it truly is an operable design and implementation. At the other extreme, rigorous a priori studies will drive the actual design to the point where the architect has little to do once the initial testing is done. That is, the major building blocks would be selected based on user needs and the design would be derived directly from the basic building blocks.

The above extremes represent the art of computer design versus the science of computer design (Figure 1.1).

These design techniques can be accomplished ad hoc. That means, as you build a computer, the build-a-little, test-a-little approach can be used, or the project can be based upon structured, computer-aided design tools to give an operable and efficient design before the building of hardware and expending of capital is begun.

Based on the above, the goal of this text is to introduce the reader to the concepts for design and performance evaluation of Distributed Computer Systems. We will start with the elementary notion of the nature of a computer. This discussion will deal with the basic components of the classic von Neumann machine, followed by introductions of concepts for other classes of computers. It will include special purpose machines such as signal processors, array processors, backend computers, data flow machines, etc. This will lead into a discussion of what constitutes a distributed computer, what its capabili-

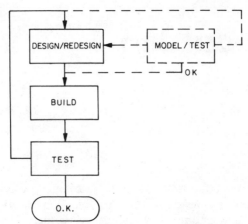

FIGURE 1.1   Approach to system design.

ties are, and what problems arise from distribution not seen in the central computer models and how they differ.

Following this the reader will be introduced to the major components which comprise distributed systems, namely networks, operating systems, and data base management systems, ending with discussions for performance evaluation and computer-aided design.

Network architecture design will deal with the description, classification, and design of protocols and hardware to allow a collection of computers or devices to converse over some geographic distance. This distance can be widely separated, as seen in ARPANET, or more tightly coupled as in a local network, as seen in a real-time control application such as paper mills, nuclear plants, ships, planes, etc.

The next section will describe operating systems comprised of a collection of Software/Firmware/Hardware responsible to provide a usable environment for user tasks to run while not interfering with one another.

Following this section a chapter dealing with data base management is provided. A data base management system provides the interface and control to global data in a unified fashion to all users. This chapter will describe the basics of DBMS followed by the issues in the design and structure of distributed data base management systems. Once this concept has been adequately covered, the text will introduce the reader to performance evaluation of computer systems via analytical models and simulation leading to discussion of design aids for users in automating the design of distributed systems.

Architecture and History of Early Computers

In this section we examine the architecture of the basic von Neumann machine and describe the historical growth and development of computers from the mid-1940s when von Neumann wrote his paper [379] dealing with the organization of the stored information computer, to the present status of distributed computers.

The first computer grew out of the need of the military to have a mechanism to quickly compute ballistic missile trajectories. The outgrowth of these early studies was ENIAC, completed in 1946 at the Moore School of Engineering under the direction of Eckert and Mauchly. It consisted of approximately 1,500 relays and 18,000 vacuum tubes and had the capability of 5,000 add/subtract instructions per second. This early computer had hardwired programs and required rewiring to reprogram. This system was used for approximately 10 years before being retired.

Modern stored program computers appeared in 1944. The idea for this class of computers is attributed to von Neumann. His first stored program computer was the EDVAC, which was never built. Wilkes, who studied with von Neumann, built the first stored program computer, the EDSAC, in 1949 in the United Kingdom. It had a prime memory of 1,024 words and secondary memory of 4,600 words. It was the first computer to use a memory hierarchy.

At the same time this was occurring, von Neumann, Goldstein, et al were working on the TAS or von Neumann machine at Princeton. This machine became the basis for all modern computers. The architecture has not changed drastically over the years, other than for technology insertion. Due to its importance, a brief description of it is included herewith. A more detailed study will be included in future chapters.

The basic von Neumann machine is comprised of five major building blocks or components (Figure 1.2) as described below.

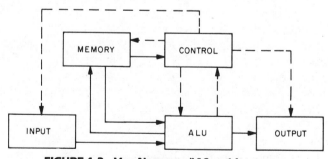

FIGURE 1.2   Von Neumann/IAS architecture.

INPUT

The input unit functions as the means upon which a human can put information (programs/data) into the computer to be acted on.

A myriad of devices have been built to date to describe these functions, as will be seen in Chapter 2.

OUTPUT

The output unit functions as the means upon which the computer provides the requisite outputs as described to it via the user's stored program (input) commands.

MEMORY

The memory unit functions as the medium which is utilized in storing instructions (programs), intermediate data, and final results of computations.

ALU

The CPU (arithmetic logic unit) is the functional unit which performs the instructions (arithmetic, logic, and redistribution operations) on supplied data.

CONTROL

The control unit interprets instructions supplied from memory and provides the needed logic signals to devices to execute the interpreted instructions.

The von Neumann architecture operates in a very structured manner. That is, it operates under a cycle called the read/execute cycle. This cycle, in general, performs as follows:

1. The control unit fetches an instruction from memory based on a pointer which is incremented through a program.
2. The control unit then decodes (interprets) the instruction into its actions.
3. Based on this decoding, the instruction is now executed. Example: fetch operand, store operand, get input, perform addition, etc.
4. Once step three is completed, control reverts to step one.

Von Neumann's original paper describes in great detail much of what is seen in today's computers. From this start computers went through various phases, but they still greatly resemble their early ancestors.

The mid- to late-1940s saw great growth in research, at various institutions, into the design of IAS (von Neumann) style machines.

During the time that the IAS computers were being built, the first real-time response computer was being built at M.I.T. It was completed in 1951. This type of computer is significant because it allowed computers to be used in fast response situations or human life critical situations such as real-time industrial simulations, air traffic control, process control, etc.

The 1950s saw the birth of the computer industry. The first successful machine was the UNIVAC I delivered in 1951 to the census bureau. Its major architectural advance was in its use of magnetic tapes for inputting and outputting and storage of large amounts of data.

Following these early machines were subsequent design modifications With each new computer some level of architecture was either refined or upgraded via technology insertion.

Following this and other earlier successes, the industry took off. The next big leap for the industry came with the arrival of core memories in the mid-1950s. This event allowed designers to replace the inefficient electrostatic storage tubes with a new, more reliable, survivable storage medium which required less space, weight, and power than its predecessor. Along with this new memory came an advance in multilevel storage systems, that is, the use of magnetic tape and disk (drum) as secondary storage. At the same time, to alleviate the burden of programming in machine languages, efforts were begun to develop various high level languages. The most noteworthy, based on its impact on the industry, would have to be the development by Bachus and his coworkers of FORTRAN during the period 1954-1957. The influence of this language is still felt throughout the industry.

The next phase in the history of computers came in the late 1950s to mid-1960s and was due to the use of transistors. These devices allowed many manufacturers to supply more computing power for the dollar.

The trend at this point was to continually develop larger and more sophisticated machines such as the CDC 6600, and the Burroughs 5000 to name a few. These machines were designed to be used with high-level languages and included sophisticated operating systems.

As time went on, the trend began to shift from large scientific computers to general purpose computers. The emergence of Digital Equipment Corporation (DEC) with its line of minicomputers and the advance of MSI (medium-scale integrated circuits) followed by LSI (large-scale integration) and presently VLSI (very large-scale integration) have aided computer designers by allowing them to provide more and more capability for the same or less cost than previous designers. This is a phenomenon not seen in other industries. These led to many markets being developed such as personal computers, microprocessors, minicomputers, super computers, etc.

Along with these strides in architectural features software also progressed through many phases. Operating systems grew from the primitive capability of one user on the system at a time (Figure 1.3), through the batch environment where job turnaround time was reduced, then on to multiprocessing where the CPU, utilizing its operating system, swaps jobs in and out, giving all users the feel of running the computer by themselves.

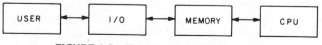

FIGURE 1.3 Single-user system, c. 1952.

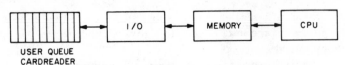

FIGURE 1.4   Batch processing, c. 1958.

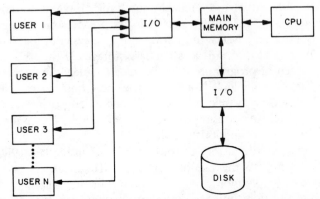

FIGURE 1.5   Time-sharing computer (absolute address), c. 1962.

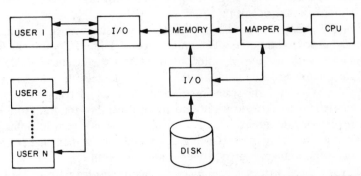

FIGURE 1.6   Time sharing with virtual storage hierarchy, c. 1972.

The early stand-alone concept of the von Neumann machine, where one user used the computer while others waited until he was done, was an inefficient use of an expensive resource (Figure 1.3). This concept disappeared and progressed, based on user need, into batch systems where the inefficiency of users' jobs being loaded and unloaded once completed was resolved. In a batch environment many users' jobs were bundled together and fed into the machine and outputted once completed. This required only one setup and breakdown between much larger jobs. This aided system efficiency, but still did not remove all the inefficiency. If a job acquired the CPU and had long idle loops for I/O, etc. the CPU would remain idle when this occurred (Figure 1.4). The next generation of operating systems removed this inefficiency by allowing many users to share the CPU at one time via interactive I/O devices. The idea here was to give each process a chunk (quantum) of CPU time to operate in. If the quantum was well selected, then users would view the computer as one dedicated to their task. The problem with this setup was that the system still required users to have great knowledge of the system structure and addressing to be able to locate their programs in physical memory (Figure 1.5).

The present operating systems supply a level of multiprocessing to users along with a virtual memory environment. That is, many users can use the computer simultaneously while utilizing a memory space much larger than the physical space. The operating system in concert with compilers, linkers, and loaders provides mechanisms to handle user virtual addresses and map them to physical hardware (Figure 1.6).

The trends in the future are clearly based on the past. Vendors will strive for smaller, faster and cheaper computers which supply the same, if not more, computing power.

This trend will aid in the development of low-cost collections of computers combined into a single system (distributed processing).

These networks will be used by personal computer users' resource-sharing networks (Figure 1.7) as well as industrial users' local area networks (Figure 1.8) performing a myriad of user tasks.

The remainder of this book will discuss the basic hardware blocks of a computer and how these are combined into collections of computers to deliver increased capability to users along with discussions of how to select the proper capabilities in support of user requirements.

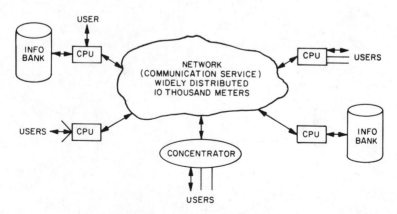

FIGURE 1.7   Resource networks.

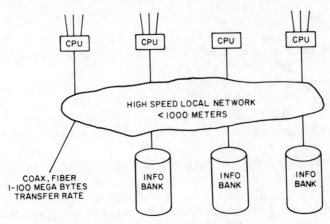

FIGURE 1.8   Local area network.

CHAPTER TWO

The Basics of Computer Architecture

All modern digital computers consist of an interconnection of central processing units (CPU), memories, and input/output devices connected together by communication buses and controlled via the control unit (Figure 2.1). This chapter will discuss and introduce the architecture of these four components and the method by which they are interconnected. Also presented will be a high-level vista of various devices built from these basic building blocks, namely associative processors, array processors, signal processors, pipeline processors and multiprocessors. (Figure 2.2).

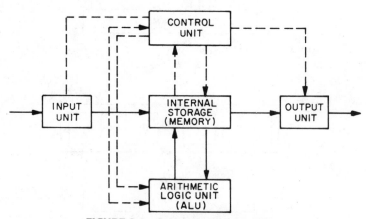

FIGURE 2.1   Control unit Interaction.

Arithmetic Logic Unit (ALU)

The ALU is the device in a digital computer which performs the actual work of computation, calculation, and comparisons. This device is composed of a shifter, adder, logical operator circuit, and an accumulator, temporary and conditional registers. This device accepts data from the internal storage memory and acts on it based on the control unit signals being supplied.

Using the supplied data the ALU may be requested to do operations such as add the content of the accumulator (ALU basic resident register for per-

CPU = CONTROL UNIT + ALU + REGISTERS

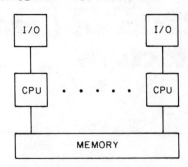

(A) MULTI PROCESSOR

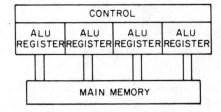

(B) ARRAY PROCESSOR

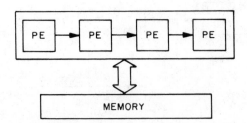

(C) PIPELINE PROCESSOR

FIGURE 2.2   Multiple-processor architecture configuration.

forming operations) with the data being supplied into the temporary register (Figure 2.3) and store the result back into the accumulator (A register).

Other operations that the ALU would be required to perform include: increment contents of the A register and store results back into the A register, neumonic code Inc A (operation code or assembly instruction), decrement the contents of the A register and store back into B register.

Neumonic dec A

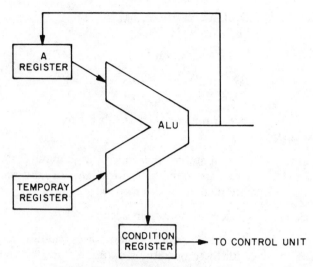

FIGURE 2.3   Arithmetic logic unit.

Load accumulator with the contents of memory location X (Figure 2.3) or store A into memory location X.

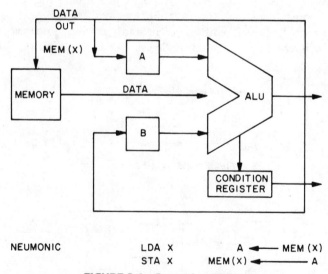

NEUMONIC		
	LDA X	A ◄─── MEM (X)
	STA X	MEM(X) ◄─────── A

FIGURE 2.4   Operation of ALU.

Neumonic   LDA   X   A<------MEM[X]
           STA   X   MEM[X]<------A

Load B register with the contents of memory location X or store B register into memory location X.

Neumonic   LDB   X   B<------MEM[X]
            STB   X   MEM[X]<------B

Add memory X to register A or add memory to register B.

Neumonic   ADA   X   A<-----A + MEM[X]
            ADB   X   B<-----B + MEM[X]

Other operations include arithmetic such as sub B from A,
Multiply A times B, and divide A by B.

Multiply,   These require either microprogramming algorithms or
Divide   extra hardware to perform and usually require many
             more memory cycles to perform.

The ALU also performs logical operations such as:

compares A with B and outputs results into condition register as well
as, and, or, etc. All these operations output a status bit into the condition register.

Outputs of the condition register are then used by the control hardware/
software to produce the proper effect on the processor. This action will be
described further on in this chapter.

ALUs are comprised of hardware capable of performing the tasks (instructions) listed above. Hardware for these units includes devices such as half adders, full adders, right/left shifters, comparator circuits, and, or, nor, etc.
connected by internal buses and controlled via the control unit's control lines.

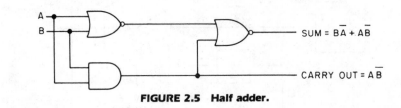

FIGURE 2.5   Half adder.

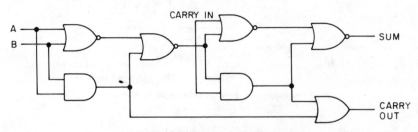

FIGURE 2.6   Full adder.

More details of specific hardware and software algorithms for the operations of the ALU can be found in [375], [376], [377], [378].

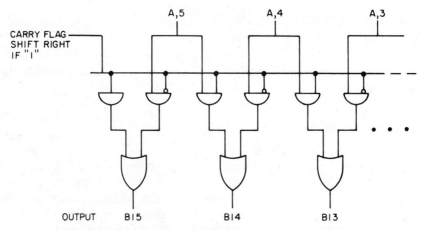

FIGURE 2.7 A simple right-shift circuit; multiple gates.

Internal Storage (Memory)

Memory architecture is the basis upon which computer system performance is measured. That is, modern computers are limited by the access speed of the memory being used. Architects have gone to great lengths to optimize the performance of memory hierarchies in order to achieve the fastest access possible.

This chapter will present the basic technology for computer memories and discuss the architectures used in constructing optimal storage hierarchies.

Computer memories are required in the von Neumann scheme of computer architecture to store both instructions and data for the application user. These computer memories consist of a large number of storage locations (bits) organized into words (memory locations) each capable of storing one word of data/instructions plus circuits to address a location and to read or write this location.

Memory Hierarchy

Computer memory in modern systems is comprised of a hierarchy (Figure 2.8) of memory devices which, when taken as a whole, represents the totality of storage available for users. This hierarchy consists of various classes of memory defined as follows [375].

> Random Access
> Direct Access
> Sequential
> Associative
> Read Only (postable and nonpostable)

RANDOM ACCESS MEMORY

This is memory which can be read/written in one memory cycle. Any address can be accessed within the same time delay. The best example of this type of memory is core or semiconductor primary memory where access time for any location is the same.

DIRECT ACCESS MEMORY

This storage is best illustrated by the magnetic disk drive systems. In this type of system information is accessed via direct addressing as in the RAM case, but access has other components which cause extra delays. These components are related to the location of physical records on the device and of the transfer mechanisms (read/write heads) position. The delays involved include sequential searching (getting to data region), waiting for markpoints, and transfer of information to the RAM memory of the computer.

SEQUENTIAL ACCESS MEMORY

The best device to illustrate this class of storage is the tape drive. In this class of storage the records do not have unique addresses upon which one can retrieve them. In order to retrieve a record, one would search the index at the head (front) of the medium, find the reference to the requested file, spin out (fast forward) to the vicinity of the record, then sequentially read records until the requested one is located and transferred. The worst case would be that you are at the last record of the tape and you want the previous one. In most devices of this type you must rewind to the index (start of tape) and search sequentially for the record.

ASSOCIATIVE MEMORY (CONTENT ADDRESSABLE)

This class of memory device has a random access capability (wired-in addressing mechanism) plus the ability to simultaneously search and compare all locations to a mask value supplied during one memory cycle. Thus, a specific address for a datum does not have to be known since one can use the contents or a portion of it to access the word. All matches are flagged and are accessible on the following cycle of memory. The best example for use of this type of memory is in cache memory systems where fast access to data is required. It is also used in paging and segmentation addressing hardware. These will be addressed in greater detail later on in the book.

READ ONLY MEMORY (ROM)

This class of memory device is used in applications where a program or data is to be produced at the time of design and embedded as part of the computer. This type of memory is non-volatile and for read only purposes. Manufacturers will commonly put selftest or diagnostic software into ROM storage for use when system problems arise. Another use for ROM storage is when a system is first designed it uses microprograms (programs written that act as hardwired messages to signal operations discussed later under control) to emulate the operations required of the final computer architecture. Before delivery these control codes are burned into a ROM which now fixes the computer's instruction set and therefore its operation and view as seen by the user.

In all of the above memory devices a designer would decide what to use or not to use based on the available dollars (sale price of memory hierarchy) and access time requirements for the system.

In optimally designed memory hierarchies, the designer aims to provide the speed of the fastest device (usually Cache) at the price of the least expensive (tape, for example). This is done by optimizing the amount and type of storage at each level of the hierarchy based on its cost versus performance ratio and its impact on overall efficiency.

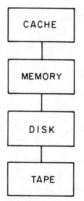

FIGURE 2.8   Typical memory hierarchy.

The typical memory storage hierarchy in use on modern computers today consists of an expensive small (<16K cache) cache memory, plus less expensive main memory (semiconductor RAM > 1 megabyte) plus secondary storage on a magnetic disk unit (usually 10 to 300 megabytes) followed by archival storage on a tape unit. The relationship between these types is best illustrated in Figure 2.9 which normalizes to costs based on cache costs.

From this it can be seen that if one follows the optimization policies as described in [377] then an optimized hierarchy with close to the response of cache with the cost of tape can be achieved.

To achieve this, the architect then must balance the size of each hierarchy element so that given the maximum storage to be required with the minimum delay, the following can be solved for:

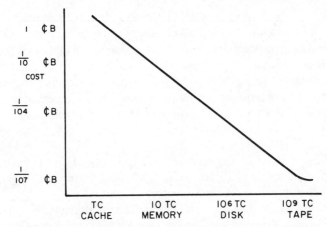

FIGURE 2.9 Memory hierarchy cost/access relationship.

$S^* =$ size of total hierarchy $= \sum\limits_{i=1}^{N} S_i$ sum of the size of all the
individual elements

$T^* =$ time on average to access $= \sum\limits_{i=1}^{N}$ $P_i\ T_i$
$P_i = I = M_i - 1$
= the probability of accessing level i times the time delay caused by
level i per access

$C^* =$ cost of the hierarchy $= \sum\limits_{i=1}^{N} S_i\ C_i$
the sum of the size of level i times its cost per bit

The goal is to provide the size wanted with the minimum T^* and C^* values
possible.

This can best be seen by graphing the C^* and T^* values for various sizes
and combinations of the hierarchies and taking the minimum achieved value.

For example: We are required to design a hierarchy of at least three levels
with user addressable memory of 150 megabytes and requiring some combination of the following technologies.

	T_i	C_i
Bipolar cache	.06	10
MOS RAM	1.00	1.00
Bubble Memory	180	.06
Disk	25,000	.002
Tape	8×10^6	.0004

We are also told to use the MOS RAM and disk. To determine the best
level to use requires the computation of the cost of the hierarchy (C) and the
expected average time $E(T) = T^*$ then the balancing factor is the $C^*\ T$ value
which is the cost versus speed value. The final computation is shown opposite.

It can be seen from this that we can determine the optimal technologies to
use given the fact we know the system requirements.

$$C* = \sum_{i=1}^{n} S_i \, C_i$$

where S_i is found from Saltzers metric which relates the miss ratio of the hierarchy element to its size.

$$\text{Miss Ratio } M_{Ri} = \frac{b}{b + s_i} \qquad \text{which yields } S_i = b\left(\frac{1 - MR}{MR}\right)$$
$$\text{where b is a technology constant.}$$

$$E(T) = T* = \sum_{i=1}^{n} \frac{T_i b}{b - S_{i-1}}$$

which relates the previous hierarchy element to the present one.

$C * T = $ the cost verse performance metric

Configuration	Total Cost-C	E(T)	C * T	
MOS + DISK	7.01m	1.19	8.34	
CACHE + MOS + DISK	7.14m	0.25	1.78 ← "BEST"	
MOS + BUBBLE + DISK	2.51m	1.06	$\overline{2.66}$	
MOS + DISK + TAPE	0.36m	14.4	5.18	
CACHE/MOS/BUB/DISK	2.65	12.5	33.12	
CACHE/MOS/DISK/TAPE	0.36	13.6	4.90	} CHEAP
MOS/BUB/DISK/TAPE	0.25	9.42	2.35	} BUT
CACHE/MOS/BUB/DISK/TAPE	0.25	8.6	2.15	} SLOW

FIGURE 2.10   Computation of optimal hierarchy.

Primary/Cache Memory

The memories at the lower levels of the hierarchy belong to the class of Random Access or Associative Access devices. Random Access devices can be characterized as consisting of N (where N is equal to the total number of devices) identical storage units each accessible via a hardwired address with each word exhibiting the same access delay for read or writes, independent of location variance from access to access.

This type of memory system must possess four basic functional capabilities, namely:

a storage medium capable of being read/written by location in unit time

the ability to address information usually via a MAR (Memory Address Register),

the ability to buffer data once read or before writing,

the ability to sense data upon read request and force data with transducers (drivers) to write data.

The above requirements drive us to visualization of RAMs as seen in Figure 2.11.

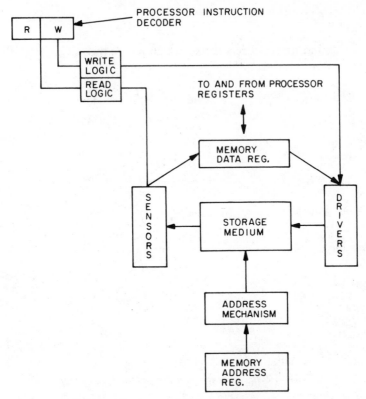

FIGURE 2.11   Random access memory.

Before discussing the organization of whole memories, we will examine how individual cells in such a memory would work.

Before semiconductor memories arrived, core (magnetic) memories were the primary source for computer instruction and data storage. Core memories store each bit by magnetizing a toroidal ferite core in the 1 or 0 direction (Figure 2.12). In order to read a core, first a pulse in the 0 magnetization direction is applied. If a 1 had been stored in the core, the resulting magnetic flux reversal would cause a current pulse in the sense wire threaded through the core, thereby providing the proper signal to the reading device.

To allow selection of only the cores wanted, say, for a word, we utilize select and inhibit currents in 2 or 3 wires threading each core. This process of threading the cores with the same wires and organizing the cores in a regular structure describes the organization of the memory. Organizations used depend on many factors, the main one being the technology in use.

2D Organization

The simplest organization for memory is the 2D scheme. The 2D memory

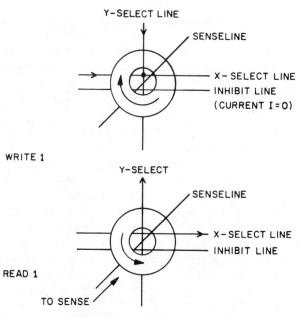

FIGURE 2.12   Magnetic cores.

organization requires that there be separate physical lines for each word and bit as seen in Figure 2.13.

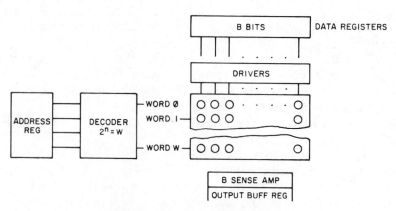

FIGURE 2.13   2D memory scheme.

Each core must be threaded with two wires, one for the selection of a word and one for the sensing or switching of bit level flux signals 1 or 0 out of or into the memory.

To access a word in memory, the memory address register (MAR) is loaded with the required address. This address is decoded in the decoding circuitry down to one address line which is then energized forcing the data into the sense amplifiers and into the memory data register, to be utilized externally. To write to the memory the opposite occurs. The data to be written is supplied to the memory data register, then the address of the word to be written into memory is placed into the memory address register. The address is then decoded in the decoder logic and the corresponding wordline and bit drivers are excited (energized) to cause the proper flux change in the core locations specified.

This organization requires W (number of words) times B (number of bits) cores to provide the requisite memory size. This implies $2^n = W$ distinct physical word lines derivable from the decoders, W drivers for the W words of memory, and B sense and inhibit amplifiers to allow reading or writing data from or to the memory cells of the memory words. It is apparent from this that if the array of cells consists of a large number of words that have few bits per word, then the memory will be long and narrow in structure and will consume much space and driver control logic, whereas if the memory could be made symmetrical (square) it would save space and wiring. On the other hand the 2D memory has the advantage of requiring less wiring and space than the 3D to be discussed later. Stone [375] has a rigorous comparison of pros and cons for these structures.

2 1/2D Organization

In order to form a more symmetrical cell arrangement, the 2 1/2D organization arose. This method allows for a symmetrical cell array to be developed that more nearly matches a square structure allowing for minimal space utilization.

The 2 1/2D arrangement allows for the separation of the memory array into groups of N bit words. That is, it allows for the memory to be divided into separate memory segments, each addressable using the same word array and enhanced via a segment address. See Figure 2.14.

This method saves on wiring for all words and allows a more structured and regular array.

To address a word in memory, the address is placed in the memory address register which will then supply N bits to the segment decoder to select the requisite segment and N bits to the word select hardware to select the proper word. The reading or writing occurs as before with the sense or driver circuits being used to access the information in the memory cells. More details of this system can be found in Stone [375].

3D Organization

The most widely used organization on early computers was the 3D Organization for memories. This method uses b planes of w cores to represent $w = 2^n$

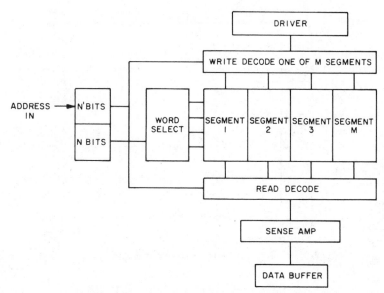

FIGURE 2.14   2½D memory organization scheme.

b bit words. What this refers to is that bit 0 of all words will reside on plane 0 and bit 1 of all words will reside on plane 1 and so on. To address data in such a setup would require the physical address be supplied to an address register which splits the address into X and Y components. These are then used to address the particular bit in all planes to supply the requested word.

As an example, if 256K logical words of 16 bits per word are wanted then 16 planes (arrays) of 256K bits each would be required to supply the required density. This would be organized as a 512×512 array of cells. The entire memory would require 16 such chips as shown in Figure 2.15. The address for an access would be transferred as a combination of 9 X and 9 Y addresses, 1 with each chip supplying 1 bit on every access.

While this organization allowed for more symmetrical structures, it required more time to access due to wire length delays, but did save on peripheral circuits count which was critical in early computers.

Transistor and Semiconductor Memory

With the advent of transistors and the development of MSI, LSI technology, the trend toward semiconductor memory use in computers began. These memories are volatile. That is, they lose their status when power is removed. Therefore, this type of memory device would require battery backup circuitry to retain their contents if power were disrupted. Aside from this feature, these memories are very desirable in modern computers. Their access speeds are

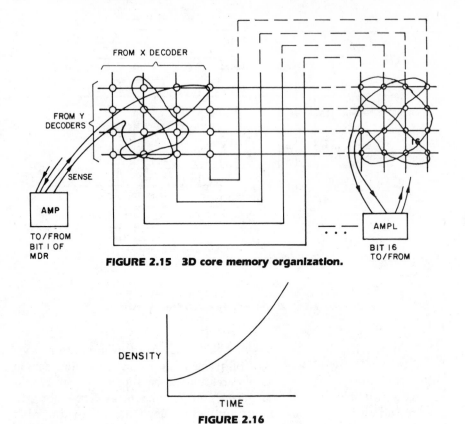

FROM X DECODER

FROM Y
DECODERS

SENSE

AMP

TO/FROM
BIT I OF
MDR

BIT 16
TO/FROM

AMPL

FIGURE 2.15   3D core memory organization.

DENSITY

TIME

FIGURE 2.16

much better than core and memory density has been drastically increased as depicted in Figure 2.16.

The basic cell in an electronic Random Access Memory (RAM) is constructed using 2 transistors and 2 resistors (Figure 2.17).

This basic cell is comprised of a flip-flop. In its simplest form, it consists of two transistors cross-connected (Figure 2.17). The two states for the circuit are defined by whether transistor T1 or transistor T2 is on. For example, if current is flowing through T2 to ground; i.e., T2 is "ON," then the voltage potential at point B is 0. The base of T1 is grounded and T1 is held "OFF." This implies that Va = A and base of T2 is also at that voltage keeping it "ON." This implies a stable state. Similarly, if T1 is "ON" and T2 is "OFF," a similar argument would hold. From this we can now discuss how the basic cell of Figure 2.17 works to store and retrieve bits of information in a semiconductor storage cell.

The basic storage cell is depicted in Figure 2.17. Recall from above that in order to write a "0" or a "1" one node, either A or B, must be brought to ground while the other node, B or A, must be driven to a high state, a "1."

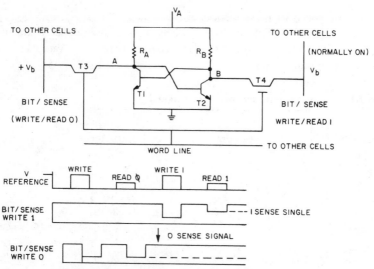

FIGURE 2.17   Basic memory cell and its operations.

In Figure 2.17 in order to write a "1," a word pulse is applied to the word line turning T4 "ON." Since its source is at ground, point B is brought to ground causing T2 to turn "OFF" and point A to increase to VA, causing T1 to turn "ON" which switches the cell to the "1" state. The same argument would hold to write a "0" into the cell.

To read a word, a small word pulse is applied without a bit pulse, causing T3 and T4 to conduct slightly. This will cause either A or B, whichever is at 0, to create a small current flow through its transistor providing a "small" drop in the bit/sense voltage. Sensors can pick this up and amplify it to retrieve the state of the cell. This is a non-destructive read. That is, the contents of the cell are not destroyed during the process.

Using the above described cell, memories can be constructed in the same organizations as the core memories and require much less space, weight, and power to produce and operate.

For further reading in this area, you are directed to Ayling & Moore [13], and Bell and Newell [370].

I/O Devices

The following discussion is provided for completeness. It is not the intent of this section to provide an in-depth view of I/O devices, but to provide a view of what classes of devices are available to system designers.

There is a wide range of I/O devices available for use in computer systems. They range from highly interactive online devices to non-interfering offline devices. The speed of these devices also covers a wide spectrum; from 10-60 CPS (characters per second) for terminals, up to millions of characters per second. Table 2.1 depicts the range and characteristics of a variety of the devices presently available.

Table 2.1   I/O devices and performance ranges.

I/O Device	Medium	Transfer Rate/Range	
Video Display Terminal (VDT)	Video Screen	10-240 CPS	Interactive
Teletype	Paper	10-60 CPS	Interactive
Paper Tape	Paper	10-1000 CPS	Offline
	Paper	10-150 CPS	Offline
Card Reader	Card	100-2000 CPM	Offline
Card Punch	Card	100-250 CPM	Offline
	Paper	100-40K LPM	Offline
Mag Tape	Surface Magnetic Tape	15-300K CPS	Offline
Cassette Tape	Surface Magnetic Tape	10-400 CPS	Offline
Drum	Cylinder Magnetic Surface	30K-2M CPS	Ofline
Disk (Hard)	Aluminum Magnetic Surface	30K-2M CPS	Offline
Floppy Disk	Flexible Mylar Magnetic Surface	25K CPS	Offline

VIDEO DISPLAY TERMINAL/TELETYPE

This class of I/O devices supplies an interactive interface to allow humans to interface in realtime with computer software/hardware interactions. This class of devices can transmit and receive information to and from a CPU on a character-by-character basis. The variety and capability of this class of device is tremendous. These devices cover the range from simple teletype input/output devices to intelligent terminal devices which, in their own right, are stand-alone computers. This type of device is connected either directly or through a modem (modulator-demodulator) which allows terminals to be connected to computers over telephone lines. This type of device is the one which most modern users are familiar with.

Typical speed characteristics of these devices range from 10 to 60 Characters Per Second (CPS) for teletypes (a device with a keyboard and printer instead of a keyboard and video display) and 10-240 CPS for video display terminals (Figure 2.18). The transfer characters are typically the ASCII character set.

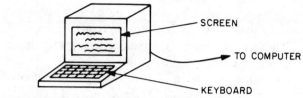

FIGURE 2.18   Video display terminal.

On early computers input/output was provided via paper tape readers/writers. This device was used to simplify the input and output of data to and from the computer. Before paper tape, input was done manually via switches on a computer front panel (Figure 2.19) which would be done a location at a time via switches for address, load memory, increment data address, etc.

Paper tapes allowed for rapid input of programs but still required teletypes, etc., to decipher and construct the tapes.

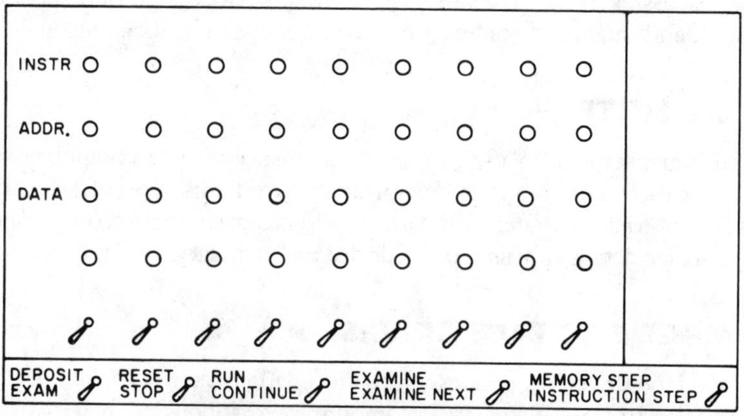

FIGURE 2.19   Computer front panel.

These devices were quickly replaced by faster devices such as magnetic tapes though users may still come across these devices for bootstrap loading of command programs for computers.

CARD READER/WRITER

Card readers/writers were very popular during the early days of computing before the inception of time sharing systems.

This class of I/O device allowed for the easy bunching (stacking) of jobs together to be run through a batch (many jobs at a time) processing system. This allowed a computer, which did jobs serially, to be able to perform many jobs in sucession without the tear-down and setup time previously seen in earlier stand-alone systems.

The medium used by this device is an 80-column punched card which is punched in the proper location to represent some character in the available set. The punched card is then added to a group of similarly punched cards to construct a program and then all are put into a card reader to be fed into the computer for processing. Again, this class of devices has all but disappeared in favor of more efficient I/O devices.

LINE PRINTERS

Line Printers are the main medium for hard copy outputs for modern digital computers. These devices operate in a spooled fashion. That is, outputs, during computation, are directed to files which, once completed, dump this data to the line printer which prints out a job at a time in sequential fashion.

Line printers all operate in the same fashion, writing a line at a time and are constructed using various technologies such as impact printing, jet spray printing, laser printing, etc.

The discussion of the technologies of these devices is beyond the scope of this book and interested readers are directed to manufacturer's manuals.

CASSETTE TAPES

Cassette tapes have been used in small, slow-speed home computers to provide a cheap means to input data/programs into this type of system. They provide data to a computer in the 10 to 400 characters per second range.

For further details of this type of device see manufacturers' information.

MAGNETIC TAPE DRIVES

Magnetic tape drives are devices which store large volumes of data, usually for archival type storage. Tapes are commonly long ribbons of mylar plastic film coated with magnetic oxide. Typically, these tapes contain approximately 2400 feet of ribbon and are 1/2 inch wide. There are 7 or 9 tracks written across the width of the tape and therefore require 7 or 9 read/write heads to store 1 character (ASCII) across the tape, using either 6 bits or 8 bits plus parity per frame.

The structure of a typical device can be seen in Figure 2.20.

The format of storage is typically via records separated by a record gap of usually .5 inches. (Figure 2.21).

The density of storage on tapes is typically in the range of 200 to 500 bits/inch for 7-track and 500 to 6250 bits/inch for 9-track systems.

Tape drives are serially accessed devices. In order to read a file on such a device requires one to rewind the tape and search a record at a time for the particular file and once found read it in. Writing requires finding the last record on the tape to be occupied and continuing to add records from that

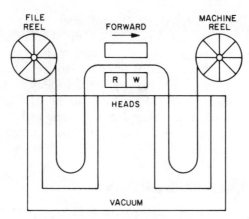

FIGURE 2.20   Typical tape drive.

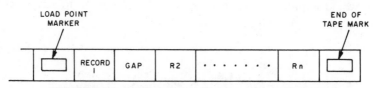

FIGURE 2.21   Typical magnetic tape storage format.

point on until either the write completes or you run out of tape. Typical transfer rates for tape to computer and vice versa range in the 15 to 300K characters per second range.

FLOPPY DISKS

Floppy disks have seen a sharp rise in popularity and use in personal computers as inexpensive secondary storage. Floppy disks are constructed of circular disks usually made of mylar (same material as magnetic tapes) and are coated with magnetic oxide. This is placed in a plastic jacket for protection. (See Figure 2.22).

FIGURE 2.22   Floppy disk.

Floppy disks come in 5¼-inch or 7½-inch sizes and can store from 128K (K = 1024 bytes) to 1 Mbyte depending on the number of tracks available and the density of bits on the diskette. Reading of diskettes occurs as in tape units. That is, the read/write head is brought into contact with the medium and transfer occurs through the read/write head's ability to decipher magnetic fields on the disk surface which represent the bits stored there.

The mechanical portion of a floppy disk drive is usally similar to a hard disk drive. There is an arm with the head on it that can be moved in and out to various tracks on the diskette.

HARD DISKS AND DRUMS

In early computers, magnetic drums were used for secondary storage. These required a head per track to access data. An advantage was that the track to be selected for reading or writing could be selected electronically and there was no seek time for a mechanical device to get to the proper track. To read a record would require an average delay of half a revolution to access any piece of data on the device (Figure 2.23).

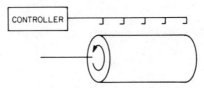

FIGURE 2.23   Magnetic drum.

This was so due to the physics of the device. Once a track was selected the worst case read would be one where the required data just passed the head. Then the access time would be approximately one revolution plus transfer time. Conversely, the best case would be where the data is right under the head and the time would be just the transfer time. So on the average, the time would be one-half rotation plus the transfer time.

In hard disks used in most systems today, the medium is a hard platter usually made of aluminum which is coated with magnetic oxide and spun on a spindle. Accessing is done in one of two ways as follows:

1. Fixed arm, head per track, as in Figure 2.24.

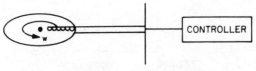

FIGURE 2.24   Fixed arm disk.

In this case the transfer time for a piece of data would be the same as that for the drum, though it is more expensive due to the extra read/write heads required to have such a capability.

2. Moving Head Disks. Most disks used today are of the latter type. They consist of a collection of platters set up in a disk pack as seen in Figure 2.25.

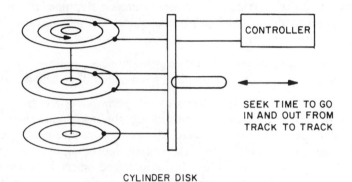

CYLINDER DISK

FIGURE 2.25   Moving arm disk.

In this setup the disk is organized into cylinders comprised of the aggregate of all tracks (one per platter surface) that the read/write heads are set to. This setup allows for much more storage in the same volume as old drums. The time to access a piece of data will be longer by a factor called "seek time." This is the time it takes for the mechanical arm to bring the read/write heads out to the proper cylinder to be read/written.

Densities of the disks are of the order of 10 plus Mbyte range depending on the number of platters and density of disk storage with transfer speeds of .5 to 10 Mbits per second.

For further information on capabilities, see specific vendor data on I/O products.

Control

Loosely discussed previously were the components which comprise the von Neumann class of computer architectures (Figure 2.1). The last remaining component to cover within this class is also the most important, the control unit. The array of hardware and software that comprises this component gives the computer its capability to read instructions from the memory, perform an operation, and determine the appropriate action to take once completed.

The collection of hardware and software called control impacts the performance of all components in the computer. The control section will be comprised of simple logic to control actions which must occur every cycle such as

clock signals, automatic increment of instruction pointer register, and enabling of memories on the fetch cycle during an instruction's sequence of execution. This unit must be able to accept data from the memory, buffer it
(instruction register), decode it into proper threads of execution, and implement these threads of execution to cause the requisite action.

As an example of this, let us look at the ALU and the Add Instruction. In
the basic mode of operation in a von Neumann machine, the instruction,
since it shares memory with data, must be fetched from memory. This happens in the following way:

Fetch instruction, decode instruction, execute instruction, or
Fetch instruction, decode instruction, fetch operand, execute instruction.

The control unit uses the address in the memory address unit as the address of the instruction; it enables this forcing the stored information into the
MDR (Memory Data Register) which drives the data into either the Instruction Register (fetch cycle) or the data register, depending upon the cycle. If it
is in the initial fetch cycle, the instruction is placed on the instruction register
and is next decoded by the control unit. This decoding will result in the generation of hardware signals to drive specific devices to cause the proper execution in the next cycle (clock period).

Execution occurs when the provided output signals are pulsed and caused
to act on the hardware as designed, causing the wanted action. For example,
in the add instruction, the Instruction Register will provide the add opcode
to the control unit which will then drive the ALU to add the contents of the
accumulator with that supplied by the lower bits of the instruction. This assumes immediate addressing. That is, the instruction consists of opcode and
data and another fetch is not required to get data for the operation.

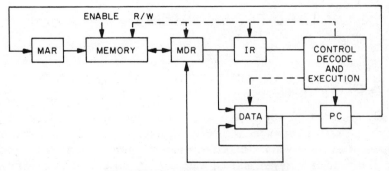

FIGURE 2.26 CPU control schematic.

The control section itself can be constructed using various techniques. The
major methods used are namely:

ROM Designs

PLA Designs
Discrete Hardware

The classical method in computer design was to define the required actions that had to occur for each state the machine could (or was required to) make transition to. The next step was to use these to define random logic that would provide the requisite responses based on the given imputs.

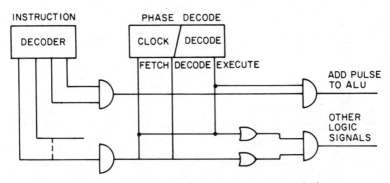

FIGURE 2.27   Example of random logic control design.

In the add example, the discrete logic would provide the decoding of the instruction to provide the signal to the ALU chip to add the two provided input streams of data.

The more common method for CPU control designs is utilizing either a ROM (microprogram memory) or PLA (programmed logic array) approach. The main difference between a PLA and a ROM is that the PLA can be made to accept only the required addresses (instructions) and can ignore the rest, thereby saving on storage locations. They are constructed from AND gates and are more expensive than ROMs, but fewer may be required in a design.

In these as in the random logic case, the required states and transitional actions must be defined and cataloged. From these a ROM (Read Only Memory) or PLA is used to take the input (address) supplied and provide an output based on this. Designers map the instruction into the number and type of required outputs as seen in Figure 2.28.

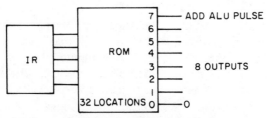

FIGURE 2.28   ROM control unit.

If the add instructions opcode (an opcode is the binary representation of the instruction) is 0101 and the required output is to raise signal line "add ALU" to a high state which is a "1" on pin 7 and "0s" or low state on all others, then in location 5 in the ROM a 10000000 must be stored. This will cause the wanted output signals when this address is requested. The storing of various codes in the control ROM defines the computer's instruction repertoire (Figure 2.29).

INST	ADDRESS	OUTPUT SIGNAL DEFINITION							
ZERO	0	0	0	0	0	0	0	0	0
INC	1	0	0	0	0	0	0	0	1
DEC	2	0	0	0	0	0	0	1	0
LOAD	3	0	0	0	0	0	1	0	0
STORE	4	0	0	0	0	1	0	0	0
ADD	5	1	0	0	0	0	0	0	0
JUMP	6	0	0	0	1	0	0	0	0
JUMP ZERO	7	0	1	1	0	1	1	1	0
HALT	8	0	1	1	1	1	1	1	1

FIGURE 2.29 Example of microprogram.

This technique of control design is known as microprogramming. By using this methodology designers have increased flexibility in defining instruction sets for modern computers. It also gives the ability to modify existing instruction sets via changing of a few components, namely the control ROMs. This allows for extremely versatile systems that can be tailored to specific task requirements.

The discussion of microprograms is beyond the scope of this book. Therefore, interested readers are directed to Wilks, M.V., and Stringer, J.B., "Microprogramming and the Design of the Control Circuits in an Electronics Digital Computer," in *Proceedings of the Cambridge Philosophical Society*, #49, 1953, pp. 230-238; Tanenbaum, A.S., *Structured Computer Organization*, Prentice-Hall, Englewood Cliffs, N.J., 1976; or Rauscher, T.G., and Adams, P.N., "Microprogramming: A Tutorial and Survey of Recent Developments," *IEEE Transactions on Computers*, Vol C-29 #1, Jan. 1980, pp. 2-20.

Putting it Together

Now that we have seen and understand the basic components that comprise a digital computer, we can look at various methods that have been used in combining these components into numerous computer designs. The basic von Neumann computer consists of a CPU, (ALU and control), a primary memory, and I/O. Using these same components and connecting them in various ways can yield a wide array of specialized processing engines.

There are many reasons for wanting to restructure the basic von Neumann architecture, the main one being performance. For reasons based on user application requirements varying the architectural makeup of a computer will aid in its performance for a class of jobs. It should be noted that the basic von Neumann machine is the basis for general purpose computers. That is, it is designed to meet a wide array of user requirements (jobs) while supplying a reasonable response time. In specialized applications such as signal processing, vector processing, etc., other architectures will provide better performance.

Other architectures such as parallel processors, multiprocessors, and pipelined machines represent efforts at increasing the performance of computers in general purpose applications.

The first category of computer architectures to be covered is those that attempt to enhance the efficiency of operation via replication of some components of the architecture.

ARRAY COMPUTERS

The first class of computers is the array or vector processor. This class of computer is best described as a computer where each instruction executed acts on an array of values simultaneously versus a single value at a time as in traditional machines.

The basic architecture for this machine is a collection of processing engines which are controlled by a central control unit and fed data from multiple data sources (Figure 2.30).

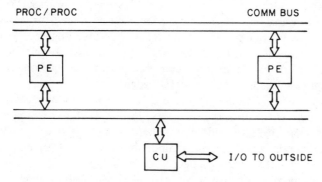

FIGURE 2.30 Basic vector or array computer structure.

Each of the processing engines (PE) has its own local memory associated with it. The cycle of operation for this architecture is very interesting. The control unit acts as a sequential machine acting serially on each instruction. Its job is to examine each instruction and determine the mode of operation (i.e., whether it is a vector instruction or not). That is, if an instruction would best be performed in the array of PEs, then it would direct the execution there; otherwise it would continue serial operations.

The best way to illustrate the performance of this architecture is to walk through an example to add together two arrays of numbers each with an array of size n. In a sequential machine it would take N iterations to perform the addition—adding the two elements and storing them in a third.

Vector case:
While all elements are not processed do

Neumonics   begin
  Loadv A1   Load from I/O elements to be added into
  Add v A2   memories of Peo to Pen:
Storev A3
end   Add the contents of vector A1 to vector A2
                              and store in vector A3;
                          end
                        end while
                      Sequential case:

                      For I = 1 to n do
                        A3i = A1i + A2i
                      end for

In the array or vector machine the algorithm would work as follows: The control unit would load the N memories with the contents of A1o to A1n into PE array, PEo - PEn. It would then take A2o to A2n and load those into the PE memories. It would then command the N PEs in one instruction cycle to add the two arrays and store them in a third array designation.

Given that the data is available in the PE's memories to perform computation, the array machine is faster by a large value (in the order of the size of the given arrays), but the balancing factor in comparing the general case to the array version is that the array processing elements require approximately 2n steps to load the values into their memories from the control unit where the general case was in the memory already.

It can be seen from this simple example that if many such computations had to be performed once the data were loaded, such a machine would be extremely efficient in performing manipulations on large arrays of data.

The instruction sets of such machines would require differentiation of array (vector) instructions versus sequential ones (Table 2.2). The instructions will be executed in parallel by each element on its supplied array elements. Examples of this class of architecture are shown in Figures 2.31 and 2.32.

PIPELINE COMPUTERS

Another class of architecture is the pipelined computer. This class of machine tries to speed up the average execution cycle of instructions through the use of parallel execution of the operations required in performing instructions. That is, a pipeline machine is comprised of a collection of hardware to perform in parallel the functions of instruction fetch, decode/data fetch, and exe-

TABLE 2.2   Example vector instructions.

Vector Instruction	Neumonic	Action All Cases (0≤K≤N−1)
Add	Add A	ACC[K]:=ACC[K]+A[K]
Shift	Shift A	ACC[K]:=ACC[K]*2
Logical	And A,B	FLAG[K]:=A[K] and B[K]
Load	Load A	ACC[K]:=A[K]
Store	Store B	B[K]:=ACC[K]
Multiply	Mul A	ACC[K]:=ACC[K]*A[K]

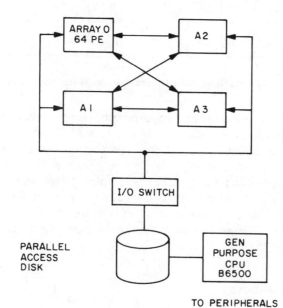

FIGURE 2.31   Illac IV organization.

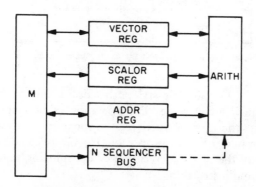

FIGURE 2.32   CRAY-1 organization.

cution. The goal of operation is to fill the pipes of fetch, decode, and execution in order to drop the average execution time down to the length of the longest operation, i.e., if the fetch cycle is the longest, then the machine will approximate this speed overall. Figure 2.33 depicts the flow of information for a pipelined execution of N instructions.

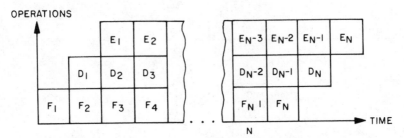

FIGURE 2.33   Pipeline execution phases for N instruction stream.

In reality, due to programming requirements, the pipe will not always operate in the optimal mode as depicted in Figure 2.33. What actually occurs in reality is that instructions arrive at the pipe that do not require additional data so they are operated on in the optimal way. That is, they are fetched, decoded, and executed, but the pipe can have holes, delays, and restarts in the pipe based on other types of instructions causing problems. Instructions that require additional data will cause delay holes in the execution phase (Figure 2.34) and jumps will cause reinitialization of the pipe (Figure 2.35).

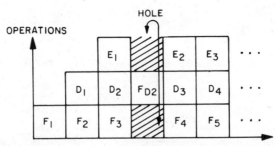

FIGURE 2.34   Pipeline: holes caused by extra cycles required for data fetch.

The restart caused by the jump-style instruction is due to the inner operation of the pipelined architecture. The operation of the pipe is one which continually extracts the next instruction from memory. If a jump occurs and the next instruction is not the proper one to be executed, it will cause a dump and restart of the pipeline execution cycle beginning at the new address supplied by the jump instruction.

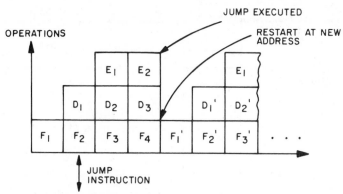

FIGURE 2.35   Pipeline: slack time caused by jump instructions.

The benefit of a pipelined architecture is to—on the average—speed up execution of instruction processing. That is, it cuts down the fetch, decode, and execution cycle to approximately the average speed of the largest term in the overall cycle.

The analogy to a pipelined computer would be the assembly line where parts come in from N locations and are put together in steps at each station. Once the assembly line is full the construction of a complete product is completed on every cycle of the longest link in the line. This principle is used in Detroit to efficiently build cars.

Many computers today use this idea to speed up the average execution of programs, the Amdahl 470 and the Cray 1 among them.

STACK COMPUTERS

The next class of computer architecture is known as stack computers. This class of computers utilizes the stack as an area of management for processes and data versus memory and registers as in the other classes of computer architecture.

The basic operation of a stack is as follows: A stack is a first-in last-out queue. That is, as elements are put on a stack they are pushed down by the next item and so on. Elements can only be accessed (removed) via the top of the stack. So all operations are oriented around the pushing and popping of items on or from the top of the stack. The stack pointer points to the top of the stack at all times and is used to manage it (Figure 2.36).

A stack machine would operate on the contents of the stack with the same instructions as previously described. In the standard von Neumann architecture the ALU acted on the contents of the accumulator and data register. Now in the stack environment, it operates on the contents of the stack in order of storage. An example will help illustrate this point. Given the equation $(A + B + C)/(BxD)$ to solve, the stack machine would operate as follows: To

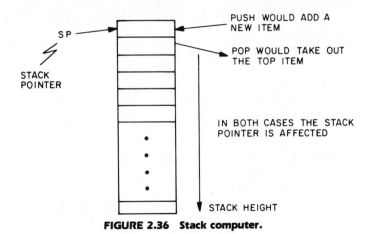

FIGURE 2.36   Stack computer.

perform the first function of adding three numbers we would have to push A, then push B on the stack. Add these two together, then push C and add (A + B) with C to give (A + B + C). Next we would push B, then push D, then multiply to get (B x D) and to get the final result perform a divide which would perform the final operation. Figure 2.37 shows the operation pictorially providing the status of the stack after each operation.

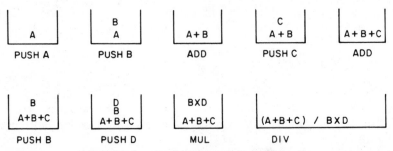

FIGURE 2.37   Equation execution, stack view.

   Stack computers have been built and include models such as the Hewlett-Packard HP3000 and the Burroughs 5500. A much more common use of stacks in computer architecture has been in the use of stacks for managing activation records, for managing procedure calls, and nesting of such procedures.

DATA FLOW COMPUTERS

So far we have seen array processors, pipeline processors and stack processors. The next class of machine to look at will be the data flow computer. This computer is different in that its control operation is vastly different from the classic computer.

In data flow computers, operations are driven by events. These events are data arrivals (data flow). The control is derived from the data flow in the system. In particular, an instruction will execute only when all the operands (data) for it are available and these instructions only cause action or transformation on the data not on the computer's control flow. These are distinctly different ideas than that of the von Neumann computer.

The organization of a basic data flow processor can best be described using the M.I.T. data flow machine (Figure 2.38).

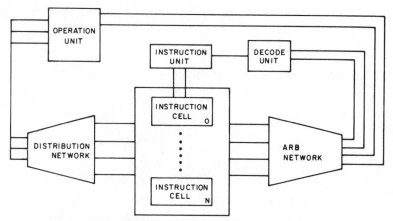

FIGURE 2.38   M.I.T. data flow processor.

As described earlier this computer is comprised of ALU-type devices (Operation Units), memory (instruction cells), I/O arbitration and distribution networks and control (decision units and control networks). The units of the von Neumann machine are basically all there, but the architecture is different.

The operation of this device is different from that of the von Neumann machine. Programs are written using a graphical language which depicts data linkage, operator actions, decoder actions, control links, splits and mergers, etc. The discussion of this language is beyond the scope of this book, but you are referred to J. B. Dennis, "A Highly Parallel Processor using Data Flow Machine Language" Memo 134, *Laboratory for Computer Science*, M.I.T., Cambridge, MA, 1977.

Using this descriptive language one can develop programs to structure the actions of the arbitration, control and distribution network units to implement the graph in the physical system. The first section is the memory or instruction cells. Each of these contain an opcode and two registers with operand values. These are the same as the operator elements in a data flow graph. When all data types coming into an operator are available, the data is sent to the arbitration network to be sent either to an operation unit for computation or decision units for branches in the graph. These go into the control net to alter flow or are directed by the distribution network data links to the proper cell.

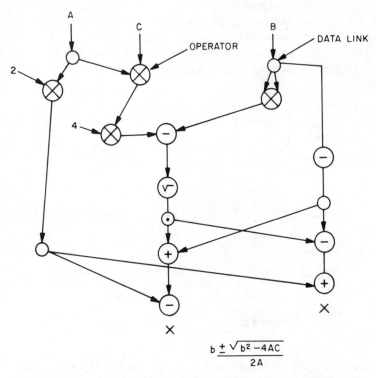

$$\frac{b \pm \sqrt{b^2 - 4AC}}{2A}$$

FIGURE 2.39   Data flowgraph representation of quadratic formula.

For more details on this type of architecture, you are directed to Glenford J. Meyers, *Advances in Computer Architecture*, 1978, and references in his text.

SPECIAL PURPOSE PROCESSORS

Many computers have been built with special purposes in mind, such as signal processors, data base processors, image processors, etc. The numbers and scope of each architecture go beyond the purpose of this text. As an example of this class of special purpose machines, I will discuss some versions of image processors. Image processors have been used in many applications such as pattern recognition, biomedical images for diagnosis, remote sensory classification, robotic vision and industrial inspection, to name a few. Most image processors consist of large arrays of similar devices which all do the same job on different data. The architecture is similar to that of the array architecture described earlier but is tuned and extended to perform a single job rather well (Figure 2.40). The job of the array processor is to take a sample of the picture provided in memory and through common commands interrogate and refine the provided image based on supplied boundaries and conditions.

Examples of this type of machine would be NASA'S massively parallel processor built by Goodyear Aerospace. This machine is comprised of three basic blocks as seen in Figure 2.40.

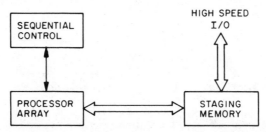

FIGURE 2.40   Basic organization of the massively parallel processor.

The sequence control is the device which interrogates programs and controls the array's operations. The array of processors is comprised of 16,384 microprocessors connected in a 128 x 128 configuration. The I/O staging memory can provide up to 320 megabytes of data/sec. to the array. More details of this and other machines can be found in the references at the end of this text.

Multiprocessors

The final class of architecture I will discuss briefly in this chapter is the class of multiprocessors which will help lead us into discussions of distributed computers and distributed computing/processing. Multiprocessing systems are comprised of a set of processing engines, each with the capability of a von Neumann machine and having basically the same architecture. The thing that makes them unique is the means by which they are used and interconnected in performing their tasks. Multiprocessors are inherently more able to handle a wider class of problems than the previous architectures, because they have a more general and extensible architecture.

Architectures for multiprocessors come in many styles. The basic one consists of a collection of processors connected to a bank of memories via some switching network (Figure 2.41).

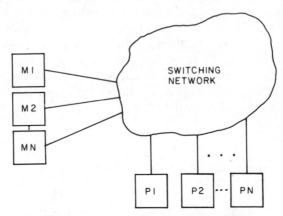

FIGURE 2.41   A multiprocessor environment.

The switching network is connected to all memories and all processors via some circuit switching hardware ([303] for examples). This hardware allows any processor to talk to any memory by forming the connection, then transferring the data over the connection. The switching network could be one like that used in CM* Carnegie Mellon University or a crossbar switching system with dimensions of N rows for the N memory banks and N columns for the N processors. Processors in this system can simultaneously write from all N memories, if they have the bandwidth to support this, but can read from only one at a time. Typically in these systems, memories can be accessed by only one unit at a time. The reasons for writing to more than one memory simultaneously would be to update a shared memory location used for some synchronizational or communications procedure between the processors.

Multiprocessors offer the ability to perform many cooperative tasks simultaneously. Jobs that previously had to be performed serially due to the CPU limits can now be performed in parallel, thereby speeding up overall execution of the job.

The problem with this type of environment is the cooperation and synchronization required by this system to guarantee the respectability and integrity of the shared resource, the memory. Means for protecting the memory from many problems in accesses have been developed. One is the semaphore which is a shared element that will tell a device whether it can use an area of memory or not. An example which uses semaphores for synchronization of a cooperating set of tasks would be the producer-consumer relationship. In this example there are two task types, namely, the producer whose function it is to produce X units of some entity into the shared buffer space and the consumer whose function is to remove (consume) X units of some entity from the shared buffer space.

The problem is to guarantee that only one consumer or producer is in the buffer area at any time. This is accomplished using a semaphore or signal/wait states. These controls will allow only one user to enter an area at a time (mutual exclusion).

Using the notion of signal (flag) to indicate that the resource is free or wait (flag) to indicate it is busy, the producer-consumer relationship would look as follows:

Producer	**Consumer**
Wait (flag)	Wait (flag)
Insert item in buffer	Remove item from buffer
Signal (flag)	Signal (flag)

The wait instruction would be implemented as a busy wait on the synchronization word flag. It would continually test until free, then set the flag to true. Signalling would set the flag to false. This type of synchronization is required in order to intelligently allow processes in multiple processes to communicate their actions and synchronize the operation of the tasks through the use of common memory.

Other methods for memory utilization in multiprocessors use the notion of allocating blocks of memory to specific tasks and reserving portions for shared data. This can be accomplished using mapping schemes in hardware to implement the allocation. Paging hardware can be used and will take the given address and map it to a physical page as follows: The supplied address is viewed in two parts. The first part is the page number and the other the displacement. The page number would point to the page in the page table which would contain the actual physical page address (upper bits). This address would be used as the base location with the displacement concatenated to it for the actual physical address (Figure 2.42)

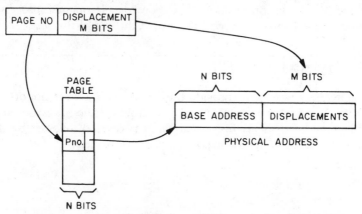

FIGURE 2.42   Virtual address calculation with page table.

This method would allow many tasks to operate in parallel, each using their assigned memory banks and, if required, communicate to each other via "shared" memory banks (Figure 2.43).

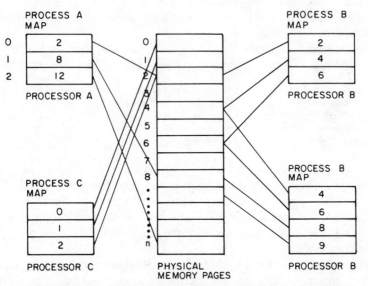

FIGURE 2.43   Multiprocessor sharing of physical memory.

Figure 2.43 depicts four processes running on three processors showing the pages in physical memory that they are utilizing. It depicts pages (physical) 2, 6, and 8 as being shared by more than one process and therefore these pages would require synchronization of processes to guarantee that no interference is destructive. These computer architectures were the predecessors of distributed computers which no longer utilize shared memory as a communication/synchronization mechanism. The new computers use message passing as the means for synchronization. For more details on multiprocessor and multiprocessor enhancements see references at the end of this text.

Summary

This chapter was written to provide the reader with a basic notion of what consititutes a computer architecture. Architecture for the basic von Neumann machine as outlined in his historic article was covered followed by descriptions in more detail for all the major components, namely:

The memory
The arithmetic logic unit
The input and output units
The control unit

The chapter concluded with discussions of computer architectures that can be realized using these basic components as building blocks. Introduced were:

Array computers
Pipeline computers
Stack computers
Data flow computers
Special purpose computers
Multiprocessors

CHAPTER THREE
Distributed Computer Systems: Introduction and Concepts

In the previous chapters basic concepts and ideas in computer architecture were presented. They were intended to supply the reader with a basis upon which to delve further into the expanded architectural world of distributed computers and distributed computing.

This new class of computer architectures represents a radical change from conventional thought in the area. The basis of this class of computer systems is no longer centralized in scope. That is, the jobs being performed are more geared towards parallel execution of processes that may or may not be required to synchronize their operations rather than the traditional processing applications that always performed their functions serially. Distributed computer systems can best be viewed as a collection of autonomous, stand-alone computers (ALU, memory, I/O, control) tied together via a communications environment whose function is to perform an overall applications job which can better be performed in autonomous possible parallel executable sections.

In traditional computers, tasks were always viewed as serially executable. The notion of parallel execution was not present because it didn't exist in the hardware world; i.e., hardware to perform parallel computing did not exist. With the advent of distribution of processors, thought processes and problem solving techniques had to be reworked in view of the new capabilities that these machines possess and supply to users.

An example of processing jobs that can be better performed in a distributed computer system would be one such as this: a large manufacturing organization which previously did all its processing jobs centrally in one computer through interactive terminals.

We could view the class of jobs required to be performed as being either tightly coupled (needing each other's data to process), loosely coupled (needing some of the intermediate or final results to process the job), or stand-alone (needing no data from sources other than its own). Given this description, a company that has a wide mix of these jobs could benefit from distribution of processing.

First, if the end users of processing are distributed over a wide area, then the terminal response times would be terribly slow for the users tied to the central computer. This would be so due to the query delays at controllers and the low priority of remote users versus local users.

46

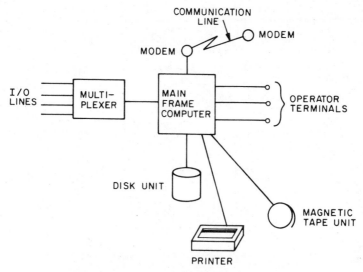

FIGURE 3.1 Mainframe computer system.

Secondly, since they must all exist in a time shared and limited resource machine (single-CPU serially executable environment), they must be content with possibly large periods of wait time in accessing resources during heavy use periods by higher priority users. Higher priority refers to jobs which have precedence—that is, must be done before all others, such as payroll on payday.

If this organization disposed of the million dollar mainframe (Figure 3.1) and purchased some high-powered personal computers or minicomputers, then they could disperse these processors to the end users who need the processing such as inventory control, payroll, accounts receivable/payable, research and development, plant maintenance, etc., giving them faster access to their programs and data through the localization of processing at the site of need.

The problem or challenge of distributed computers (Figure 3.2) is to supply a unified architecture to support these users in a logically viewed centralized fashion while supplying them the benefits of distribution. These issues will be covered in greater detail later in the text.

Claimed Benefits of Distributed Computers

What will a distributed computer system supply to users that would make them desirable? Many authors have addressed this question in technical papers and most, due to the lack of clear representation of what constitutes such a system, have made wide claims of benefits derivable via distribution. The

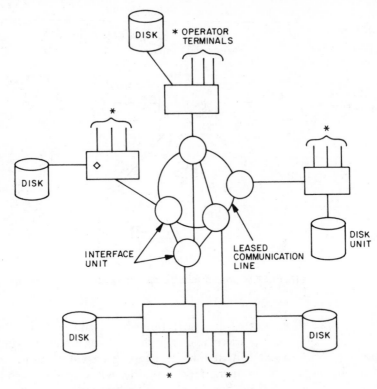

FIGURE 3.2   Distributed computer.

claimed benefits for distributed processing or distributed computer systems include:

Increased system performance
  Increased throughput
  Reduced response time
  Increased capacity
Improved resource sharing capacity
Improved reliability and availability
Graceful degradation/growth
Ease of expansion/enhancement

Each or any of these claimed benefits can be achieved only if a truly distributed system architecture is realizable. That is, new architectures must possess a unified global control mechanism. They must have an operating environment which supports all of the above by possessing greater capability for synchronization and monitoring of global resources, thereby allowing a global operating system to make prudent decisions in support of the above beneficial features.

Each of the above benefits is derived via the distribution of processing and control. Increased throughput comes from the ability to break processing into more processors, thereby allowing for more code to be performed per unit time. Increased capacity is derived directly from the increased number of processors and memory now available. Reduced response time is derived through having the processing capacity brought to the user via a dedicated processor. By not sharing a processor one can see intuitively how response time would drop.

Increased resource sharing is derived via the ability to have more and wider variety of devices available for use by anyone in the system. This allows for a larger volume and mix for the operating environment to manage and supply user needs.

Improved reliability and availability is realized through the use of extra hardware (processors, memory, etc.) that is available for use when another is lost due to failure, etc. If one unit is lost the processing can be moved to another unit and suffer only a short delay due to reloading and restarting. This is different from the traditional environment where a failure in the computer would cause the loss of all processing.

Such a system would allow for graceful degradation of service under failures. As processors and devices are lost, the load can be taken up by other processors and devices causing a reduction in processing capacity/throughput due to processes sharing a processor, but there is still the ability to do work whereas the centralized computer loses all processing capability. The opposite is true for expansion. As more applications are added the system has the increased capacity to expand and take on more. If more processors are required and if the network (communications environment) can support growth, then one just needs to add more processing engines to support the increased load.

The above features describe the capabilities wanted in a distributed computer system. The realization of these capabilities tends to come somewhere in between the optimum level and the traditional centralized system.

The differentiating factors deal with the number and distribution of computer resources (CPU, memory, I/O) the mode of control supplied from centralized to multiple full cooperating operating environments, as well as the distribution of information and microprograms within the system. These will be described further in later sections.

Distributed computer systems come in many configurations covering a wide spectrum of processor and topological sophistication. The range of devices included in this category include ARPANET (Figure 3.3) which is a widely geographical distribution of varying computers connected over telephone lines. In this system the only uniform link is the IMPs or interconnection processors. This is usually classified as a resource sharing environment. This style of network is utilized as an extension of your present computer resources. It allows you to borrow someone else's spare processing capacity when needed. This network allows you to ship jobs (like batch systems) to another computer anywhere on the network and have your job processed

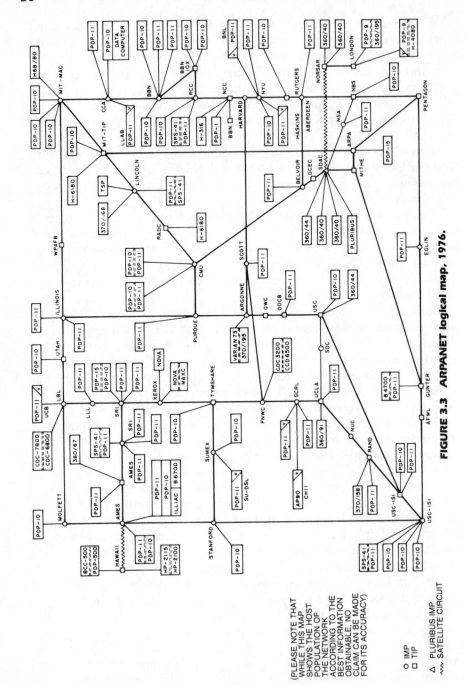

FIGURE 3.3   ARPANET logical map, 1976.

there. This allows, for example, someone at MIT in Cambridge, during the early morning hours, to use a CRAY-1 computer not in use at Berkeley to perform complex vector computations, thereby adding to MIT's ability to perform their applications more effectively. This methodology can be utilized by any organization to have the services of a CRAY-1 when needed, but could not justify or afford the purchase of such a machine.

The idea of resource sharing came from early operating system work. It was found, during early operating system studies, that it would be better to allow more than one job to run in a computer simultaneously, thereby utilizing more of the system's I/O and processing resources. This work showed that jobs went through cycles of heavy CPU utilization, then periods of wait, due to I/O functions, etc., followed by other periods of lean use. This led operating system designers to conclude that the expensive resources could be better utilized if jobs were scheduled in and out of the CPU or I/O processors based on their usage requirements which led to better utilization of the overall resources.

In a distributed computer system, the same holds true, but on a larger scale. In a distributed resource network there may be many special-purpose devices such as data base computers, array processors, signal processors, image processors, super computers, minicomputers, and microcomputers, to name a few. The object of the resource network is to more effectively utilize their resources by allowing others to use them when they are not in use. The problem with this class of distributed computer system is that users of one computer do not have interactive control (real time) of their jobs. They only have a capability of remote resource utilization. At the other extreme, a distributed computer system could be comprised of a collection of microprocessors connected via a high-speed fibre optic network which provides a very tightly coupled and integrated environment.

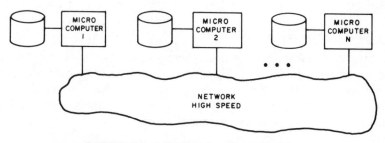

FIGURE 3.4   LAN (local area network).

In this extreme case the idea would be to provide an interconnection network architecture capable of supplying processor to processor message passing at close to the speed of the internal data paths of the local computers. In this case, a user on one computer would have the illusion (given a tightly coupled operating system environment) of having a computer with much more processing power than is available on his single microcomputer and also will have control of the other processes he spawns in "Real Time" (perceptual sensory case).

An example of how such a computer would operate is as follows: A user would begin his application such as control of an automated (robotic) assembly line. The user starts the process by commanding the remote robotic arm processor to prepare their station for operation. All the N devices go through a self-test (diagnostic) process and report back to the command device. The user perceives one computer responding to him, not N computers. The N computers complete the self-test diagnostics much faster than if one central computer did the testing. The user could then begin the assembly process and, based on operational requirements, converse with any of the remote computers to give command or receive status as though he were tied directly into the remote device. The notion just described introduces the reader to the idea of real-time control or real-time processing. This will be discussed in greater detail later in the chapter.

Topology

The array of topologies (interconnection architectures) and the classes of computers used are extensive. The limiting factor is based on user requirements and technology. Anderson and Jensen's paper [9] on computer interconnection structure—taxonomy, characteristics, and examples—discusses the classification for interconnection of computers in a distributed environment. From this paper one can see that the types of interconnection architectures possible are extremely extensive.

GLOBAL BUS

Examples of major interconnection schemes would be the Global Bus (Figure 3.5) which consists of nodes (a collection of hardware to interconnect to the communications network and the computer system that is connecting into the distributed system) connected to a shared communications path. Each device utilizes this shared path to converse with others.

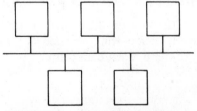

FIGURE 3.5 Global bus topology.

STAR

The next major class of interconnect would be the Star or Central Switch Configuration (Figure 3.6). This type of interconnect is comprised of nodes which must communicate to the others through a central switch which is usually controlled by some central arbiter.

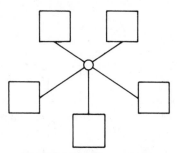

FIGURE 3.6   Star topology.

RING

The next class of interconnection topology is referred to as the Ring (Figure 3.7). In this topology units are strung together on a ring-configured communications link and converse via trains of messages which rotate in the ring.

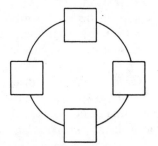

FIGURE 3.7   Ring topology.

GRAPH MESH

Another class of interconnect topology is the Graph Mesh or irregular style network (Figure 3.8). In this type of topology there is not usually a regular structure. It is comprised of a number of links that in totality connect all the nodes together. This topology requires more mechanism than the previous three in routing (directing) messages from node to node in the network. These topologies and attendant communications control protocols will be discussed in greater detail in the following chapters.

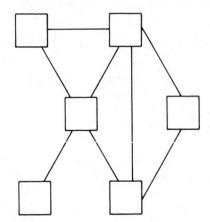

FIGURE 3.8   Mesh or Irregular topology.

As there are many ways to interconnect computers into a distributed computer system, there are also many types of computers that have been utilized in these systems. There are homogeneous systems in which all the computers are of an identical class and therefore utilize the same software during execution. Systems of this type include multi-microprocessor systems, vendor networks such as Prime Net, DEC Net, and Wang Net, which are all networks developed to interconnect the computers developed by the particular manufacturers. The other class of network is the non-homogeneous. In this system computers of different types are connected together providing a wide array of capabilities. This type of computer network is much harder to develop due to the differing requirements for interconnection and conversation with the various machines and their operating environments.

Also utilized in computer networks are many special-purpose devices to supply extra efficiency in overall system performance. As an example, a system may be comprised of various sensors and data processors which extract information from raw external stimuli and convert this into usable system data which is then provided to a distributed data base management system. This system would handle information management for the system. Another component of such a system would be general processing engines for handling user requirements for program processing or data extraction, and there are a wide array of user devices to support the end user's visual informational requirements.

Figure 3.9 represents a quick snapshot of some of the capabilities and characteristics of a distributed computer system. Next will be a more formal discussion of what a distributed computer system is, what distributed processing is, and, finally, a classification of the level of performance from real-time computers to resource-sharing networks.

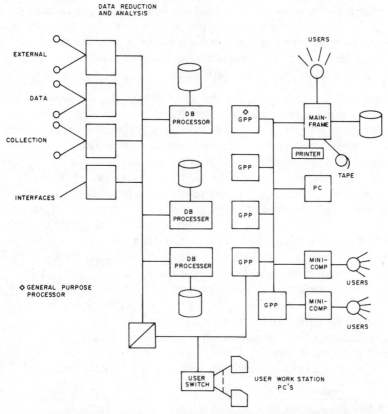

FIGURE 3.9 Example of a distributed computer system.

What is a Distributed Computer System?

From the previous discussions the best description of what constitutes a distributed computer system is as follows:

Dispersion: There must be a physical distribution of processing resources in a distributed computer system.

Interconnection: The processing resources must be connected via a communications network and all communication is via the passage of messages in the network.

Resource Sharing: Resources are spread throughout the network and can be utilized in some way by remote devices (either in batch mode or in real-time). Transparency of these resources must be provided (users need not know where resources are located).

Control: Control (Global) is concerned with how to synchronize the operations of the entire system in performing a mix of jobs whose requirements may not be totally known a priori. Global control is concerned with the cooperative interaction of user processes (user applications) with the underlying system structures.

There is still much room for variability within this definition. The major features (from a user's viewpoint) are that the system is transparent. That is, he views it in the same light as a centralized mainframe computer where he accesses devices and processes (programs). In such an environment cooperating tasks have the capability to run in parallel and communicate via message passing methods. This is similar to ADA's rendezvous capability that holds up one task until the other gets to the proper rendezvous point. This is different from earlier multiprocessors where interprocess communication would occur via shared memory locations. In one case it causes a more tightly coupled system, one that can be controlled via semaphore-type operations (test and set) to extreme levels of cooperation. In the distributed case while sharing is not present, synchronization and cooperation still are, although in a looser context. There is no single physical location or place where the cooperation is achieved. It is achieved through the usage and enforcement of protocols in the execution of the remote cooperating tasks.

Enforcement of the protocols will allow for cooperation and synchronization of the runtime system. These protocols exist at different layers in a system to control and synchronize different aspects of the system.

Protocol

The number of these layers and their respective functions are not as yet generally agreed upon. Figure 3.10 shows the relationship of physical devices to logical protocols. The protocols presented do not follow the ISO model as described by Tannenbaum in his book *Computer Networks* [398], but do possess the same capabilities. These protocols represent the layering this author has seen in recently developed systems. Figure 3.11 shows the architecture and the protocol layers and Figure 3.12 represents the ISO model of protocol layering. The description of the functions of each layer will enhance our ability to grasp and understand the concepts embodied in future chapters and delineate their impact area on the overall architecture of distributed computer systems.

PHYSICAL INTERFACE LAYER

The physical interface layer is concerned with the physical transmission of signals across a communications channel. This layer deals with the mechanical and electrical characteristics and operation of the interface. It must handle the representation of "0" and "1" via a set of voltage levels, etc. and must handle

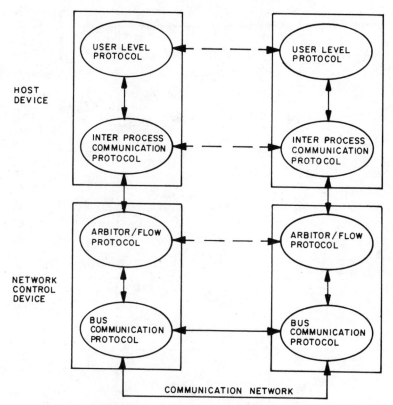

FIGURE 3.10 Bus communication hierarchy.

timing of the data bits over the channel as well as implementing the physical mechanisms of control in the network. Control at this level is viewed as procedural. That is, this is how it is done to control computations physically and to guarantee one entity is communicating over the channel. The protocol is simple at this point. It may be as simple as the sending and comparison of bits as they are sent out over the channel to detect conflicts, the recognition of a bit sequence to begin or acquire control, or the request signal from a device requesting service. From this it can be seen that the main function at this layer is to handle physical interfacing issues without regard to the meaning of any information sent. Information is viewed as bits only at this layer.

NODE TO NODE PROTOCOL LAYER

The function of this layer is to supply an error-free transmission environment to the upper layers. This layer covers the data flow over the physical circuits provided by the lower level previously described. This layer implements the true control protocols in the network. It utilizes the medium to implement a wide array of potential control protocols as will be seen in the next chapter.

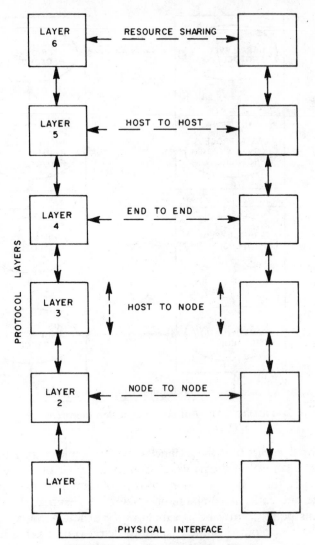

FIGURE 3.11 Communication layers.

Examples of such mechanisms would be the following: The control of the medium; i.e., which device is going to be allowed to transfer may be determined by sectioning up the time on the bus into frames (time periods) and using these as monitors for control cycles.

Control at this level may be implemented via detection of collisions of messages which would cause none to be allowed to transfer, but cause all to delay and retry (CSMA carriers, sense multiple access schemes [154], [155], [159], [160], [162]), or control, using frames that could be implemented by sequencing a physical/logical token (unique sequence of bits) across the medium and having each device detect and count the tokens. Once you reach

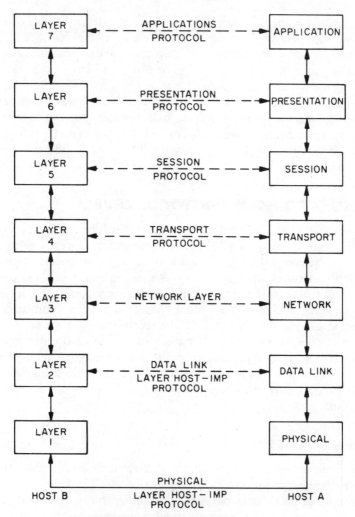

FIGURE 3.12   ISO reference model.

your node's value in memory you get control. As will be seen later on, there are a multitude of methods for implementing the low-level acquisition of the transmission medium. Another function of this layer of protocol is to handle the routing (addressing) of packets (subsets of a message) which can be sent in one frame (time unit) through the network. This entails the sending of the packet to the addressed unit in the system either directly, if the medium supports it, or via a store and forward action. The store and forward action entails taking the packet, looking at its address and determining via table lookup, etc. where the packet is to go. If not direct, then send to the designated intermediary who would then send it on to the final destination. A further requirement at this level is to provide an error-free transmission facility for packets. This breaks down into providing for detection and correction of errors in transmission. Techniques may include basic encoding and decoding of packets to perform detection and correction or the retransmission of packets that do not reach their destination or reach it in error. This may involve a protocol that requires each packet be acknowledged to determine if, A, it arrived, B, it did not arrive, or C, it arrived but in error and finally D, if nothing happens and a time-out occurs. It is possible that the protocol would continue to retransmit some predetermined number of times before it would report a problem to upper level software. This level is the basis upon which networks are constructed.

HOST TO NODE PROTOCOL LEVEL

This protocol layer performs the interfacing between the logical end-to-end protocols and the lower level physical protocols. This layer is given messages which may be comprised of many packets that are the smallest units for transfer over the network. Its job is to break these messages into the packets and add the control overhead. This function includes the formatting of the packets for transmission which includes adding header and trailer information and the encryption or encoding of packets to be sent over, either for error control or access restrictions. The control of transfer of the packet over the network, includes retry, leveling, and sequencing. On the other end at the receiver node, this layer must decrypt or decode packets and assemble them back into the full message before routing it up to higher protocol layers for user applications.

END TO END

The purpose of this layer is to connect and manage logical circuits or channels between cooperative processes within the network.

This layer of protocol in the network supplies the capabilities of communication to the network processes. It supplies message control in terms of what type of message passing is required. For example, there is broadcast, which implies sending this message to all nodes and coordinating its sending; point to point, which is sending this message from node 1 to node 20; and one to many, to send this message to nodes 1, 3, 5, 7. This is the layer which removes the physical aspects of the system from the upper level processes. Processes must not know where things are stored, just logical names. Another function of this layer is to link processes into the network and manage these links. Here also is the notion of a logical port or channel. These represent conduits by which the processes can send their messages to one another. This level manages the operation of these conduits. It may be required to open, close, and share ports between processes based on system loading requirements. The last function which this layer must provide is the ability to route messages (vice packets) through the network. This is done though the establishment and maintenance of logical vice physical paths through the network. The underlying physical path could be altered by failures, etc., but the upper level logical paths would remain intact. User applications software would not be aware of the underlying physical transitions occurring due to fluctuations in the hardware. This implies a level of isolation and invisibility or transparency of the actual system layer.

HOST TO HOST PROTOCOL LAYER

This layer deals with the creation and maintenance of dialogue between resources on one computer and another. This layer allows resource-sharing protocols to link up to available resources on another node and maintains these hookups as long as a user process requests it. This layer is similar to what would be required of an operating system to provide a log-in service to get into a computer in order to do useful work. This layer would establish the "session" (period of usage) for users and provide the mechanisms for acquiring needed resources as required, as well as holding on or timesharing those that have already been allocated. This layer provides the link betwen the network and local user processes.

RESOURCE SHARING PROTOCOLS

This level of software is greatly neglected in the description of the ISO reference model for protocols. Software at this layer gives a computer system its characteristics and provides services tangible to the applications programmers. It also supplies the transparency to network-induced requirements that users need not know about in the performance of their tasks.

Software that exists at this level is similar to that which a user would see when logging on to any computer. That is, we would have file transfer capabilities that resemble those on centralized computer systems, but allow for more varied operations such as a transfer from port A to port B, editors, compilers, and debug software, etc. could be found at this level, which would aid a user in his ability to use the variety of resources available. Also at this layer could be support software such as the data base management software with the capability to link data bases on one machine with those on another. Finally, software to unite these capabilities across computer boundaries would exist at this level. Command protocol services such as the ability to assign priorities, print files, provide time and date information, status setting and monitoring, and user level support such as virtual scrolling and terminal protocols which render remote devices to appear as local to the user's location. Beyond this layer would be the myriad volume and variety of user application coding which would use these services in performing their tasks, oblivious to the volumes of data and decisions being made below.

DISTRIBUTED PROCESSING

Distributed processing or distributed computing is a very misused, overused, and misunderstood term. If one looks at vendor sales literature one can find voluminous claims as to the capabilities of distributed computing or processing systems. In reality, they may be supplying a multiprocessor and claiming it possesses some new capability. Due to misinformation, users may buy one distributed processor system and actually get a different capability than they thought they wanted. So if this is the case, what is distributed processing?

Distributed processing and computing implies, by its name, the notion of computation being performed in multiple locations. But what does this imply? Does it imply breaking down a problem so as to solve it in multiple pieces running concurrently? Or perhaps demonstrating the ability to do many jobs simultaneously as in a multiprocessor?

This author believes that the term describes a system capability. Distributed processing and computing refers to the collection and aggregation of system hardware which must be distributed as described earlier, and communications software which supplies the capability to allow the hardware to transfer messages and system services which supply the environment in which execution of applications is performed.

Taken together, these supply the capability to perform computations in multiple locations, all in support of a unified system goal. This system specification or goal must span the entire collection of devices and services. The "system" is used in support of the specified goals—whether they be as complex as supplying a real-time control environment for a computer-controlled production facility down to linked personal computers to provide a corporate shared information environment. They are linked into a "distributed computer system" by the nature of the overall task and the implementation that realizes it.

The most important aspect is the unification of goal via the operating environment. This environment is the link which performs the task of supplying a single system view to all users. As part of this view, the system must supply all utilities, resources, and services via generic names not dealing with their physical location or redundancy level of the entities. This generic naming convention will allow the system to be viewed as a single element (transparency of network), not as a collection of shared resources. Beyond this, the operating environment is comprised of a collection of autonomous units of control (physical network, nodes, CPU, memory, I/O, and interface unit to network), which interact cooperatively utilizing management policies expressed by the philosophy of the total system's executive control.

The goal of this distributed system is to provide all network services to users in a transparent fashion allowing for multiple processes to run concurrently and in synchronization via the network architecture and its protocols. This operating environment allows the distributed hardware to be viewed as a virtual machine with capacity N for computation. This allows users in the idealized case to develop their applications without care for exceeding capacity on the machine they physically reside on. In reality, jobs are spread over the network allowing for a greater level of load balancing and parallel execution of tasks to be performed.

As can be seen from the previous discussions, there are not any clearcut methods by which to determine what is distributed processing/computing, since the best attempts at defining this term have fallen short due to the dynamic nature of the terms. The true term would be best delivered as representing a capability. The capability allows users to use as little or as much of the distributed resource-sharing capability as they deem fit in their application. This leaves the definition of distributed processing/computing as the capability of applications to distribute their processing jobs in order to achieve a higher level of performance. An example would be that an organization has applications which require processing of incoming orders and outgoing shipments and maintaining billing and inventory. In order to increase productivity of the cycle, the organization implants the process over a network of computers integrated into a distributed computing facility. The system possesses a distributed data base capable of supplying shared data to any of the processors, invisibly. Also, it possesses an operating system which supplies a unified system view to all users. The applications can be loaded to any processor in the network for processing and the users will see an overall increase in performance of their application due to dedication of resources.

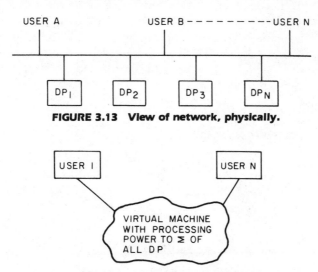

FIGURE 3.13   View of network, physically.

FIGURE 3.14   User view of machine C.

This example points out the difference in user view (Figure 3.14) versus system implementation (Figure 3.13), with the difference being supplied by system services at the resource-sharing level insulating the user from the distributed dependencies of the system.

REAL-TIME PROCESSING

Within the notion of what a distributed computer system is or what distributed processing is, there is also another definitional problem: namely, what is distributed real-time processing. As technology has grown into distributed computing, so too has the application of this technology grown into more diversified areas. Originally distributed resource-sharing networks were developed and a large body of information and technology ensued. Using these new ideas, researchers extended the basic idea into local area networks and finally into high-speed local area networks with highly integrated control of the entire environment. This increased capability allowed increased user applications to more varied and demanding environments such as real-time processing.

Before we can tackle the definition of distributed real-time processing, we must first define the term real-time in its proper context. What do the words "real-time" represent as defined by the dictionary? Webster defines the word "real" as "actual" or "true" and "time" is defined as "the period during which something exists, happens, etc., a set period or term as of work, confinement, etc." From the above, we could postulate a meaning of "real-time" as the actual or true period during which a physical process transpires. What does this mean in terms of computer systems and in particular distributed computers and computing? In terms of computer operation we could view this definition as follows: Real-time is computer operations in which the ratio of the time interval between two events (TE 1) in a simulated system (computer processing time) to the time interval between the corresponding events (TE 2) in the physical system is unity.

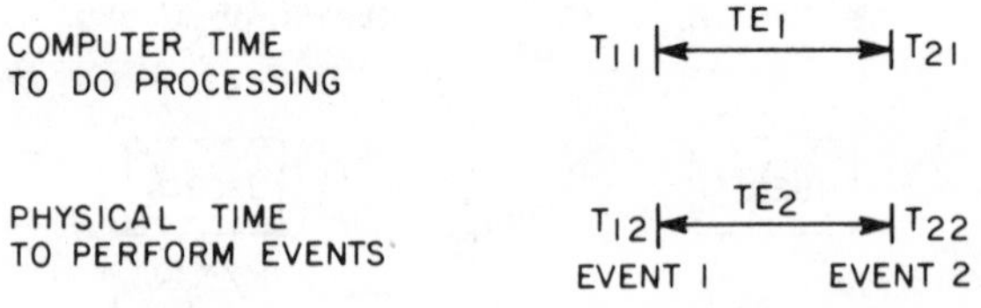

COMPUTER TIME
TO DO PROCESSING

$$T_{11} \longmapsto \overset{TE_1}{\longrightarrow} T_{21}$$

PHYSICAL TIME
TO PERFORM EVENTS

$$T_{12} \longmapsto \overset{TE_2}{\longrightarrow} T_{22}$$

EVENT 1   EVENT 2

$$RATIO = \frac{T_{21} - T_{11}}{T_{22} - T_{12}} = \frac{TE_1}{TE_2} = 1$$

FIGURE 3.15

In pictorial form, the ratio can be viewed as depicted above. This ratio represents the realization that the physical system events are followed by the simulated system events or vice versa.

Real-time computation typically in a real-time computer is defined as performance of a computation during the actual time that the related physical process transpires so that results of the computation can be used in guiding the physical process. This constitutes the notion of real-time control. That is, the function of the computer using data fed in from sensors in the real environment to a computer results in effectively guiding the operation of the physical process.

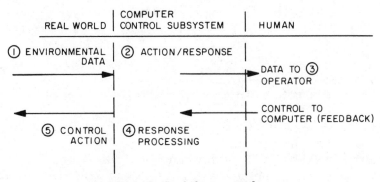

FIGURE 3.16   Real-time control process.

Classes of real-time computer systems can run the gamut of applications. A real-time system could be one which controls the activities of a nuclear power plant or a process control system in an automated manufacturing facility, all the way up to the banking machines that we use in our banking transactions. All represent real-time computing devices, but the difference is in the requirements placed on them for response and the level of feedback. In one case, it is extremely important for stimuli to be reacted to immediately, whereas in another, reaction within the tolerance of human perception is adequate.

In real-time control environments the distributed computer system is required to perform control functions (actions) at certain fixed time intervals—or based on events (the extraction of data from sensors triggers the recognition of an event), or via user (operator) interaction. Examples of these actions would be to sample the output flow rate and temperature of a reactor's cooling water every five minutes. This would be a fixed interval timing activity in which, if we said that when pressure at a certain valve is more than its tolerance then you should activate that valve, we would be performing an action based on event occurrence.

In this type of system, computing devices are required to perform data acquisition and reaction tasks in a continuous or periodic rate based on the application. This class of system requires real-time control algorithms to calculate the changes and react to them in real-time.

Many times such systems are organized "logically" in a hierarchical fashion (Figure 3.17) with the lowest levels performing the time critical data acquisition and direct control of the physical system along with the more complex time-consuming functions such as performance optimizations, scheduling, program monitoring, and fault localization being done in the upper levels.

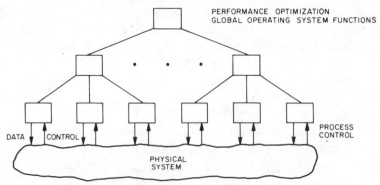

FIGURE 3.17   Distributed system hierarchy of control.

Physically these systems are organized as a distributed computer system in order to provide the high reliability, availability of processing, and graceful degradation under failures required in a real-time environment. These systems must function properly under adverse and high load conditions and still supply the requisite performance. In order to provide this service the network must be reliable and high speed, and the software modules must be constructed so as to be able to permit almost any combination of modules to be brought together for execution in any processor. Such systems, due to physical requirements of control of specific devices, require much redundancy (multiple copies of the same processor, I/O to devices, etc.) to provide the requisite levels of availability and reliability, especially in life-critical applications where such systems are applied.

LANGUAGE REQUIREMENTS

Beyond the above discussions, in order to provide this service, a distributed processing system imposes new requirements on software. The software must be able to provide:

True parallelism; that is, the ability to run tasks concurrently
Real-time task execution (time and event scheduling)
Intertask communications
Programmed support of fault tolerance
Control of real-time events
Synchronization of distributed tasks which may not know about each other

Not many languages exist that can be classified as true real-time programming languages or distributed programming languages. The best example of a language designed to meet the requirements of both real-time and distributed execution is ADA. ADA was developed by DOD for real-time distributed control applications. The language has many constructs that lend themselves to support of the above requirements.

The following section will attempt to just highlight some of the major features. More interested readers should consult the following references for additional details on ADA and its capabilities.

Grady Booch, *Software Engineering with ADA*, Benjamin/ Cummings Publishing Co, Inc., 1983.

A. N. Habermann and D. E. Perry, *ADA for Experienced Programmers*, Addison Wesley Publishing Co., 1983.

Peter Wegner, *Programming with ADA and INTRO Systems of Graduated Examples*, Prentice-Hall, 1980.

ADA supports the construction of modules of software which can stand alone and have specified interfaces to the outside world. This greatly enhances the capability to construct applications code to support the real-time programming requirement of real-time systems and provide the proper representation of data to the outside world. ADA has the capability to set up a priori the access to various data types using the access type. This allows for sharing of objects from program to program that may not have the same name.

ADA allows tasks to be run concurrently and to synchronize or communicate via the rendezvous mechanism. This mechanism causes a task to suspend execution once it hits this point (entry) until the other cooperating tasks reach their corresponding entry point. At this time the service code is run and once completed the tasks continue on their own. Using this mechanism, synchronization of multiple tasks can be achieved by message passing. This mechanism would be used to construct a simple producer/consumer process over many computers as follows:

```
Producer Task Loop          Consumer Task Loop

Produce (X)                 Consume (X)

Put (X)                     Take (X)

End loop                    End loop


            Synchronizer Task
                entry    Put (Z)
                entry    take (Z)
            loop
                Accept put (X) do
                    B: = Z
                end.
                Accept take (Z) do
                    Z: = B
                end
```

In this example the two tasks, producer and consumer, run in parallel when either hits the code in their routine for Put (X) or Take (X). They wait until the third task the synchronization hits either accepts Put (Z) or accepts Take (Z). In this example a producer will get access first—then a consumer—and it will continue to loop forever in this loop.

An example of ADA in process control actions would be as follows in a nuclear plant. A task is running in a microprocessor and is monitoring the pressure on a reactor cooling system and is controlling the pressure release valve. The following ADA code would support such a function.

```
Task Cooling-pressure monitor;
Task Water-temperature-monitor;
Task Body cooling-pressure-monitor;
    pressure: float;
begin
   loop
       Get (pressure) <———Data acquisition command
       If pressure > max-pressure then        >
          begin
          open pressure-release-valve; > Real-time control
          Activate-pressure alarm;           > algorithm
       end If
    end loop
end cooling-pressure-monitor;

Task Body Water temperature-monitor;
    Temperature: float;
Begin
  Loop
      Get (temperature); <——Data Acquisition
      If temperature > max-temperature then
         increase-cooling. flow:
         activate-cooling. alarm;
      end If;
   end loop;
end water-temperature-monitor;
```

ADA also has the ability to cause interrupts on events to low level service routines (assembly code) for extremely time-critical functions where high-level code may cause too many processing delays.

ADA has other features for causing task initiation and termination based on timing requirements using the delay command. This would allow processes to cause a task to wait a fixed period of time between checks on a control variable or some other system requirement.

Example: In our previous example, if we insert a delay of 60.0, statement into the pressure task after the end, we will cause the never-ending loop of testing the pressure to be invoked only once per minute; this allows an effective way to monitor real-time events while not tying up processing resources.

When the delay is encountered the task is put to sleep for the specified period, to be awakened by a timer.

Another feature of ADA that is relevant for distributed and real-time computer system operations is the notion of exception handling (or error handling). This feature allows us to sense some condition, an error in processing or hardware failure, and to take action to either correct the condition or degrade the performance of the interrupted service based on the encountered condition. In the code, one would cause the invocation of an exception handler by the statement raise followed by the exception name. This would cause control to shift from the present task to the exception handler when this statement is encountered.

From the above brief examples and discussions, it can be seen how ADA supports the distribution of processing and the control of real-time activities. ADA and other languages developed for real-time environments possess powerful mechanisms for control and synchronization not found in other languages. For more details of the above and other ADA capabilities, the reader is referred to references previously provided.

Summary

This chapter should have conveyed to the reader the definitions and breadth of distributed computers, computing, and real-time systems. The following chapters will now focus on some of the components, capabilities, and implementations of these systems.

This chapter provided descriptions of what constitutes a distributed computer system, what distributed computing is, and how real-time computer systems have evolved into distributed computer environments.

CHAPTER FOUR

Communications Networking

In order for any distributed computing system to operate or to be classified as a distributed computing system, it must have communications between distributed system resources. This chapter will discuss the low-level protocols and topologies which have been developed to support communications/linkage between resources in these systems.

Topologies for distributed computer systems are as many and as various as the protocols that drive them. Early works by K. Thurber and E. D. Jensen [9], [270], [271], [272], [273] were aimed at defining the variety of interconnection structures and categorizing them by common features. Figure 4.1 represents a view of taxonomies for hardware interconnection architectures and goes beyond to list some systems that may fit under these categories.

In geographically distributed systems, the development of the topology may require the solution of very hard graphical problems to minimize the size and dispersion of the links to connect the autonomous computers into a network. This problem can be categorized as consisting of the following:

Given the location of the hosts and user devices and given the traffic loads from all points to all other points and given the cost of leasing lines from all points to all other points, the problem becomes one of minimizing the cost of supplying interconnections and communications with the constraint of supplying a given level of reliability and throughput with as minimal delays as possible. Problems of this type usually allow the variability of topology (connectivity), line capacity, and flow assignment.

This class of network deals with packet-switched communications utilizing a store and forward type of protocol. That is, messages are sent into the network utilizing some routing function (shortest path or least cost routing) and ultimately arrive at the destination in a hop from place-to-place fashion. Examples of such networks are ARPANET, constructed to interconnect large computer systems, Tymnet and GE net, commercial time-sharing nets, and Sita network, which is the worldwide airline reservation network. An example of network topology for such a network is given in Figure 4.2. This is the ARPANET as it existed in April 1976.

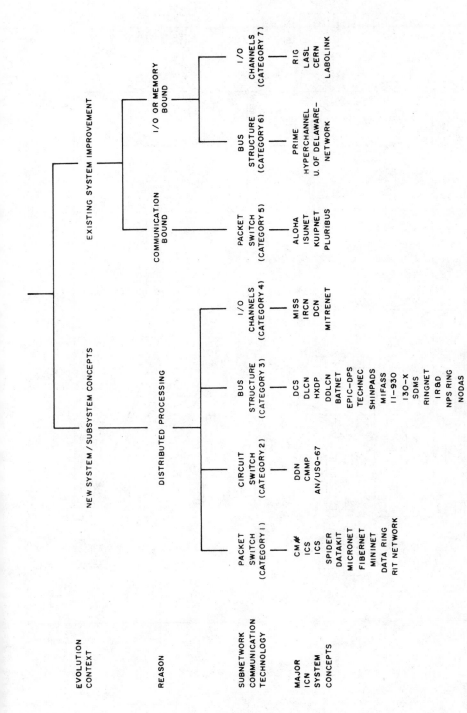

FIGURE 4.1 Taxonomy for hardware interconnection.

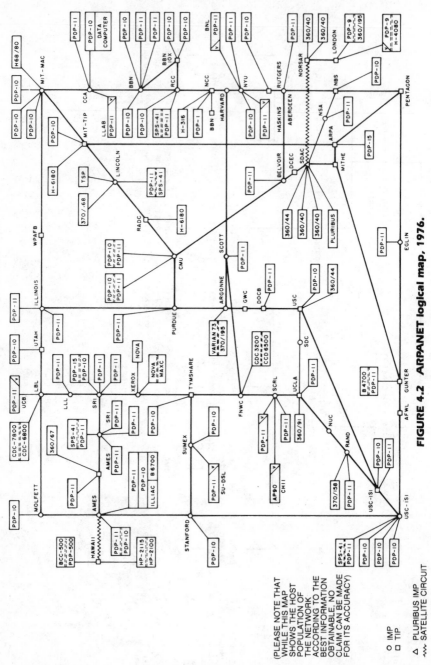

FIGURE 4.2   ARPANET logical map, 1976.

To determine the optimum topology for such systems would require much computation, as the following example will show. If you have N nodes and you require point-to-point connectivity, then you could have potentially $N(N-1)/2$ links. This represents potentially $2^{N(N-1)/2}$ topologies that must be examined. This is derived from the fact that a line can either be there or not. As the number of nodes rises, say above five, the problem becomes extremely hard and time-consuming to solve.

Many algorithms have been developed to address the problem of how to connect the nodes of a graph (network) to provide a minimum cost network. The most rigorous are in the class of dynamic programming algorithms which search for an optimum configuration through the search of all possible combinations. The problem with this approach is that it quickly becomes intractable when the network rises above a few nodes. An example algorithm of this type would be the all pairs shortest path problem.

In this algorithm you are given a graph $G = (V,E)$ vertecs and edges and a cost matrix $C(i,J)$ with the cost of edge (i,J). The problem is to determine the shortest paths that connect the points together. Using this result, a connectivity of the shortest path from node to node can be recommended and a topology derived. The problem is that this algorithm requires on the order of N^3 time complexity to perform the optimization which becomes excessive as N increases.

Another class of algorithms which has been used in the solution of network topology design is the divide and conquer technique. In this technique the problem of finding the "best" topology for N nodes is broken down into smaller pieces until more simple techniques can be used. Once a solution to the smaller subsets are performed, the subsets are rejoined using the condition of connecting the subsets by the minimum distance between the subsets. Using this method the solution can be arrived at quicker than the previous method; it may not be an optimal solution, but it is a good one.

Another class of algorithms used in solving this problem is the Greedy algorithm. This class of algorithm attempts to solve a problem by doing as much as it possibly can on each iteration. That is, the problem is broken up into stages and a feasible solution is either found or not determined in each phase. From this stage a next feasible solution is found. If not available, then try another avenue and so on until completed. Completion occurs when some bound on improvement per stage is not met.

An example of an algorithm which can be used to solve the problem of how to interconnect the nodes is the shortest path problem by Dijkstra. This algorithm is a Greedy technique that operates as follows. It maintains a set S of vertices whose shortest distance from the source is known in some cost function. Initially S contains only the source vertex. On each iteration we add to S another vertex V whose distance is the shortest to S. Once S has all the vertices (nodes) we have solved the problem. The algorithm is given in Figure 4.3. The algorithm assumes we are given $G = (V,E)$ where $V = 1,...N$ and vertex 1 is the source. C is an array of costs. $C(i,J)$ represents the cost from node i to node J as previously defined.

```
Procedure Dijkstra
    begin
       S: = (1)
       For i: = 2 to N do
          D(i): = C (1,i) initialize D
       For i: = 1 to N-1 do
          begin
             choose a vertex W in V-S such that
                D(W) is a minimum
             add W to S;
             For each vertex (v) in V-S do
                D(v): = min (D(V), D(w) + C(w,v))
          end
    end Dijkstra
```

FIGURE 4.3   Dijkstra's algorithm.

Many other techniques are available to solve the problem of how to interconnect nodes with minimum cost. For the more interested reader I direct you to reference [380], [381] and to algorithms such as Prim's, Kruskal's and the add or drop algorithm to name a few.

The previous discussion was mainly presented to spark interest in readers who may have an interest in analysis and design of wide area network topologies.

The thrust of the remainder of this chapter will be in the presentation of topologies and protocols utilized in local area networks where higher speed communications allow for tighter control (timingwise) of resources than in the geographical networks.

Local computer networks come in many kinds of topology and protocol for communications. From Figure 4.4 we can see the wide variety of possible topologies and in more detail Figure 4.5 shows the view of what these topologies could be, given the physical implementations. The topologies come in a few basic modes, such as the star topology where we have a centralized hub to which point communication lines from the nodes converge for communication services. Also, there is the mesh (irregular) topology where nodes are connected in an arbitrary pattern; each of the nodes can have multiple paths to other nodes. This topology is closest to that seen in the geographically distributed systems. Also this style of topology requires a more sophisticated routing control mechanism due to its connectivity. The next linkage covered is the ring topology. In this topology the communications path is a loop with each node connected to exactly two other nodes in a given loop. Routing is simpler as is control in this architecture. The final major type of topology is the bus. In this configuration the nodes are connected along line segments.

This topology is found in many local computer networks, and with a wide variety of control protocols.

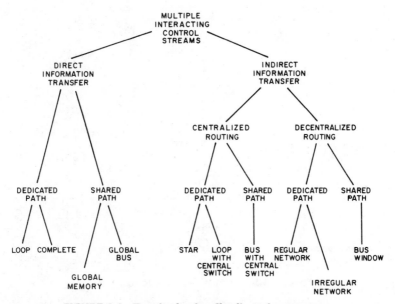

FIGURE 4.4 Topologies for distributed computers.

The differences in the four basic topologies described above and those depicted previously in Figure 4.5 is the method of control. The global bus and bus with central switch are essentially the same topologically, except that control data flow is implemented via the interaction of distributed vice centralized mechanisms. The mesh architecture is similar to the irregular network; regular networks and complete interconnects structurally are the same, but the method of control for each has distinct differences. The loop and loop with central switch are examples of the same topologies, but with distributed vice centralized control.

The following discussion will cover major control schemes and follow with discussions of particular implementations to further clarify the methods that are utilized.

Control Protocols

As shown in Figure 4.5 there are many variations on how to interconnect a local computer networking system. Just as there are multiple methods to connect the units physically, there are also multiple methods to provide control of the resources in such networks.

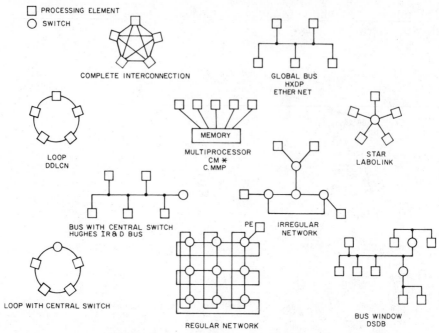

FIGURE 4.5 Various network topologies.

TABLE 4.1 Dimensions of distributed control.

Control Level	Physical Needs
• Single Fixed	Single CPU
• Master/Slave Fixed	Single CPU with Peripheral Devices
• Master/Slave Dynamic	Multiple CPU's Tightly Coupled
• Replicated Totally Autonomous	Multiple CPU's Loosely Coupled
• Multiple-Cooperating on Sub-Tasks	Multiple CPU's
• Replicated Cooperating	Multiple CPU's
• Multiple Fully Cooperating	Multiple CPU's

As seen in Table 4.1, control has various levels of decentralization. It runs the gamut from a single fixed control point to the wide extreme case of multiple control points cooperating in the execution of a task.

The different control techniques can be classified roughly as being either centralized or decentralized. Various bus control techniques will be outlined below in general terms using ADA as the descriptive language and hardware control ideas to depict the mechanisms for clarity. Most realistic methods encountered tend to use equivalent functions by transferring coded control over the bus data and/or control lines. Examples of real systems will be discussed to aid in the description of the protocols described.

Bus Control Protocol Techniques (Centralized)

With centralized control, a single unit is designated to recognize and grant requests for use of the system bus and resources. Three schemes are outlined below with variations noted.

DAISY CHAINING

In this control protocol implementation we require a physical realization of connectivity in order to realize this mechanism in its pure sense. This protocol requires a central cognizant control device which can recognize where service is required and initiate the control process. Two realizations of this are shown in Figure 4.6 and Figure 4.7.

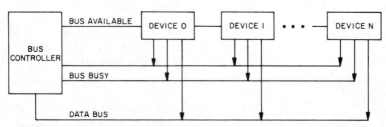

FIGURE 4.6   Global bus implementation of centralized daisy chain.

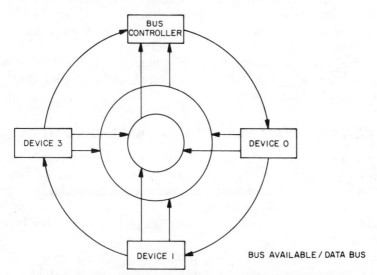

FIGURE 4.7   Ring implementation of centralized daisy chain.

```
Procedure Centralized Daisy Chaining
    Begin
      Device = 0
        If bus request is valid then
        begin
        while bus busy = false loop
          If device req[device] = true then
            begin
              Bus request: = false;
              Bus busy: = true;
              Data bus user: = device;
            end
          else
            Device: = device + 1;
          end if
        end;
      end if
  end; Centralized daisy chaining
```

Procedure 4.1   ADA procedure representative of centralized daisy chaining.

The generic operation of this control protocol is depicted in the ADA procedure of Procedure 4.1. This procedure shows how a device requests service and is granted it based on closeness to the controlling device. This method represents a physical prioritization of devices based on distance from the control node.

Control signals in this method can be passed logically vice physically on a single bus via control messages. The advantage of this type of control protocol is that it is simple (the controller may just be a flip flop), which raises bus available or bus request and reset on bus busy. The addition of devices just requires the additional stringing of the device to the three control lines.

Disadvantages of this method include low reliability. For example, the loss of the central controller brings down the entire network. Secondly, the physical connectivity forces priority of service onto the devices that cannot be changed dynamically. This prioritization could lock out other (farther removed) units from ever getting service.

CENTRALIZED POLLING (GLOBAL COUNTER)

This protocol is based on a central unit that has a counter which sends out the counter contents on receipt of a request for service. Individual units compare this to their local count codes and once a match is found, a bus busy signal is raised to indicate that the requestor has been found. Figure 4.8 depicts the control signals and action involved in this protocol, and ADA Procedure 4.2 clarifies the process.

The difference from the previous protocol is that this protocol will allow for a variation of which poll gets control by varying the poll codes stored or assigned to the devices. Priority will not be set due to proximity to controller.

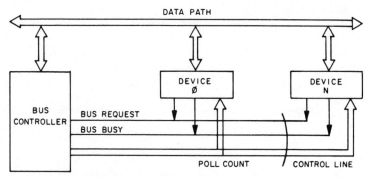

FIGURE 4.8 Centralized polling protocol.

This mechanism will allow either round robin (circulating poll code, wrap-around) or prioritized (start from 0 each time) allocation of the bus resource. As in the previous case, reliability/availability is solely based on that of the central node. If it fails, the network also fails.

A variation of the above technique simplifies the central node by eliminating the centrally generated poll code and request lines. This method utilizes distributed control software and hardware at each node which can sense an update signal, compute a new code, and determine which is being awarded the control. The simplification is depicted in Figure 4.9 and the operation of this mechanism is shown by the ADA code of Procedure 4.3.

```
Enter with bus-request set to true and device-req(device) true
only at the device who is requesting service.

Procedure centralized-polling-W-global-count-is
type

Max-count, count, data-bus-user, device: integer;
bus-request, bus-busy, device-requesting (device); boolean;

begin
   device: = 0;
   if bus-request is valid then
      begin
         While count 1 = man-count or bus-busy: = false loop
            count: = count + 1;
            if device-request(count) = true then
               begin
                  bus-request: = false
                  bus-busy: = true;
                  data-bus user: = device
               end
            end:if;
         end;
      end if;
end centralized-polling-W-global-count-;
```

Procedure 4.2

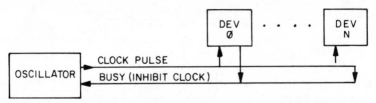

FIGURE 4.9   Polling with distributed control code.

```
Procedure polling-w-dist-counters is;
    type inhibit : Boolean ;
        clockP : integer

    Entry send (clock:integer)

    Task clock;

    begin
        While inhibit 1 = true then
            send (clockP);

    end;
    end clock task;
    Task device;
    Type counter, loc-pri:integer;

    Task-body device is

    begin
        Loop
            Accept (send (clockP));
            count: = count + 1:
            If count = loc-pri the inhibit : = true
            call service-routine;
            end;if
        end loop;
        end device
    end pollingw-dist-counters;
```

Procedure 4.3

This control protocol method allows for a round robin (logical) allocation of the communications resource, if all counter spaces are used by one for each unit. Or the allocation can be variable (tailored to requirements) if the number of units is less than the maximum count size. The limiting variable on the number of devices is the counter size. Using this scheme, the reliability can be increased by building in the ability of any device to provide the count signal to the bus users. This can be accomplished via a master/slave relationship between an active counter node, requiring that another be designated as secondary.

CENTRALIZED INDEPENDENT REQUEST

This control protocol utilizes a centralized arbiter to determine which will be able to utilize the data bus for communications. This method operates as follows: A unit or units requests use of the communications resource. The central arbiter then, utilizing some arbitration protocol, selects a user for the communications system, and tells all others it is assigned and inhibits other requests. The winning unit uses the resource, then completes the cycle by allowing requests again. Figure 4.10 represents the physical realization of such a method and Procedure 4.4 is the ADA control program that represents it.

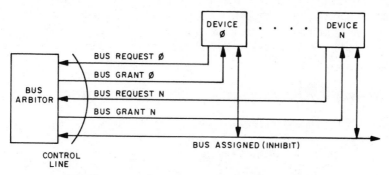

FIGURE 4.10   Centralized independent requests.

Procedure centralized independent request is :

```
type  bus-req:integer
      bus-req-list: array (1..N) of integer;
      bus-assigned: Boolean
begin
while bus-assigned = false loop;
begin
            collect (bus-req)              Call routine to collect
                                           all requests
            select (bus-req-list)          select a requestor from
                                           the bus-select-list
            bus assigned: = true
            end
        end
    end central independent request.
```

Procedure 4.4   ADA representation of the arbiter.

In this control protocol many varied methods of control could be used. The selection routine could poll the requestors and select the first, last, highest priority, etc. It could form them into data structures and select based on some minimization or maximization of utilization criteria, or it could be required to have the requestors send in some coded information about the message and the physical device and it could decide based on this data. This approach could have lower delay in performing the allocation of communications resources and leaves complete flexibility to the control arbiter as to what selection procedure to use. Again, as in the previous cases, this method's reliability is low because it is dependent on the reliability of the central node.

Decentralized Control Schemes

In a distributedly controlled system, control logic is (primarily) distributed physically throughout the devices on the communications resource. As was seen in the centralized case there are three basic schemes; daisy chaining, polling, and independent requests, though in the distributed case, the variations are much wider. Some will be described in this section.

DAISY CHAINING (REQUEST DEPENDENT)

In this method of decentralized control, users requiring use of the communication resource send out their request onto the control medium. This request is then sent back into the requesting units as bus available in priority order (daisy chain). The first requesting unit to get the signal takes control of the communications network and inhibits bus available from continuing. Once it is completed, if others are still requesting, the signal will be regenerated and move on until the next unit gets control and so on. Figure 4.11 depicts the physical control flow and Procedure 4.5 the ADA representation of the same.

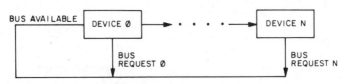

FIGURE 4.11   Daisy chaining.

```
Procedure regenerative daisy chain is
type
    bus-request, bus-available: Boolean
end
begin
    while bus-request = true loop;
        begin
            if bus-available = true then
        P-bus-available
            use-bus-resource
        V-bus-available
            end if
        end
end regenerated daisy chain
```

Procedure 4.5   Regenerative daisy chain.

The ADA program would use a P and V semaphore-type operation, using a semaphore task as shown below to allow only the user requesting service and having the bus-available signal to use the resource.

```
Task semaphore is
    entry P-bus-available;
    entry V-bus-available;
end;
begin
    loop
        accept P-bus-available;
        accept V-bus-available;
    end loop;
end semaphore;
```

Procedure 4.6   ADA semaphore synchronization task.

This control type will cause periods of high use and idle time on a control bus since it is not a continuous control action. It is more robust than the centralized case because control is not dependent on any one device. In order to make the system resilient to failures, the control signal must be able to bypass a failed unit to keep the daisy chain united. This is easily accomplished by a relay which can be initiated upon device hard failure or by network operating system control.

DAISY CHAIN ROTATING

This control mechanism is one of the most common in use for ring topologies. In this protocol the bus available signal is constantly rotating from device to device. When the signal is received by a device it can either use the communications resource or not. If it does not, it sends the bus-available signal on to the next device in the chain.

The pictorial representation of this protocol method can be seen in Figure 4.12 and the control program is described in Procedure 4.7.

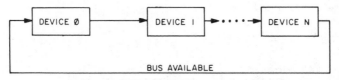

FIGURE 4.12   Rotating daisy chain control.

This method is independent of the number of devices in the chain. The control can be passed either by a signal pulse or via coded control messages (tokens) that rotate through the network. This token can physically move from device to device such as in a ring topology or can logically do the same via coded address tokens which move from logical unit 0 to logical unit N. Many systems have been developed that use this method of communications resource arbitration.

```
Procedure rotating daisy chain is
type
   bus-available

begin
   while bus-available = true loop;
            P-bus-available;                       acquire control
            use resource;                          use resource
            V-bus-available;                       relinquish control
      end;
   end rotating daisy chain
```

Procedure 4.7   Rotating daisy chain.

POLLING

This method of decentralized control protocol requires that each unit be able to respond to some predetermined set of "addresses" or logical names in order for bus control to be effective. This method allows designers to tailor the workload (bus resource utilization) based on known user communications usage patterns or to allow all users equal use of the resource.

The operation of this method is depicted physically in Figure 4.13 and logically in Procedure 4.8 ADA representation.

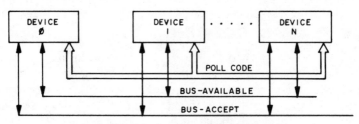

FIGURE 4.13   Decentralized polling.

```
Procedure decentralized-polling is
type poll-code;my-poll-code:integer;
my-poll-code: = constant;
entry poll-code;

begin
   accept P-(poll-code);
   if poll-code = my-poll-code or old-poll code not taken then
      begin
         use-communications-resource;
         compute-next(poll code);
      end
   end if
P-(poll code); send out new code
end
```

Procedure 4.8   Decentralized polling.

This control protocol will operate as follows: The unit which just relinquished control (P(poll-code)) sends out the next poll code computed in compute-next (poll code); the other devices will be monitoring the communications resource and if the new poll code they acquire via accept P(poll code) is equal to their known code words, that device now has control of the network communications resource. It uses the resource and goes back into the mode as described above. If the sender does not get an acknowledgement or reception it will compute another code and continue until someone takes control of the resource. This method requires that at any time one user device is the master which will send out the poll code once he is done. If he fails before he does it, there is an a priori determined sequence of unit status by which the control cycle can be restarted.

The new poll code that initiates control can be as specific as a physical designator or a logical address or even as simple as an indicator to tell everyone to update their global counter which is used as the poll counter. Examples of this will be shown later.

DECENTRALIZED INDEPENDENT REQUEST

This control protocol method is one of the richest for versatility and for variety of implementations. The basic notion for the control protocol is that all users wanting use of the communication resource must fight for use of it based on the available control method implemented. It could be based on priority resolution, collision, detection, etc. The basic structure of such a system is that depicted in Figure 4.14. In this figure we show a bus request line and a bus assigned line. This indicates that this method of control has two phases: the contention and the resolution of control.

Procedure 4.9 depicts a generalized representation of the procedure required in determining who gets control of the resource.

Procedure independent request is;

```
Begin
   request-myid): = true
   message (pri): = priority
   if bus-assigned-false then
      contend (message(pri));
   else
      delay (message(pri));
   and if;
if contend (message(pri)) = true then
   bus-assigned: = true;
   use-comm-resource;
end if
```

Procedure 4.9   Independent requests.

Dependent on how sophisticated in hardware and software one is prepared to be, the contention scheme can be simple or very complex and supply either a low-level use or high-level of use of the resource.

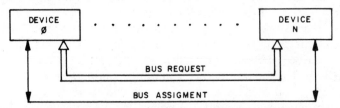

FIGURE 4.14   Decentralized independent request.

EXAMPLE OF CONTENTION-BASED SYSTEM

A well-known form of contention in control protocol of this type is the aloha network and the carrier sense multiple access schemes or CSMA as they have been called.

In these control protocol schemes, users view the communications environment as a shared medium that is available on demand independent of other users or is slotted, broken up into fixed timeframes, and available on slot boundaries, as in Figure 4.15.

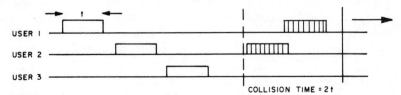

FIGURE 4.15   Examples of collision in pure aloha communication system.

In the pure aloha configuration users send out their messages of maximum length T over the communication medium (radio space). If they are received properly an ACK is returned. If during the period of transmission another message is sent, a collision occurs. If this happens, then the entire messages from both are lost. In aloha, to recover from this, each user whose message collides goes into a randomization algorithm which delays each retransmission for some random time in the future.

In the pure aloha case, if the maximum throughput in time T is G and Po is the probability that a packet (message) will avoid collision, then the successful traffic throughout S is equal to P.G.

$$S = G\,Po$$

If we assume a poisson distribution of access requests, then the probability of avoiding a collision becomes e^{-2G}. Therefore, from the above,

$$S = Ge^{-2G}$$

which supplies a maximum throughput of .184 of the available channel bandwidth. In the slotted aloha the period of collision drops to t vice 2t and S is now given as:

$$S = Ge^{-G}$$

In this case the maximum available capacity is 36.8% of maximum which is twice that of the pure aloha. Both of these are called persistent CSMA protocols.

The problem with both of these techniques is that they are very unstable when heavy loads ensue. The realizable throughput under a maximally interfering load of transmissions and retransmissions will degrade to zero.

Many proposals to alleviate these problems have been postulated. The main one is to sense when someone is transferring on a line in order to avoid collisions. These mechanisms are known as P-persistent CSMA. In this case the protocol is designed to monitor the bus and based on its P value it will either send immediately or upon sensing channel not busy (P = 1) delay with some probability less than 1. As the probability of immediate transfer decreases, the overall performance increases, as in Figure 4.16. Other modes of CSMA include non-persistent CSMA. In this mode of control protocol the user senses the channel. If it is busy it does not wait. It does not continually sense the channel waiting for it to free up such as in persistent CSMA. It waits some random period of time and then repeats the algorithm. This method intuitively must increase the throughput (due to fewer collisions.) This method can be formulated as a slotted or unslotted version. In this case, the slotted version will realize a greater possible theoretical limit on throughput than the unslotted. The comparison of the various CSMA protocols are shown in Figure 4.16.

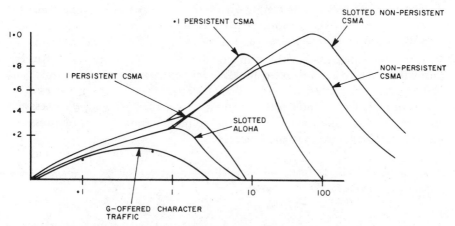

FIGURE 4.16 Comparison of performance for various CSMA protocols.

Another well-known contention resolution system is Ethernet. Ethernet was developed at the Xerox research center in Palo Alto, CA. It was developed using a coaxial cable as the transmission channel. In this implementation, user nodes monitor the channel continuously during their transmission. If a collision is detected, transmission immediately terminates. This method wastes less of the available bandwidth.

The algorithm for control is as follows:

Procedure Ethernet is

```
begin
  If link-busy = false then
    begin
      transmit (message);
      while time / = 2* prop-delay loop
        If listen(message) / = message then
          Randomize (message)
        end if
      end while
    end
    Transmission OK
  end if
end; ethernet;
```

Procedure 4.10   Ethernet procedure.

The Ethernet protocol can achieve channel utilization rates that are above 90% for packets of 1/100% of the maximum capacity and with bus lengths of up to 1 kilometer.

Another interesting contention-based protocol is described in [95]. In this paper a large distributed computing system is described that utilizes a contention resolution scheme to allow for extremely high utilization of bus resources.

The physical network is comprised of fibre optic data and control paths (separate data and control lines) that are used in providing real-time high speed communication to users over a series of buses (Figure 4.17).

This communication environment provides up to 16 megabytes per second throughput per bus with up to 63 BIU (bus interface units) per bus. Communications are packetized and utilize a slotted view of the resource. The protocol looks to use the resource optimally by always filling up the next data bus slot with a message to send. The communications protocol is implemented on the control bus and operates as follows:

```
Procedure DOT-OR control protocol is
BIT: [0,1];
Bit-position, first-bit, last-bit, r bit position)
B   is array of first-bit to last-bit of bit;
Loop
  begin
    For bit-position in first-bit to last bit loop
      transmit (B(Bit-Position))
      accept receive (B)Bit-Position
```

```
            If B(Bit-position) / = B(rbit-position) then exit;
        end if
    end for
    Transmit -message (frame + 1,)(message)
  end;
end loop
```

Procedure 4.11   ADA DOT-OR control protocol.

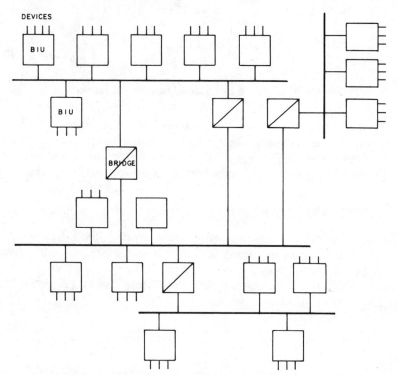

FIGURE 4.17   DSDB configuration.

For this protocol each device is autonomous and performs control calculations as such. The bus is organized in a slotted fashion (called frames). During each frame period the control mechanism determines who will get to transmit a message in the next period. Each device BIU which has a message to send is involved in the protocol. Starting at the sensing of the beginning of a frame each unit sends its bits one at a time and listens. If the bit received does not equal the bit sent, this device will drop out for the remainder of the contention period. The bit pattern used for contention is comprised of 6 bits of message priority, which may be the same for many devices, and 6 bits of address, which are unique for each device.

Figure 4.18 depicts DOT-OR contention resolution frame and indicates who has won the right to send in the follow frame. With this contention res-

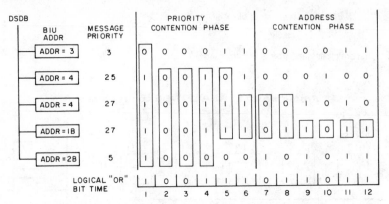

FIGURE 4.18 DSDB distributed contention resolution.

olution mechanism there is no notion of collision and in all cases only one device will acquire access of the communications medium. In the best case, the bus can attain 100% utilization of the data communications resource. Further chapters will describe other features of this unique architecture.

RING ARCHITECTURE

Ring networks typically use the daisy chain style of control protocol. The daisy chain is implemented using a rotating token which, when acquired, allows a user to append his message to the tail of the message train.

There are four major classes of ring architecture control protocols, namely token, contention, slotted, and insertion.

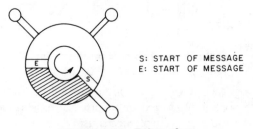

S: START OF MESSAGE
E: START OF MESSAGE

FIGURE 4.19 Token ring.

The token ring was described in [81], [82], [83], [84], Figure 4.19. In this structure round-robin (daisy chain) control token circulates around the loop allowing only one device at a time to acquire the medium and transfer a message. This method allows for transfer of variable-length messages, but restricts the transfer of messages to only one unit at a time.

The contention ring [382] differs from the token ring in that when there is no traffic there is no token circulating. In this protocol, if there is no traffic on the bus and it wants to transfer, then it just does so. When the message comes around it takes the message and the token it put on the ring off it. In the other case if it notices a message on the bus, it waits for the token, converts it to a connector and adds its message to this, then puts the token on the end of the message string. Under heavy load this ring acts like the token ring. The problem with this is that if the message doesn't have information about the sender or if two or more send out messages simultaneously on an idle link, there will be more than one token. When the other devices see the message and token, they may remove it without it being their message. In the worst case, the messages would be put on and removed at the next node causing "collision" and loss of the messages. In this case, they will time out, then randomize and try again (Figure 4.20(a) and (b)).

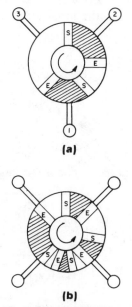

(a)

(b)

FIGURE 4.20   (a) Contention ring; (b) insertion ring.

If node 1 transfers and node 2 decides to transfer at the same time, then when node 2 sees the SOM of node 2 it will remove the message and token. When node 1 sees node the SOM of node 2 will do likewise, causing a collision.

The next class of ring is the slotted ring [383]. In this protocol the loop is logically divided into fixed size time slots. Messages are formed into packets which fit into these slots, one slot per packet. Messages are broken up into packets and sent in order over the link as follows. When a unit wishes to send a packet, it looks at slots coming by. When one is sensed that is marked empty, it marks it full, then puts its packet in. This scheme allows multiple devices to be simultaneously transmitting—but in order to do this devices must perform extra processing (Figure 4.21).

The final method of loop control protocol was described in [384] and is referred to as the insertion ring. The transfer of messages is accomplished through the use of a register insertion technique allowing for the loop to carry multiple messages of variable size at any time (Figure 4.22). In this protocol, the ring interface has a hardware shift register that has two buffers, an input buffer and an output buffer. Incoming messages are buffered and relayed out of the unit. If the output buffer has a message in it, it is allowed to transfer its message only if the length of the message is smaller than the remaining space in the delay (input) buffer. This condition of having at least the same number of bits left in the input buffer as those being sent out is done to guarantee that while I am transmitting my output if input arrives, there will be enough buffer space available to hold it until I am completed and can continue shipping out the input buffer contents without losing any data.

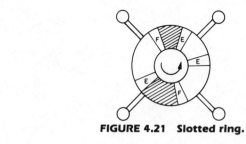

FIGURE 4.21   Slotted ring.

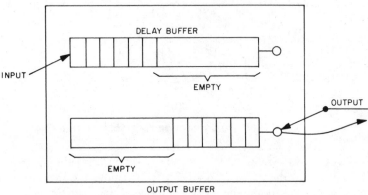

FIGURE 4.22   Insertion ring delay register.

This scheme allows for a higher possible bus utilization than the other mechanisms without the problems. Messages are taken off the ring by the destination sites, thereby acting as an acknowledgement of the message.

STAR ARCHITECTURES

This class of architecture is best represented by a central switching (controlling) environment used to connect multiple computers together. Two examples of systems that support this type of interconnection are Cm* [266] and Labolink [385]. Cm* is a modular multi-microprocessor system developed at Carnegie Mellon University in which all of the processors share access to a single virtual memory space (Figure 4.23).

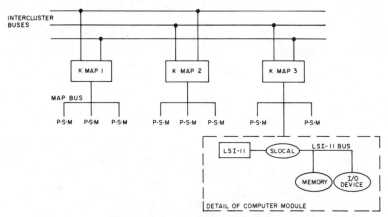

FIGURE 4.23   Cm* configuration.

A computer module consists of a DEC LSI-11 processor, a local switch (slocal) to direct references from the processors selectively either to local memory or to map bus, and to accept references from map bus to the local memory. Up to 14 computer modules (P-S-M) and one mapping processor (KMAP) form a cluster. The KMAP consists of three major components. Microbus, Pmap, and linc. The K-bus arbitrates and controls the map bus. The Pmap is a microprocessor; with the basic configuration having 1K x 80 bits of writable control store (microprogram space) and 5K x 16 bits of RAM for holding mapping tables, etc. The linc provides the interface to two intercluster buses which allow communications between clusters. The protocol for transmission of messages involves the use of addresses. When the address is supplied, the central controllers KMAP perform the mapping and accessing of the information utilizing a packet-switched message transfer strategy. The KMAPs are the centralized controllers for the cluster.

The other system, labolink, is a local network developed at Kyoto University (Figure 4.24). It is a "network" designed to interface terminals to several mainframe computers via a minicomputer controller. This minicomputer is the central (star) switch which implements the control protocol.

Labolink is primarily oriented toward two requirements:

1. Supports user access to a variety of computers from terminals in a laboratory.
2. Permits high-speed file transfers between remote computers and local computers.

The system consists of a PDP 11/40 switching computer connecting the remote networks and computers and a microprocessor-based switching system supporting terminals connected into the network.

There are several unique system features in labolink:

1. The network support software executes as user programs.
2. An automated theory model was used as the design basis for the PDP/HITAC interface.
3. A very interesting connection concept, a single-line multiconnector, which was developed to allow ease of replacement of communication channels in response to technology improvements.

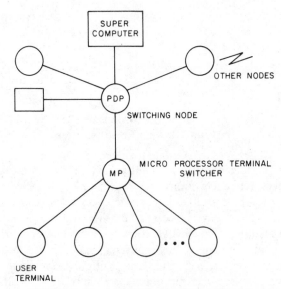

FIGURE 4.24   Labolink computer network.

Summary

Introduced in this chapter were the ideas of network topologies from arpanet-type, geographically separated networks to the local ring, bus, star, and irregular network structures.

Also included in this chapter was a discussion of some major communication control protocols, their implementation, and operations as well as examples of some actual networks which have used some of these control protocols.

CHAPTER FIVE

Operating Systems

In order for readers to more fully understand Global Operating Systems we must first step back to describe classical operating systems. In the past the need for operating systems grew from a desire to more fully utilize the capacity of the computer and not waste resources. Operating systems grew from simple stand-alone machines with minimal support up to the present time-sharing systems of today. The most interesting area of operating systems, development has been in the timesharing arena. This class of operating systems has seen the hardest and, once solved, the most rewarding problems and solutions in early computer systems software developments.

The following discussion will introduce some of the basic components of local operation systems, namely the idea of mutual exclusion primitives, states of operation, memory management, process management, and I/O management.

In order for an operating system to realize any capability of controlling diverse operations, we must possess the notion of mutual exclusion. Mutual exclusion refers to a particular entity by which only one process at a time uses a resource and excludes the other and vice versa.

Examples of this capability would be a hardware memory with dual ports. It would possess a hardware arbiter which would select only one of the two requestors at any one time to access the word for writing. Another example would be a computer instruction called test and set. This allows a set of user processes to use a particular element as a test point to perform mutual exclusion. Users would test the location and, if available, set it in the same instruction cycle, thereby locking out others from accessing it. The user process that wins can then perform its critical section of code, then relinquish control by unsetting the test point, thus allowing others to access the critical section. This leads us to the question of what is a critical section? A critical section is defined as a section of code which must be accessed by only one user at a time to avoid conflicts and erroneous operations. An example of a critical section would be the use of a buffer in the producer/consumer relationship. It is the goal of this process to not allow consumption of an element until production of an element has occurred. To better describe this example, the idea of a semaphore (mutual exclusion) primitive is now described. Dijkstra [70] derived the notion of semaphores to guarantee the mutually exclusive use of critical sections for computer systems.

A semaphore is an element that can have two states, either true or false, and no other states. Dijkstra devised operations on a semaphore as comprised of one of two types, namely P(S) as a request to acquire the semaphore (right to use critical section) or V(S) as a release of the acquired semaphore. The following code represents the operation of a generalized semaphore and a counting semaphore.

P(S)   If S = 0 then S: = 1 else enqueue;
V(S)   S: = 0; if queue<>null then dequeue;

General Semaphore Operation

P(S)   If S =max then S1 = S+1; else enqueue;
V(S)   S: = S-1; if queue<>null then dequeue;

Counting Semaphore Dijkstra

Using these semaphores one can construct solutions to problems such as the readers and writers problem, the monitor problem [69], and the producer/consumer problem. We will describe the producer/consumer problem presently.

First, let us restate the problem. In simple terms, we want to allow the production of elements and the consumption of these elements in a noninterfering fashion. These elements are stored in a shared repository and therefore mutual exclusion is required to let just one process access the item at any one time. The process is shown below:

```
Initialize with S = O and (produce first element S(1) = 1
    P(S)                            P(S1)
        Buffer = Buffer + 1         Buffer = Buffer -1
    V(S1)                           V(S)
  Producer                          Consumer
```

This method would allow for the use of a general or counting semaphore to be used to supply either a singular ability to produce then consume, or a counting version allowing many productions of elements followed by consumers of elements or a combination of the same.

The importance of the previous example is in the concept of mutual exclusion and the ability of it to provide use of critical sections of code safely. This allowed the construction of many higher level OPSYS constructs that manage data and processes in present computer systems. Readers who wish to get a richer perspective on semaphore use are directed to [70].

States of Operation

Now that we have the notion of a semaphore and have seen how it can be used to construct control mechanism for operating systems, we now need the notion of states of operation for operating systems. The basic states that a process (unit of work) can be in once created are ready, running, or waiting. Ready is the state in which a process has a process control block and is ready to be scheduled and dispatched to run. Running is the state in which the process has control of the queue and is executing code. When either a running process encounters a situation in which it must wait for some action or resource or if it runs out of its CPU slice (quantum), it is blocked and put in a wait state. When it awakes it returns to the ready queue to be restarted based on the scheduling scheme utilized. Figure 5.1 depicts the states of operation and Figure 5.2 the processes that support these states.

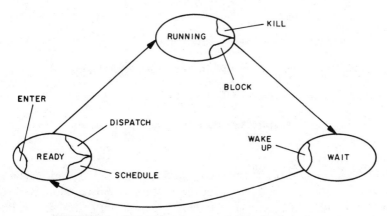

FIGURE 5.1   Operating system states of operation.

This is a very simplistic view of process states of operation and the more energetic and motivated reader is directed to [69] for further information.

Another problem that local operating systems must address is that of deadlock. Deadlock is the condition where one process holds a resource A and wants resource B, while another process at the same time holds a resource B and wants a resource A. In this case neither can complete their processing because they cannot fulfill their resource requirements; therefore we have a deadlock. There are four reasons why deadlock is possible: they are allowing mutual exclusion, not allowing preemption, allowing hold and waits, and circular wait. In order to not have deadlock, operating systems must guarantee that one of the four conditions does not happen. We must allow mutual exclusion or a meaningful operating system cannot be built. Therefore, one of the three remaining conditions must be corrected. The levels of deadlock correction include detection, prevention, avoidance, and recovery.

In detection the notion of a resource allocation graph (rag) is used. The operating system builds a graph which indicates what resource is held by what process and what resources are being requested by which processes, as in Figure 5.3.

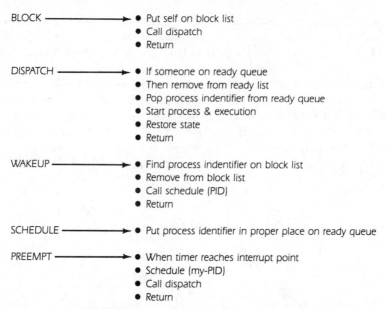

BLOCK ⟶ ● Put self on block list
● Call dispatch
● Return

DISPATCH ⟶ ● If someone on ready queue
● Then remove from ready list
● Pop process indentifier from ready queue
● Start process & execution
● Restore state
● Return

WAKEUP ⟶ ● Find process indentifier on block list
● Remove from block list
● Call schedule (PID)
● Return

SCHEDULE ⟶ ● Put process identifier in proper place on ready queue

PREEMPT ⟶ ● When timer reaches interrupt point
● Schedule (my-PID)
● Call dispatch
● Return

FIGURE 5.2   Operating system functions.

The basic method of detection is to look at the rag and reduce it by removing all processes that just have allocations and no wait requests from the rag, return their resource, reallocate it, and reiterate until this can be done no more. If only resources are left then there is no deadlock. If there are processes left, then deadlock is present and recovery must be initiated.

Recovery consists of selecting one of the remaining processes as a victim, preempting it, and removing its resources for use by the other processes, then reiterating this until the graph has been totally reduced (Figures 5.3 and 5.4). The preempted process can either be restarted later or aborted based on system sophistication.

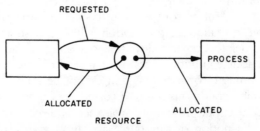

FIGURE 5.3   Resource allocations graph.

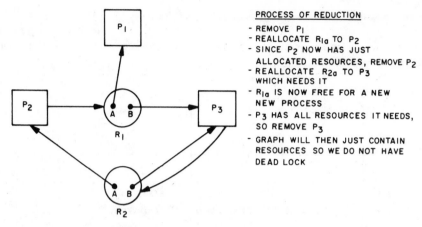

PROCESS OF REDUCTION
- REMOVE P_1
- REALLOCATE R_{1a} TO P_2
- SINCE P_2 NOW HAS JUST
  ALLOCATED RESOURCES, REMOVE P_2
- REALLOCATE R_{2a} TO P_3
  WHICH NEEDS IT
- R_{1a} IS NOW FREE FOR A NEW
  NEW PROCESS
- P_3 HAS ALL RESOURCES IT NEEDS,
  SO REMOVE P_3
- GRAPH WILL THEN JUST CONTAIN
  RESOURCES SO WE DO NOT HAVE
  DEAD LOCK

FIGURE 5.4   RAG reduction technique.

The next area is deadlock avoidance. In this case the objective is not to find it then correct it, but to avoid the occurrence of it. The best example of a method that does this is Dijkstra's banker's algorithm [390]. In this algorithm there exists the notion of safe and unsafe states. The idea is to allocate resources only as long as a safe state exists. That is the safe state with its remaining resources which allows all units to complete.

State 1	Current Loan	Max Needed	State 2	Current Loan	Max Needed
User 1	1	4	User 1	8	10
User 2	4	6	User 2	2	5
User 3	5	8	User 3	1	3
Available 2			Available 1		

The example shows that the State 1 is a safe state because it is possible for all processes to finish. If user 2 is given the remaining two it will finish and free up six units of resource. Then three resource units can be given to user 3 and three units to user 1, allowing them to finish also.

In the other case there is only one available unit of resource. None of the current allocations can meet their maximum need so none can complete. This is, therefore, an unsafe state.

Another area of interest is the area of deadlock prevention. This area attacks the deadlock condition of hold and wait, no preemption, and circular wait conditions. The techniques are as follows: First, to avoid the problems of waiting for resources, processes are required to acquire all they need and hold them until completed. This is inefficient, so the idea is to break up the process into pieces and acquire resources on a piece-by-piece basis and release once done with the piece.

For example, a process requires six tape drives to read, sort, and store files. By breaking up the requirement for total resources, one can have periods of holding two units at a time but no more, thereby freeing up four others for use by other processes (Figure 5.5).

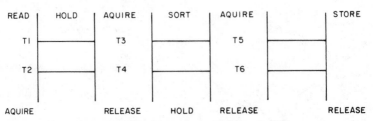

FIGURE 5.5   Example of hold and wait.

The next area of prevention is to allow preemption. This means that if a unit cannot complete its processing due to the inability to acquire all its resources, then it should be allowed to preempt (override) a lower priority user and acquire its resources. If a process cannot preempt another, it will go into the pool of available resources to be preempted itself. By doing this the system will ultimately be able to complete all processes through preemption. The problem is that once preempted a process should be reinserted into the ready chain at some other time to insure that it is eventually completed.

The final method of prevention is to avoid circular waits. Circular waits are the condition in which one process wants a resource held by the other and vice versa, as in Figure 5.6.

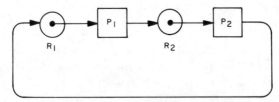

FIGURE 5.6   Circular wait condition.

The corrective process here is to provide all resources with a sequence number and require all units to acquire resources in order. That is, you cannot request a resource of smaller sequence value than is now available. This will prevent the possibility of the circular wait. It may cause some processes to get long wait times, but they will still ultimately complete.

I/O Management

Operating systems must manage the access to the various I/O devices that are connected to them. These devices include tape drives, disk drives, printers, terminals, etc. In each case the controlling sequence may differ. In a printer, the transfer is one way and must be sequential. Most operating systems use a spooling approach for printers. The output is spooled (to a disk unit) and once all outputs are inserted the entire file is dumped into the printer for output.

Tape units are controlled in a sequential fashion. To write, the operating system supplies an address and block size to the tape controller which will find the last record, then write out the physical memory block starting from the given address. To read, the operating system supplies an address to put the record and a record name for it. The tape controller will sequentially search for the requested record until it is found, then place it in the proper location in memory.

The operating system also controls access to the disk systems. This is usually of the basic queued style. By this it is meant that access is to the bare machine level. An example may be: read record 5 sector 3, etc., or query by a logical access with commands such as get employed. PAS which is a request to get a logical record. Services done by the operating system are to initiate the disk access either directly or queue them up and handle them by the scheduling scheme utilizing FIFO control mechanisms.

Another important function that an operating system must provide is local memory management. The major functions that a memory management mechanism must provide are placement of files in memory, management (use) of file while in memory, and replacement of files in memory. Placement strategies attempt to provide mechanisms to place files in an "optimal" (based on requirements) manner. Typical methods include best fit (select the operating area that wastes the least space), worst fit (select the largest that is available), first fit (select the first one encountered that will fit in), etc.

Page replacement is the mechanism used to replace pages in memory that must be forced out due to space limitations and loadings. There are two basic methods to decide when to replace; demand (replace only when forced to) and anticipatory (try to guess the next one to drop out. The problem is that the guess can be good or bad). Under these mechanisms various algorithms have been developed to determine which to drop. Some include LRU (least recently used page is shipped out), FIFO (first page in is first page out).

The operating system must also manage how the memory is used. To provide this, most modern computers use a mixture of paging and segmentation to provide the requisite management. The virtual space is broken up into segments which each have some number of pages. The operating system keeps track of which segments and pages are in memory and their status. It uses this information to implement the replacement and placement strategies previously described.

Stepping farther back from these low levels, the next area of operating system interaction is process management. A local operating system must possess some algorithms to control and manage the use of the CPU resource by the user processes. This is referred to as process scheduling. Basically, an operating system selects a process to run from the ready list, of active processes, allows it to either run to completion or gives it a time slice (quantum) and then reiterates until it is shut down or has no more work to do.

Examples of algorithms used include FIFO (the user processes are ordered by arrival point and are processed in first come first served order). Another technique is least time remaining. In this case the operating system orders the scheduling queue based on time remaining to complete. Or they may order the queue based on most time remaining to complete. An example implementation is multics. In this scheduler the operating system splits the runtime into differing size quantums (time units) and it utilizes a multilevel queuing setup to manage the active processes. Processes enter at the highest priority queue which has the smallest quantum time and propagate down to the lower levels until they complete being able to use one quantum at each level they visit. The lower levels have a lower priority but larger quantum slices. See Figure 5.7.

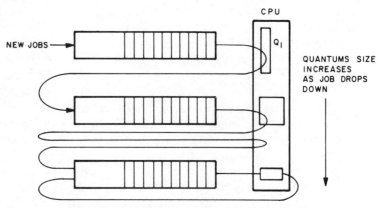

FIGURE 5.7   CPU scheduling with quantums.

The previous section attempted to provide the reader with a quick outline of the function and structure of a local operating system environment. Included were discussions of operating systems primitives such as semaphores, states of operation and requirements/mechanisms to allow the operation system to manage resources and protect integrity of operations. More interested readers are directed to the end of text references for further details.

Network Operating Systems

A distributed computing system as described earlier is one in which the hardware and software are brought together to provide a unified, cohesive and transparent view to users. To perform this integration the concept of a high-level operating environment must be provided [307], [77]. The majority of the functions which a distributed operating environment must deal with include naming, protection, synchronization, heterogeneity, resource sharing, and interprocess communications, to name a few.

The impetus for developing these high-level operating environments has emerged from the needs of users for more processing beyond the capability of the present technology to provide the requisite capability. That is, as users' preferences led to an increased need for processing, designers looked at alternatives to provide this service. This led to the development of distributed computers and from this the need for an operating system sprouted. But why was a unified distributed operating system environment wanted?

Reasons cited include the requirement to connect existing host computers into a network to provide services and capabilities such as resource sharing, increased processing, enhanced host to host communications, increased reliability, increased availablility, and increased performance in a consistent fashion.

But what is a distributed operating system environment? How can we tell if we have one available? How can it be classified? Operating systems for distributed computer systems have evolved in two ways. The first is to take existing local operating systems and build a network operating system (NOS) on top of this. The other approach is to throw away everything and build an operating environment from scratch with a single homogeneous distributed operating system (DOS).

From the above classifications we can look at some of the capabilities that comprise a network operating system. A network operating system is defined as a collection of software and associated protocols which allows a set of autonomous (stand-alone) computers which are connected together to be used in a convenient and cost-effective manner. This definition describes the capability added to existing local operating systems to unite them into a network.

But we may ask the question, what does a NOS do for you? Given the context of autonomous, possibly nonhomogeneous, processor and operating systems, a network operating system will provide the capability to smooth over the differences in implementation and operation between the various distributed system components. See Figure 5.8. The NOS will supply the capability to interface with the various local operating systems' protocols. This type of network may still possess centralized control features, central critical elements (sections of code, as well as centralized data), but the NOS will be utilized in providing a more global view of local information.

The NOS is implemented as an application code callable from the local operating systems. This NOS application allows user processes to use the network and its resources. For each resource a NOS process will be required to manage it from a network viewpoint. That is, the communications network will require a NOS component, the distributed data base manager will require a NOS component, as well as the reconfiguration manager, to name a few.

The major emphasis for this level of service, in the overall environment, is the management of global assets, such as network components including to-

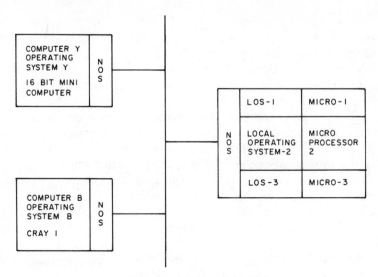

FIGURE 5.8 NOS environment.

pology, data base, global deadlock detection, global interface to local resources, etc. It is still the job of the local operating systems to provide and manage local file transfer, protocols, and service, mail (message passing capability in local host), local resource allocation and management, memory management, process management, I/O management, etc. The problem with this approach is that the NOS must "force fit" over the local environment and be cognizant of and provide access and transparency to many varied local services and resources.

This type of approach has been used in early systems designs such as in ARPANET. In this type of system, users must request use of the network operating system resources and be cognizant of some level of commands to utilize the NOS capability.

The capabilities provided by a NOS include:

User access to various network resources which includes the network and any new network resource such as a Distributed Data Base Management System.

Controlling of the access to these components which include proper access authorization, management of links, error detection/correction, etc.

Network transparency. This service is not as thorough as that which would be seen from a distributed operating system, but allows users to be removed from the requirement to know all about the network and hosts that it is requesting service from.

This same capability is utilized to make remote resources appear local in terms of usage requirements to the requestor.

A NOS must also supply the capability to uniformly apply and implement accounting procedures to assess cost for use of the network resources. It must also supply to users consistent and up-to-date information on the network configuration and user-required documentation. The most important and significant capability supplied by a NOS is that it supplies a more reliable (from an overall system view) service to the entire collection of users.

Low-Level Primitives

In order to provide these capabilities, a NOS must possess certain low-level primitives that provide the capabilities to initiate and control the movement of programs and data between the network hosts. Many researchers have referred to the low-level mechanisms as migration primitives. Four major categories of primitives have been defined: user communications primitives, job migration primitives, data migration primitives, and system control primitives. These represent the major components or agents that a NOS must provide to realize the requisite network capabilities.

USER COMMUNICATIONS PRIMITIVES

User communications primitives refer to capabilities that allow user applications to utilize the information known by the system for their own uses. Services supplied by this class of primitives include the capability of users to converse with other users they are cognizant of. This is commonly referred to as a mail facility. An example of this would be given two user processes, process A and process B. Process A wishes to converse with process B. It initiates this by calling the mail service, calls up B who, if available, may also respond back through the mail/phone service. A then begins his message and signs off once B has indicated that all is well. This is the interactive mode. Another class of mail would be where A forms a message, then addresses it to B and signs off mail. B gets a flag saying it has mail and when it has time, it may go out to get it, read it, and act on it if process B deems it important. This mail could be in the form of process data, conversation between people, program transfers, or any other imaginable form.

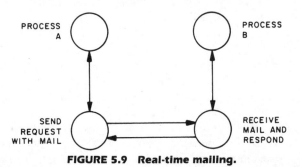

FIGURE 5.9 Real-time mailing.

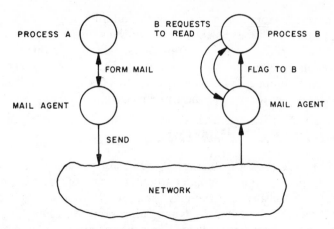

FIGURE 5.10   Delayed mail service.

The user under the communications primitive may be required to converse with the system (NOS software modules) to get information on specific system components. This is classified as a user-to-system primitive. An example of this class of service would best be described by a user forming a request (query) for information available in the global data base. A user would form a query, then invoke (call) the distributed data base manager agent to process the query and provide the user with the requisite data.

Another class of usage would be system to user. This class of communications primitive would be used in situations where the user process requires certain information when it is available. An example would be event data derived from some action causing an interrupt to some point in the system. If the system-to-user primitive is activated, this event will force an exception or call which will send the proper information to the user's process. Procedure 5.1 represents an ADA piece of code which could represent such an activity.

```
PROCEDURE SYSTEM-USER COMM-PRIMITIVE
  MONITOR
  IF TEST-POINT IS TRUE THEN 1
    ELSE 2
  SWITCH
  CASE i OF
    1:   CALL PROCESS X, ENTRY POINT
    2:   CALL PROCESS Y, ENTRY POINT
END
```

Procedure 5.1   ADA event call example.

This class of service is very important in a NOS environment in which all monitoring of Global activity must be done by user (application) level code. It is not embedded in the operating system kernel. This is so because the entire NOS is constructed on top of the local operating system as a set of application procedures.

The final class of user communications primitives can be classified as status testing. This class of service would be used by applications procedures to perform a health check of hosts and network resources which are required by it to perform its tasks. This level of support could be as simple as status indicating the network is able to provide specific information about loading of hosts/network links and status of hardware, and are available.

JOB MIGRATION PRIMITIVES

The next major class of NOS primitives in our discussion are called job migration primitives. Job migration primitives are the mechanisms that provide the capability for users and NOS to move jobs (collections of user application code) from one physical piece of hardware to another. One may ask why we wish to do this? The answer is that to utilize the increased capability in the distributed computer architecture we would want to be able to place pieces of a job (problem) where they can be done most efficiently. An example would be that given that we have the problem of manipulating some large matrices in order to derive some wanted subsolution of a larger problem, we would like to do this task on a piece of hardware more adept at it, such as a vector processor like a CRAY-1, for example.

Another reason for wanting to move a job or a piece of a job from one machine to another is for load balancing. That is, we wish to fully utilize all processing engines to the same level. We do not wish to saturate any one device causing waiting queues on its processing tables. So we ship out jobs or pieces of jobs to more fully utilize other less loaded devices and to more evenly spread out the overall processing loads in the network. The feature of languages that support this class of service is the ability to fork (split up tasks) and join (reunite the results) at some later time, thereby allowing for parallel execution of a job that can use this feature. The NOS primitive must be capable of recognizing this type of request, be able to assess how to split it up through use of communication services that supply loading information and utilizing data transfer capability to transfer programs and data to the local operating systems to load the new tasks and initiate their processing.

THE DATA MIGRATION PRIMITIVE

Another required NOS primitive is the data migration primitive. This service is required in order to allow the transfer of programs and data over the network in an efficient and reliable manner. This piece of code would be added on top of the low-level network protocols to manage the reliable transfer of data from one node to another in the network.

The function that this level of NOS must provide includes the support of transmission of data using the network protocols, transformation of local host formats to remote formats and vice versa, and error detection and correction of the transmitted information. This is the workhorse component of the network. All others rely on this service to work properly in order for the remainder of the system to function.

THE CONTROL PRIMITIVE

The final class of NOS primitive is the control primitive. This set of mechanisms are supplied to provide control and unification of the entire network into a singularly viewed entity. Functions that are supplied by this primitive set include enforcing of subnetwork control. This may indicate that the network has a communications manager who enforces the rules of protocol for efficiency, while fairly and reliably using the network communications and data transfer primitives. It also must control how and who can access and be allocated use of the communications resources. Finally, it must provide the capability to control the interaction between the network and its hosts. That is, it must maintain cognizance of the network's configuration and status and control the reconfiguration and reinitialization of the network, if failures occur.

More details of these functions will be covered in the following section on distributed operating systems and in discussion of particular systems developed.

Distributed Operating Systems

A distributed operating system (DOS), as previously described, is an operating environment for a distributed computer system developed from scratch. That is, all components from the local computers to the network level are developed together and have consistent or unified interfaces.

The motivation to develop a distributed operating system is the same as for the NOS architecture, but to a "higher," more sophisticated degree. The problems of having to force-fit structures and mechanisms is not as prevalent due to better control of the entire specification, design, and implementation. The DOS is typically a cleaner (more consistent, flowing) and more user-friendly environment. Again, this is due to not having to force-fit the network and local components together. Important aspects of this structure are that the operating system is spread over N hosts evenly. There is no central control or data and based on these features, there is no practical limit on the extensibility of such an environment. In reality, there are limits, as we will see in upcoming examples. A DOS has all the functions of a NOS/LOS combination, but extends these to a fuller context.

Generally, a DOS is expected to provide capabilities such as:

Interprocess communications protocols
Resource monitoring and allocation
Job/process scheduling

Command language
Error detection/recovery
Deadlock detection
Local memory management
I/O management
Intercomponent translations
Access control and authentication
Debugging tools
Performance modeling
Partitioning and assignment
Synchronization primitives
Exception handling
Distributed file/data system

These capabilities represent the core functions that must be implemented for a DOS to operate.

Distributed Operating Systems, being postulated and/or built, have embraced one of two model types: either the process model or the object model. The difference is basically in the view of how the previous capabilities become available to system user processes for service. In the process model, all resources, e.g., file, disk, peripheral, network, etc., are managed by a specific service process. This process is requested to perform a specific service based on system state. The key to correct operation of this model is the notion of interprocess communications. Process-to-process communications is used to synchronize and control all activities in the system, processes spawn other processes and synchronize with each other via messages. An example would be that to synchronize the producer/consumer relationship we would use a message passed between them to perform a semaphore mutual exclusion operation. This would operate by having the producer produce into some data base, then tell the consumer to go. The consumer would consume from the data base then notify the producer that the location is free and this could continue ad infinitum. A language well suited to this type of operation is ADA. With its separate notion of tasks and rendezvous DOS can be built easily.

The other model is the object model. This model views the world as being comprised of "objects." Objects consist of type, representation, and a set of operations that can be performed on them. Objects can be passive (data) or active (processes). In order to do any operation applicable in the system, e.g., read/write to a file, a user process must either possess or acquire a capability for the object. Capabilities are the controlling and synchronizing entities in this style of DOS. Capabilities exist for each process in a network and can be replicated by the "owner" of the capability. A capability can be best viewed as permission to use an object. From this one can see that the basic function of this class of operating system is to manage the distribution and use of these capabilities. To better describe this method of DOS control an example is presented in the following section. Also included is a discussion of a network operating system and two DOS of the process method.

EXAMPLE NOS DDLCN (DISTRIBUTED DOUBLE LOOP COMPUTER NETWORK)

The DDLCN NOS is build on top of the present LSI 11/23 operating system. It was developed to provide system-transparent operation to users, maintain cooperative autonomy among local computer systems, provide a reliable and robust system operation in the face of failures, and to provide an extensible and configurable environment in order to allow for resource sharing and distributed computing.

The NOS developed for DDLCN has been named MIKE [374] (Multi-computer Integrator Kernel). MIKE is comprised of a set of replicated kernels each residing in the loop interface units of DDLCN (Figure 5.11).

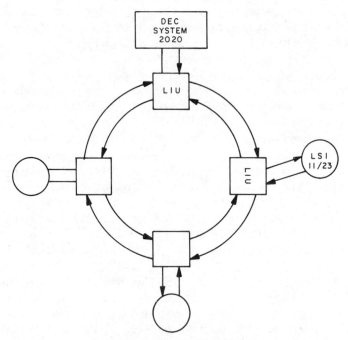

FIGURE 5.11   DDLCN architecture.

MIKE is comprised of three layers of software: the inter process communications layer, the system support layer, and the virtual machine layer. Each layer is devised to provide specific functions (Figure 5.12).

Virtual Machine Layer	High level application-oriented services. Basic NOS service
System Support Layer	Task templates Basic Ops Guaranteed session protocol Reliable session protocol Unreliable session protocol
IPC Layer	Guaranteed multi-destination protocol Reliable multi-destination protocol Unreliable multi-destination protocol

FIGURE 5.12   MIKE software layers.

The IPC layer provides software to allow guardians (the NOS (MIKE) Network Interface components) to provide either not guaranteed, guaranteed within limits and totally guaranteed message transmission. The next layer is the system support layer. This supplies the interaction sublayer (session control) and the abstraction sublayer dealing with reliability and extensibility. The final layer is the virtual machine layer where distributed data base management, resource sharing tasks, etc., are available.

TSAY [374] developed a "task" concept which enabled the object model to include LOS and MIKE regardless of internal structures. MIKE consists of a set of entities which are typed and managed. These entities can be broken down into two types: active called processes and passive called objects. The lowest entity that NOS recognizes is the task. A task consists of one or more processes and possibly some objects. Each task has one process called the guardian whose job it is to enforce local policies including naming, protection, synchronization, exception handling, accounting, etc. Tasks in MIKE are one of three classes: type, service, or operating system tasks.

Type tasks define a guardian and passive object types such as files. Service tasks are those tasks which provide network-oriented service such as the virtual resource service task which provides transparent use to network resources. The last class of task is the operating system task. This is the local operating system components with its user processes. Operating systems tasks are treated by the rest of the system as producers and consumers of resources.

Due to the NOS structure, synchronization and control information flows either by message for intertask communications and either via procedure invocation or messages for intratask communication.

Guardian names are the only names known network-wide and these are the points of all network message initiation and termination. Protection of resources in MIKE is done by tickets which is the capability to access a resource. You must possess this in order to be allowed access [374].

Synchronization in MIKE is accomplished by a combination of abstract data types (type task), message passing, and a synchronization template.

By having a guardian concept with the type task we have a protected re-source environment. The synchronization template is a specification of the re-source, synchronization variables, conditions, operations, and priority. The synchronization variables provide the structure for synchronization queues and are used in specification for operations and priority ⌊374⌋. More details of this NOS (MIKE) can be found in [374].

DOS EXAMPLES: OBJECT MODEL

SODS/OS [386] is a distributed operating system developed by W. D. Sin-coskie in his Ph.D dissertation. It is developed on a network of series 1 16-bit minicomputers developed by IBM GTD. In SODS there are two basic entities in the system: active entities (processes) and passive entities (data). As in the previous discussion of the object model SODS has objects. In SODS there are four basic object types, namely processes, exchanges, messages, and capabili-ties. In SODS processes are the active and executable entities and are com-prised of two parts, code and "context". Code is the instructions executable by the processor; context is a separate memory area from the code and is the place where the capabilities task resides. In SODS processes cannot manipu-late their contexts except via system calls allowable only when a capability ex-ists to get to it. All processes in SODS communicate via areas called "exchanges." Exchanges are separate I/O queues for processes to get at mes-sages. In order to utilize an exchange, a process must possess the capability on that exchange and in the proper state. Processes communicate between each other utilizing exchanges and via messages. Messages represent data sent to exchanges by processes and represent one of four classes: data, exception, in-terrupt, control.

Data messages convey user program information from point to point. Ex-ception messages are triggered by errors and represent vectors to processes to handle exception conditions. Interrupt messages are means to prioritize ex-change queues and jump messages to the front of queues for next service. The final message type tells process what to do such as resume, suspend, kill and start a process. The controlling mechanism in SODS is the capability. A capa-bility is required in order for a process to get data from or put into an ex-change. Capabilities contain the following: an exchange name and a set of permissions for operations allowed on both the exchange and capability.

Processes running under SODS have five system call categories available to them:

Privileged
> Read, write, get parm, set parm. These are used only for access to spe-cific I/O devices and are process dependent.

Process Oriented
> CR Proc. Allows a process to be created. This is a child process and the parent gets control of a capability to it.

Exit. All children of a parent are killed and death certificates are sent to all capabilities on this object indicating its state.

Exchange
CR Exch. — Creates a new exchange and gives capability to created process.
Flush — Empty exchange.
Note: When capabilities disappear exchanges also disappear.

Capability
DLCAP — Delete capability
SWDCAP — Duplicate capability at some other node.
GETCAP — Add capability - to capability table when one is sent to you.

Messages
TRAP — Set vector address for exception control and interrupt messages.
RCVMSG — Tells system to dequeue message and send to calling process (caller will block if no message there)
SWOMSG — This will send a message to the exchange with control variables dealing with time allowed to complete operation, class, type, location, and size of data.

Processes run in the capability environment; that is, they may communicate to processes they have capability with. When they need outside direction, they acquire a capability to converse with the outside exchange, communicate and then relinquish the capability if no longer required. In this case the exchange acts like a semaphore—use of it allows processes to not have to know the name of other processes. It allows the role rather than the process to be specified.

To converse, each process must have capabilities to two common exchanges. The initiator can send the capability to its exchange to the intended parties and vice versa. Process management is done via use of creating processes and capabilities and management of them thereafter. This system represents a novel approach to implementation of the object model.

Another example of a DOS is Chorus [387]. Chorus is an example of the process oriented model of DOS design. Chorus was built as an architecture for distributed systems as part of the French industry—government university-wide project in the area of distributed processing technology.

In Chorus, the system operational state is comprised of active entities (processes) called Actors. These Actors can create or destroy other Actors. These Actors communicate with each other through ports with messages to other Actors. See Figure 5.13. On each site in Chorus the DOS provides distributed service and a local kernel operating system, as in Figure 5.13, to application Actors for use in performing their applications.

In Chorus Actors (processes) execution occurs sequentially and is controlled via message passing. Actors are additionally broken down into separate

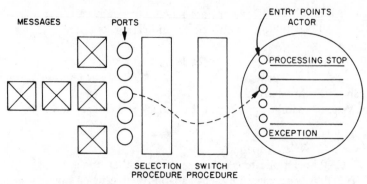

FIGURE 5.13   Activation of an actor's processing steps.

sequential sections called processing steps (on the idea of a task in ADA). Each of these processing steps can be viewed as a separate action stimulated via message input. The processing of a message, done sequentially for each Actor, is called a processing step and is triggered by the reception of a message. The processing step in an Actor is activated via a message entry which points to an entry point in the Actors list of known tasks. This feature is similar to possessing a collection of rendezvous accept statements in ADA with code segments (tasks) attached with them and embedded in a select statement as shown below:

```
SELECT
   WHEN CONDITION 1 = TRUE
      ACCEPT MESSAGE
         PROCESS STEP 1
      END
   .
   .
   .
   OR
   WHEN CONDITION N = TRUE
      ACCEPT MESSAGE
   END PROCESS STEP N
END SELECT
```

ADA example of process step activation.

Selection of the proper entry point in Chorus is handled by a selection procedure which selects which port is active and a switch procedure which determines which entry point to select based on the input stream and the Actor's supplied parameters (Figure 5.13). These two procedures run in the site's local kernels.

Another novel feature of Chorus is its built-in exception handling for message errors, etc. This feature handles problems of lost, timed out or erroneous messages automatically. This is similar to ADA's capability for exception handling. One could append to each Actors list of entry points an exception handling point which could be constructed to handle errors for the Actor.

```
PROCEDURE ACTOR X
    SELECT EPOINT
        WHEN ENTRY POINTS
                    .
        OR    .
                    .
    OR WHEN OTHER
        EXCEPTION
            WHEN CONDITION              > Exception handling list
            FIRST HANDLER               >
    END
```

ADA exception handling example.

Actors only communicate via messages and through "ports" even with Actors on the same site in Chorus. Actors can consume or produce messages with other Actors and ports allow them to send or receive these messages (Figure 5.14).

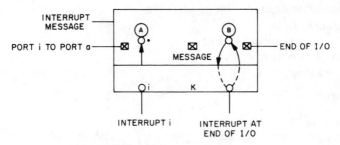

FIGURE 5.14   Interrupts In chorus.

Actors need not know of other Actors' sites but only need know that a port exists to some they wish to converse with. Ports are created with Actors when they are born and stay with the Actor if it migrates to another site. Ports require creation and opening before they can be utilized by an Actor and upon failure will be physically reassigned to where the failed Actor is revived.

Interrupts and I/O devices are viewed in Chorus also as ports. Interrupts are handled by special ports and are usually directed to the kernel for faster service. I/O is handled by kernels on devices but still utilize ports (Figure 5.15).

Chorus has two levels of DOS services. They are the system Actors and the kernel Actors.

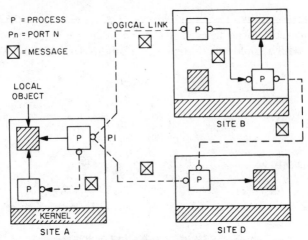

FIGURE 5.15 Message communications in chorus.

System Actors include:

Creation/destruction of Actors
Creation/destruction/opening/closing of ports
Distant communication
Creation/destruction of objects (data sets)
Management of links to objects
Memory management
Management of port names
File management

Kernel Actors include:

Selection of message port to processes
Switching to corresponding entry points (like task switch)
Management of time outs
Local transport of messages
Partial management of interrupts
Partial realization of I/O

The most striking aspect of the Chorus DOS is that it totally utilizes message passing for aspects of the system operations. The interested reader is directed to [387] for additional details of this unique design.

NOS—PROCESS MODEL EXAMPLE

NOS [95], [96] is a distributed operating system developed for use in high-speed, time critical, real-time process control systems. NOS software resides in distributed elements of a local network consisting of one or more DSDB (see Chapter 4). NOS software supplies service in support of sharing of network resources and manages the operation of concurrent application processes.

The primary functional components of NOS include:

Communications component
NOS initial process loading component
Device support component
Configuration management component
Data base management component
Operator interface component
Process synchronization component
Performance monitoring component
Fault localization component
Debug component

Processes in NOS communicate using the process model of DOS design. That is, all communication between processes, whether in the same device or otherwise, are accomplished via message passing. NOS has the ability to continually add or extract processes with no effect, other than loading, on operational processes. New processes in NOS log on to the network, are provided a unique identifier, and can now begin to link up to logical processes that they are cognizant of. This linkup is accomplished by the use of ports. As in Chorus NOS must create ports at the request of a process, and link this port to the other processes, ports being requested. Processes need not know where other processes are as NOS will find them utilizing a search algorithm, and then connect the ports together utilizing a virtual circuit mechanism.

PROCESS TO NETWORK INTERFACE

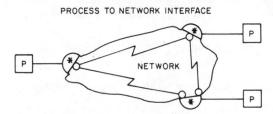

FIGURE 5.16 Logical NOS connections.

As an example of the port linkage, the following example is defined. Process A wishes to output data concurrently from two buffers to three processes, B, C, and D. In order to do this process A must create ports 1 and 2 with virtual links pointed to process B and (C and D), as in Figure 5.17. Processes B, C and D will create port/virtual link combinations identically complementary (input) for process A.

As a result of the above creation of ports and links, the network will establish connections between process A and process B, process A and process C, and process A and process D.

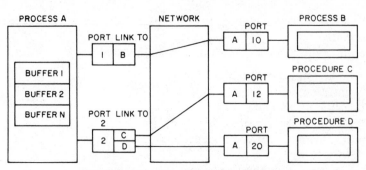

FIGURE 5.17   Port linkage in chorus.

The command available for processes in the network include:

Create port—defines port identifier, port type, operation (I/O), number of connections allowed, queue access.

Create link—causes the creation of a connection from source port to sink port(s).

Connect—connects the links into a virtual circuit or check if it is still active.

Perform operation—initiate a predefined set of operations in the network.

Query—allows processes to extract information on an active network command.

Null—processes issue this to simulate an internal timer.

PM report—send PM report to log information with PM control hierarchy.

Disconnect—drop a link but continue to hold virtual link.

Eliminate link—drop logical association between given source and sink ports.

Eliminate port—drop specified port.

Delete queue.

NOS supplies some additional hidden services to user processes as partially shown below:

Basic communications service—this function provides the store and forward nature of message communications. This is the logical/physical interface and provides the capability to, based on loading, determine the ability of a message to be handled (guarantee communications) by the network in its time period.

Process server—this function allows processes to interface with the network. It processes and cooperates with other process servers in performing the aforementioned process/network commands.

Local process locator—this is the function which searches for and locates processes on its bus interface unit or local bus.

Network route finder—the function of this process is to set up routes in the network.

NOS initial program load allows for predefined loading of processes into processors to quickly bring up the entire network into a known state.

Other major components include the network communications manager (NCM). In NOS the NCM provides system level communications resource management in support of the system availability manager and the basic communications servicer. Processing provided by NCM will perform network communications feasibility analysis (can the link support this extra load), bridge/bus failure impact assessment (what is affected by this failure), bus interface unit (communications wise) bridge (bus to bus link) reset control, and bus/biu switching control (reliability reconfiguration).

System Availability Manager (SAM) is another piece of NOS code. This piece of software is responsible for controlling the assignment of hardware resources to software processes. Throughout the period of use, the real-time systems set of available hardware will vary due to hardware failures, routine servicing and repairs. Also, as the requisite processing job changes, so will the underlying base of processes. SAM's responsibility is to maintain the desired functional capabilities in the face of changing environmental conditions.

In concert with SAM is the Configuration Manager (CM). This function controls the loading and removal of processes as requested by SAM. This process distributes the load/kill type commands to the responsible local operating system kernels to actually acquire the data and perform the task. Each device in the NOS environment has device support components which provide the interface between the device and the process-oriented NOS world.

The next major component is the data base management component. This function responds to requests for data base information and provides service to processes the query or update the underlying information base.

NOS, in this environment, also provides mechanisms to monitor system functionality, detect abnormalities, and determine affected components (hardware/software) and recommend and take action dependent on criticality of condition.

As in the Chorus system, NOS leaves process synchronization up to the individual process. The message passing capability provided by NOS allows individual cooperating processes to synchronize their activity using messages like semaphores.

Another critical issue in the overall system implementation is the notion of deadline scheduling of processes. All messages in the NOS environment have hard deadlines for completion which must be met in order to provide the real-time response to real-world occurrences. Messages, as in Chorus, are used to start, stop, and interrupt processes thereby providing responsive control of processes in the network.

Summary

This chapter introduced some basic concepts from traditional operating systems theory. Introduced were the ideas of synchronization using semaphores, deadlock detection, process management, and memory management.

Also covered were the concepts required in developing network operating systems and distributed operating systems.

The chapter concluded with examples of the major classes of operating systems discussed.

CHAPTER SIX

Data Base Management Systems

The information explosion is upon us. With every passing day organizations add volumes of new data to present data base systems. This is due to organizations' continually increased reliance on data base information for aiding in the decision-making process and in handling all levels of business, social, academic, and governmental information. Data bases also supply many benefits to organizations that utilize them. In particular, they support the reduction of redundantly stored and managed data, avoidance of inconsistencies (mismatched or contradictory data items), sharing of data, standards for data specification and change, security of data, integrity (accuracy) of the data, and conflicting requirements to some extent can be balanced.

Clearly, computers play an exceedingly important role in the storage, manipulation, retrieval, and security of data and as such have spawned a specialized area of computer technology called data base management. This new area has grown by leaps and bounds since the early days of file systems to the present mode of distributed data base management systems. One might ask what is a data base management system? In its basic structure it is merely an automated method for information management, a means to free people from the tedious and inaccurate methods of paper files and cabinet storage and retrieval. An automated data base management system consists of four major components or entities: namely, hardware, software, data, and users. The hardware is the collection of processing devices, I/O devices, storage hierarchies (Chapter 2), and communication devices that support the automation (Figure 6.1). The software represents a collection of routines (algorithms) to provide control of the underlying hardware and shield users from its dependencies. At the same time, this software component supplies easier methods by which to use the stored information and manage it effectively. Data is the usable information of an organization stored in the data base system and is controlled by the underlying hardware and software. Users are the final component and come in three basic varieties: applications programmers who access data via data manipulation language mechanisms embeddable in applications code, end users who use the data base management system directly from an interactive source, and finally the data base administrators, who manage and adjust the collection of hardware, software and data in support of the end users. The collection of the above represents a somewhat simplistic view of what comprises a data base management system.

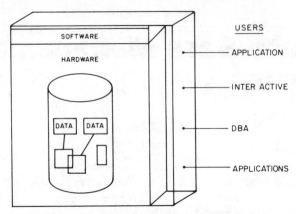

FIGURE 6.1   Logical view of DBMS.

The major area of interest in a data base management system is the software mechanisms which are designed to control the hardware interface to the users. This software is comprised of mechanisms to provide users the ability to define their data structure (data definition languages within the structure of data models, in particular the relational, hierarchical, network, and entity relationship models), to access their data (data manipulation languages such as SQL, QBE, QUEL, SDMS, forms, ICON, etc.), for data currency (accuracy of the information content), data consistency, update synchronization, security, reliability, availability, recovery, and invisibility of structure/storage (I need not know where or how my data is stored).

Architecture

The logical architecture of a data base management system has three principal levels: the internal, conceptual, and external (Figure 6.2).

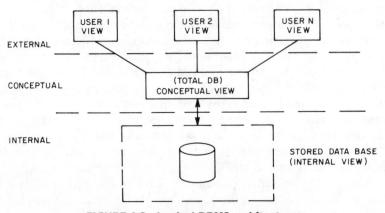

FIGURE 6.2   Logical DBMS architecture.

THE EXTERNAL LEVEL

The external level represents the user's view of the data. Each individual user will usually be interested in only a subset of the entire (conceptual) data base and therefore his view is a subset of the entire data base. Also this subset view may not necessarily represent a one-to-one correspondence to the items in the conceptual data base. They may be grouped and utilized in a different manner than that of the conceptual data base (Figure 6.3).

Conceptual View	User's Views
Employee	Manager might have view of
Employee number	where he wants to see project
Employee name	name, job type requirements,
Job skill	parts requirements and
Salary	supplies of these parts,
	status.
Part	
Part number	His view spans portions of
Part name	all these "base" relations on
Part description	the left.
Quantity on hand	
Quantity on order	
Supplier	
Supplier number	
Supplier name	
Location	
Part(s) supplied	
Project	
Project number	
Project name	
Project description	
Job type	
requirements	
Status	

FIGURE 6.3   Part(s) supplier, project, employee relationships.

CONCEPTUAL

The conceptual data base level is a view which is comprised of the aggregation of all user views. This view represents the entire information content of the data base. This data is in a form which is still logical and is abstract in relation to how the data may be physically stored. The conceptual data base can best be viewed as the interface to the distinct user views and the internal system representation of the data. This level in the hierarchy is also required to perform authorization and validation checking on requests because it has cognizance of all occurrences of a piece of information. In order to define the conceptual level in a DBM, tools exist which allow a data base administrator to construct the conceptual view (schema). These tools are referred to as data definition languages and are based on the underlying DBM logical structure (relational, heirarchical, network, and entity relationship).

INTERNAL

The internal level is the closest logical entity to the physically stored data. The internal view is comprised of internal records (ANSI/sparc term). This internal view is still once removed from the actual physical records or blocks as seen on a device. This level of the data base interfaces to the access methods (ISAM, VSAM, DSAM, etc.) of the devices leaving the actual physical interface to devices up to this access method. The internal level supplies to the DBMS a stored record view of the physical data; i.e., a collection of stored files. Through this mechanism, user operations, via a logical view, access physical data which they need not know anything about.

Below the internal level exists the access method for delivering the capability of requesting data for read/write access. The physical access method is the lowest level of software and is considered more a part of the Operating System for a computer than part of the DBMS. The access supplies the logical to physical mapping and performs the actual reads and writes from or to the physical devices (tapes, disks, etc.); see Figure 6.4.

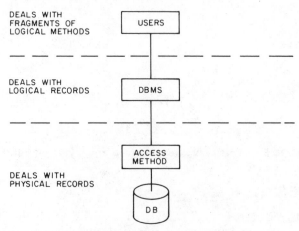

FIGURE 6.4   Access method role in DBMS hierarchy.

Physical Data Structure

The problem to be addressed is how to structure the underlying storage to service the internal level's view of the data base "records." First, we must define the problem by specifying that the storage medium is most likely to be disk storage. Using this device we can think about its structure as the basis for discussions. A file system using a disk usually will be comprised of N equal-sized "physical blocks." Each one of these blocks can be uniquely defined and has an absolute location on the device with identifier information in the header of its structure. Our logical data structure will be stored on this device as a collection of physical records which are subunits of a block.

DIRECT

Now that we have this definition of storage how does one map this level to logical structures? The most obvious method for file storage is to sequentially store the records in as much space as required. This method is easy, but it may waste space if one of the records has many similar entries. The direct method forces onto the access method interface to provide a mechanism to determine physical storage location from the logical key supplied. In systems that use an index method or hashing method of storage, the physical device in hardware provides this service, thereby simplifying the access mechanism. By utilizing other structures, you can maximize the available space.

Other methods for accessing files on secondary devices use the notion of a "key." A key is an identifier that uniquely defines the class of entities in a record or file. This implies that the key can be used as the pointer to the start of a record of similar items. Using this idea of key, we can discuss ways of using it to access items in a data base.

HASHING

Through using a hash function we could distribute the records of the data base by hashing on the key values. The location on the device is immediately available by computing the hash function for a given key. The advantage of the hashing method is that access is fast. A disadvantage of hashing is that it may waste space and could cause collisions (calculation of the same physical address). This would require a method to compress the memory utilized to not waste space and for the second some technique to find free space beyond the collision area is necessary. The problem is that this complicates retrieval and degrades the overall performance of the hash technique.

INDEXING

Indexing techniques are probably the most widely used method for organizing records in secondary storage. Many methods exist for structuring the indexes to provide a variety of logical interface structures while allowing for efficient use of the underlying storage medium.

One method for secondary device indexing based on keys is the idea of utilizing the first track of the disk unit to store the indexes for the logical key values. The disk unit looks up the key on the track, then acquires the actual physical address for the logical record from the next location after the key. (See Figure 6.5)

TRACK Ø START

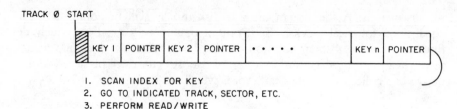

I. SCAN INDEX FOR KEY
2. GO TO INDICATED TRACK, SECTOR, ETC.
3. PERFORM READ/WRITE

FIGURE 6.5

The problem with the above method is that if the number of keys gets large, the sequential search through the keys will cause a degradation in performance. A solution is to go back to your analysis of algorithm texts and discover some marvelous data structures to aid in searching. The structure most used in searching algorithms is found to be the B-tree. B-trees (binary-trees) are structures comprised of nodes of such type that each son of a node is distinguished as either a right son or a left son and that this node has no more than one left and one right son. (See Figure 6.6.)

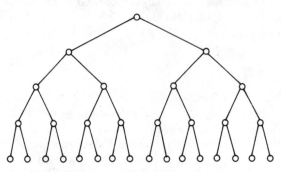

FIGURE 6.6 Example of binary tree.

A key notion from analysis of algorithms is that to find any item in a binary tree will take at most 0 (logn) comparisons. That is if the height (depth) of the tree is 3 then at most 3 comparisons ($\log_2 15$) must be done to find the item.

Many storage access methods utilize this basic notion of binary trees and binary searching to construct a wide range of access strategies. B-trees access is fast and since the records are stored in sorted order based on keys they can be accessed in order. The problem is that blocks tend not to be solidly packed due to tree structure. For further details on B-trees and other storage techniques, the interested reader is directed to [389], [381], [281].

Data Models/Structures

In order to construct data base management systems, there must exist a way upon which to visualize the information content. This way or method is the data model. A data model is a method of viewing data and structuring it for the data management system and users. The best known data models in use today are:

The entity-relationship
The hierarchical
The network
The relational

The following four sections will discuss each of these models, providing a brief introduction and comparison of them using the same example for clarification of issues.

ENTITY-RELATIONSHIP MODEL

The Entity-Relationship model (E-R) is comprised of entities and relationships and operations that can be defined and performed on them. An entity is a "thing" [399] which can be distinctly identified. An entity could be a company, an employee, or a truck, for example. A relationship, on the other hand, is defined as an association among entities. An example from the above three entities could be company-employee or product-employee, or company-product. In the entity relationship model these two descriptions are functionally represented by a rectangle and a diamond respectively. The previous example could be shown as in Figure 6.7.

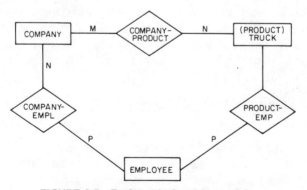

FIGURE 6.7   Entity relationship model.

The values N, M, P represent the type of mappings namely 1:M one to M (M being 0, 1, 2,.....), 1:N (N being 0, 1, 2, ...) M:N, M:1, N:1, etc.

Beyond the basic structure shown above the entity relationship models additionally possess, for each entity, attributes and value sets which describe the lower conceptual domain of the E-R model of an enterprise. (See Figure 6.8.)

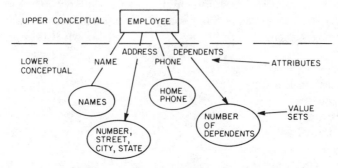

FIGURE 6.8   Example attribute definition.

Attributes are the mapping method between a value set and the entity. The value set represents a group of values of the same type. As an example, refer to Figure 6.7. Address is an attribute which maps entities from the entity set employee with values provided in the value set NO-ST-CITY-STATE.

The E-R model represents value sets as circles and the attributes for them as arrows directed toward the mapped value set.

The value sets can be single items or collections of like items. Example: A collection of phone numbers for students in a class entity as part of a school's information of classes. The entity-relationship model is relatively new and at present no constructed data base that closely follows this model is known to this author.

A similar data model called the entity function model was described in [390]. This model encompasses the notion of an entity as being the same as previously defined and instead of a relationship indicator it possesses the notion of function. The function when applied on an entity returns a property associated to it. The underlying structure is similar to that of the entity-relationship model with the function replacing the relationship. The more interested reader is directed again to [390].

THE HIERARCHICAL MODEL

The hierarchical data model is very easy to conceptualize. It is comprised of hierarchies of records with the characteristic that each record type can have several "children" record types, but each child can have only one "parent" record type. Using the previous example of Figure 6.6, the hierarchical version of this structure could be shown as that in Figure 6.9.

The hierarchical data model most closely mimics real world organizations that exhibit naturally the structure of a hierarchy. Organizations are always depicted as tree structures with one or more upper-level roots, each root having its underlying tree.

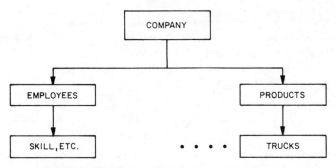

FIGURE 6.9 Hierarchical data model structure.

Many presently implemented data base systems are based on the hierarchical model. IMS is one such system. IMS is an IBM DBMS product. IMS structures data in a hierarchical fashion as described previously. Much more detail of this model and its internal structure can be found in [60], [281].

THE NETWORK DATA MODEL

The network data model is basically a generalized and more liberal version of the hierarchical data base structure. It allows a given record to possess any number of immediate superiors and any number of immediate subordinates. This flexibility allows for easier modeling and representation of many relationships, whereas with the hierarchical model such a capacity would be cumbersome to support.

The previous example used can be shown in the network model as seen below in Figure 6.10.

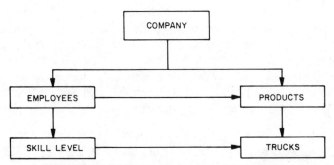

FIGURE 6.10 Network data model structure.

In the example it can be seen that the network model will allow the modeling of relationships between items not supportable clearly in the hierarchical model. In particular, notice the ability to relate the subordinate products to both company and employees and specific products to specific skills, etc. This structure allows for a more natural interrelation between entities to be modeled and supported in the data management system. More details of the network model can be found in [60], as well as Coverage of the Hierarchical, Network and Relational System's Architectures. Interested readers are directed to this text for more specifics in these areas.

THE RELATIONAL MODEL

In the relational data model information is organized into tables called relations. These tables can be directly accessed by their table name (relation name) and consist of rows and columns. The rows in a relation are called "tuples." Tuples represent the unique occurrence of the items in the relational table. The columns are called "attributes" and represent the occurrence of some unified quality for all items in the column. An example relation is shown below in Figure 6.12.

The relational model has many advantages over the previously defined models. The relational model allows for the representation of data without superimposing additional structure for machine representation or interrelations. It allows for the changing of structure without drastically impairing the operations of already coded applications. This is not true in the network and hierarchical models where using the data base implies traversing the links and following the fixed paths. If a path changes or structure changes, the code must change. This is not as prevalent in the relational model.

The relational model utilizes the power of relational calculus operators to access and manipulate the relations. The basic operations allowed in relational systems are select, project, join, union, intersection, difference, product, and divide. Figure 6.11 represents the outcome for some of the above relational operations on relations.

Our previous example in Figure 6.10 can be shown in relational format as follows in Figure 6.12.

Using relational operations we can look at or combine these to have practically any view of the data we wish to have. Additions or changes require lengthening or widening tables and will not cause an impact on operational applications code utilizing the data base system. Many systems have been developed utilizing this data model, for example, the Ingress system developed at the University of California, Berkeley, and the IBM System R system. Additional information on these systems and others can be found in [60], [281].

Recovery, Integrity, and Security

The following section will cover the definitions and basic methods used in providing recovery, integrity, and security in centralized data bases. This is done to provide the reader with some background in these areas before we continue on into distributed data base management issues of the same nature.

TRANSACTIONS

In order to discuss the above concepts we first must determine what the basic unit of work is in a data base system. In a program it is a line of code be-

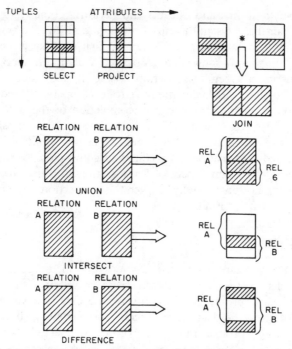

FIGURE 6.11   Example of some relational operations.

COMPANY

COMP #	C NAME	PRODUCT	LOC
C1	FORD	CARS	MICHIGAN
C2	G M	CARS	MICHIGAN
C3	TOYOTA	CARS	JAPAN
C4	PLYMOUTH	CARS	JAPAN
C5	DATSUN	CARS	JAPAN
C6	MAZDA	CARS	JAPAN

C NUMBER	C NAME	COMP #	PRICE
CR1	LTD	C1	10K
CR2	KCAR	C4	15K
CR3	TERCEL	C3	5K
CR4	B210	C5	7K
CR5	626	C6	12K

E #	E NAME	SALARY	COMPANY	SKILL
1016	GAMACHE	25K	TAYLORS	STICHER
1025	FORTIER	50K	JP TOOL & DIE	MACHINIST
2001	KIRK	75K	FEDERATION	CAPTAIN
2010	ROGERS	50K	DIRECTORAT	PILOT
0001	GOD	INFINITE	PEARLY GATE	MASTER

FIGURE 6.12   Relational tables example.

cause it has specific inputs and outputs and performs some function or unit of work. In a data base system a unit of work is defined as a transaction. A transaction is similar to a program subroutine. That is, it has a specific beginning and an ending with some state associated with it. In specific terms, a transaction consists of a begin transaction operation, and based on the internal operation and state, either a commit or rollback operation ends the transaction. Commit represents the successful completion of the unit of work (a read, write sequence, etc.), while rollback indicates an unsuccessful completion for the unit of work. The rollback could be caused by the inability to acquire some needed information or a failure in some piece of the data base system. The most important aspect of a transaction in a data base system is that it is an all or nothing activity. Either the transaction is completed successfully or it is not done at all.

INTEGRITY

What does integrity mean in terms of a data base? In the context of a data base integrity refers to the accuracy, correctness, or validity of the data under data base control and protection. Integrity from a data base viewpoint is the problem of protecting the data base contents from erroneous updates such as out of bounds inputs, programmer errors, or even deliberate sabotage.

The integrity checker component of a data base system can be viewed as a knowledge base system which utilizes a set of rules, to check the validity of a user's update based on the values of the rules. The rules can be broken down into a few basic categories. They are either bounds-checking type rules, such as seen in Figure 6.13, which look at an update to see if it is between some specified range of allowable values, or it could be structure-based rules that check the update to see if it adheres to the structure of the updateable entity, such as that seen in Figure 6.14.

```
TASK  RULE 1 IS RANGE OF PRODUCT NUMBER
         100 > P. PRODUCT NUMBER > 0
         ELSE;
                  EXCEPTION 1
                  RETURN "ERROR IN BOUNDS, VIOLATION"
              END
      END
```

FIGURE 6.13   Rule for bounds checking.

```
TASK  RULE N IS - STRUCTURE OF PRODUCT
         IF N ATTRIBUTE > N THEN EXCEPTION X
         ELSE IF N NUMBER OF TUPLES > N THE EXCEPTION X + 1
         ELSE FOR I = 1 N ATTRIB DO IF MISMATCH OF ATTRIB
                         (N) . TYPE WITH UPDATE THE EXCEPTION
                         X + 2, N
         END IF
```

FIGURE 6.14   Example rule for structure checking.

The rules in an integrity component are to be applied to update actions when they are presented to the data base. This could be either at compile time, if it is a compiled-based system like system R, or at run time. The level and impact of integrity rules will be driven by user requirements to guarantee integrity of the data in the data base. More details on integrity issues can be found in the references.

CONCURRENCY

Separate from the previous problem of verifying that a particular update is correct in terms of accuracy of bounds or structure, concurrency deals with the problem: Is this update correct in relation to all others. That is, if this update was executed in total isolation would it guarantee a correct update? Concurrency control deals with methods to guarantee that supplied transactions return correct results even when they are operating with other transactions. Figure 6.15 depicts two transactions and the problem of lost update due to no concurrency control.

Transaction 1		Transaction 2	
	—		—
	—		—
ReadA	Balance of checkbook 100	ReadA	=> 100
	—		—
	— processing withdraw 50		— Add 50
	—		
WriteA	=> 50 New balance	WriteA	=> New balance 150.00
	—		
	— Trans 1 Update lost here	This is invalid, it should be 100.00	
	—		

FIGURE 6.15 Lost update-trans 1 and 2 read the same value and therefore do not operate on the value the way they should.

Various concurrency control algorithms have been postulated, developed, and implemented. The major two mechanisms used in implementing systems are locking and time-stamp ordering. Locking refers to the acquisition of exclusive use of an item (record) until the transaction completes. This will guarantee that the update in transaction 1 is not lost, but is used by transaction 2 to perform its function on. Figure 6.16 is an example of locking and how it affects the above transaction of Figure 6.15

The acquisition of locks can be viewed as a semaphore operation performed on some level of a data base contents (this level is referred to as granularity of locks), and as such the acquisition of the lock can be executed via use of a test and set type instruction or some busy wait method as used in operating system designs. This implies that the data base system must maintain an area in memory to hold the locks and to be used by the DBM system to determine what holds what. Locking will force the serialization of updates (re-

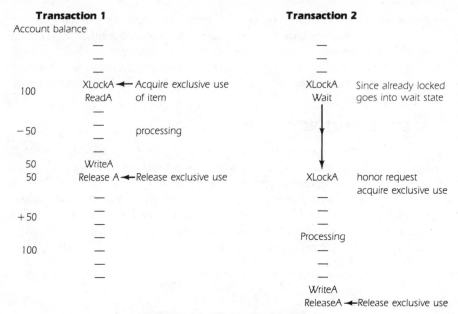

FIGURE 6.16   Example of locking.

ferred to a serializability) in a data base, thereby maintaining concurrency (correctness) of the updates.

Most implemented systems using locking have two levels of locking allowed, namely, read locks and write locks. Read locks will be acquired in order to allow more than one transaction to read an item, thereby allowing more transactions to complete and less to wait. Write locks are acquired only for items that require updating and will only be given when no read locks are pending. This allows for exclusive use of an item when writes are to be done, but does not restrict items if only reads are performed.

Another method of guaranteeing concurrency of transactions is time stamp ordering. Time stamp ordering refers to a method which enforces a specific serial execution of transactions based on transaction time stamp or sequence number. The time stamp order is derived from the actual chronological order of the transaction. In time stamp ordering the basic premise for conflict is the following: If transaction A wishes to read record R, it must check to see if a younger transaction B has already done so. If this is true, a conflict occurs and transaction A will be restarted. If transaction A wishes to update R it must check to see if some other, younger transaction has read or updated the record it wishes. If it is true then there is a conflict and transaction A will be restarted. If there is no younger transaction in conflict, transaction A will do its action and update the objects counter to indicate it is the youngest (most recent) entity now accessing this item. In order for this to work changes are only done at final commit time. All updates are deferred to the end of the transaction to guarantee that the transaction can be restarted, if conflicts arise without having perturbed the actual data. The ADA procedure (6.1) describes the operation of this basic time stamp ordering technique. Reference

```
PROCEDURE BTO (TIME NOW, TRANSACTION NUMBER)
  SELECT OP
    READ
    BEGIN
        IF TIME (TRANS #) > = MAX-UPDATE-TIME-ON OBJECT
        THEN "OK PERFORM THE OPERATION"
            READ-MAX-TIME-ON OBJECT: = MAX(TIME(TRANS),
            READ-MAX-TIME-ON OBJECT
        ELSE RESTART TRANSACTION # "CONFLICT"
    WRITE
    BEGIN
        IF TIME (TRANS #) > = READ-MAX-OBJECT- + AND,
        TIME (TRANS #) > = WRITE-MAX-OBJECT
                THEN "OK PERFORM OPERATION"
                WRITE-MAX-OBJECT = TIME (TRANS #)
        ELSE RESTART T "CONFLICT"
    END IF
  END SELECT
END PROCEDURE
```

Procedure 6.1   BTO ADA procedure.

[61] has more details of this and other concurrency control techniques.

SECURITY

Security in a data base system is meant to convey the idea of protection of the data base and its contents from unauthorized access, change, or destruction. In the context of the data base management system the security component's job is basically the job of determining if the person getting in is allowed to have access to this system or piece of the system. The job here is to identify and authenticate (to make sure it is who it is supposed to be) the individual attempting to access this information and determining if this person is allowed access to this data. Identification is done by the user through use of some user number or name and authentification is done by the user supplying some information to the system known only to the system and that user. Using this information and authorization rules (analogous to memory protection mechanism or integrity rules) the data base management software can check to see if this user has access authorization to this piece of data, thereby protecting the data from unauthorized manipulation.

RECOVERY

Recovery in a data base system is the mechanism by which the data base is returned to some known consistent state after some failure has corrupted the present state. This is accomplished in the following manner: When a failure occurs, depending on the severity, the recovery mechanism will use some known state (saved periodically to maintain recoverability) and the contents of a log file (record of all changes made to the data base since the last state save) to redo all the changes that were previously made since the last update. The above procedure would be required if the data base itself was damaged (by a head crash), or if there were some other problem that corrupted the data base then the log is used to undo all unreliable changes. The major method for recovery depicted here is redundancy (multiple copies). The redundancy exists at the state save level and update log level. These ensure the capability to recover a data base to its proper consistent state. The actual actions of redo and undo as well as the specifics of recovery are beyond the intended scope of this section. Interested readers are directed to [601] for a more detailed presentation in this area.

Distributed Data Bases

A distributed data base may best be described as a collection of local data base managers who interact together in providing a total picture of an enterprise's data across some distance connected together via a network (Chapter 4). But why do we want a distributed data base management system? The main reason is to provide data to end users in their most cost effective and efficient manner. A distributed data base allows organizations to make decisions based on total corporate knowledge available rather than just a specific local subset. It allows data to be located where it is used most, allows for sharing of resources (remote access), and allows for local control of local data where it is best understood. Additionally, distributed data bases supply additional capacity (storage and processing) while providing a means to grow more easily than a centralized system. Distributed data enhances the reliability of an organization's information base. If one site fails, the entire system need not be affected, only the failed site and others who rely on that piece of the data base for service. The distributed data base not only distributes the data base throughout the system, but also replicates (copies) portions of the data base. It enhances availability of the data for reading and even further enhances reliability by providing on-line copies for recovery from failures. Such benefits provide enhanced efficiency of use and flexibility to handle changes in usage patterns and requirements.

A distributed data base can provide many benefits to organizations who invest in them. The problem is that distributed data base management systems are still in research and much work must still be done in order to realize all the benefits previously described. The basic problem with distributed data base management systems is that they are distributed. In order to provide the goals of transaction atomicity (serializability) plus transparent access while providing good performance, it requires much additional work on the part of the distributed data base manager. Problems arising due to distributed data base systems include:

File placement
    Where and how to place files in a distributed architecture.
Query processing/optimization
    How to efficiently access the distributed data.

Update synchronization
How to maintain the copies of data distributed over many sites.
Concurrency control
How to guarantee the correct execution of transactions (serializability).
Commit protocols
How to guarantee that transactions at multiple sites all go one way or the other.
Directory management
How to store, manage, and use directories of the system data base.

FILE PLACEMENT

In order to provide data to user locations that require it, while trying to minimize the adverse affects on system operations, researchers have for many years been looking at methods to optimally place files in a distributed computer architecture. This is referred to as the file allocation problem. In distributed data base management systems files can be split up in two major fashions: either by geographical location or by function of the data. In a geographically split data base all files that are derived at a site and are used by it are stored locally. An example of geographical distribution would be to break up a company's sales office data base by region. This implies that all the accounting, sales, inventory, etc., files be split by regional boundaries (Figure 6.17).

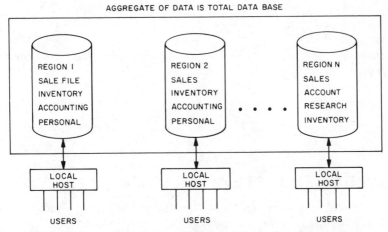

FIGURE 6.17   A data gauge partitioned by regional occurrence.

This method of distribution is also referred to as being split by occurrence. This method causes fragmented files as viewed from a global distributed data base sense. Such fragmentation or split files can cause many problems when users require an overall view of some file. For example, if Sales in Boston is directed by corporate headquarters to collect and analyze the last six months of sales for product Z, the Boston office would first have to collect all the fragments into one place, then process them to find the sales figures for product Z. If the totality of sales files were in one place, all processing could have been done there. This fragmentation allows for local autonomy and efficiency of operations at the expense of global operations.

The alternative method of splitting files is referred to as splitting by function. In this case the file components are grouped together by function, such as sales, and are united into one file for that function, and this is repeated for all major functional requirements. The previous example will be shown differently in this case. The functional files of each location are grouped and then distributed based on some requirements. An example of this form of splitting would be to have sales grouped and stored in Boston, accounting files grouped and stored at Des Moines, etc. This allows the files to be grouped together where they are functionally related and where the major function can be performed. This optimizes efficiency for global users at the expense of local users. Local users lose autonomy and control of their generated data. In order for allocation of files such as the above to be performed, organizations must have an in-depth knowledge of the structure of information and usage requirements. Given that these two elements are well understood, there are many probable distributions of the files and methods to perform the same. Ways to distribute files include:

Centralized
    All files in one place with access from decentralized sites.
Replicated or fully distributed
    All files are copied at every site.
Partitioned or factored
    Each site posesses a different piece of the overall data base with no overlap.
Hybrid
    Some overlap of files (partial replication), some centralized files.

Each of the above methods has merits and will be discussed in the following four sections.

CENTRALIZED FILE ALLOCATION

When using centralized file allocation, the entire data base is stored at a central site (Figure 6.18).

The central site is the point into which and out of which all global data flows. This strategy has the effect of minimizing storage costs because only one copy of the data base exists and is stored at only one site, thereby minimizing secondary storage costs because only one disk or group of disks exists for the entire data base system. There are some problems with this approach. The reliability of the system is dependent on the availability of the data base to service users. If it has low reliability the system also suffers from the same malady. For example, if there is a failure in either the hardware or the soft-

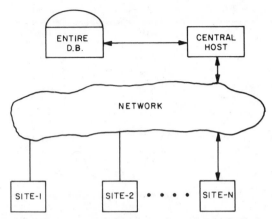

FIGURE 6.18 Centralized data base in a network environment.

ware associated with the central site, this could result in a catastrophic failure of the system if it relies totally on the data base for its functioning. Another problem with this approach to file allocation is that remote users will be subject to high retrieval costs in terms of network communication delays and contention for the limited control sites processing resources to answer queries. For example, refer to Figure 6.17. If all users request information from the central site, they will be queued up for service based on the priority of their request. The central site only has the capacity to service these units serially and as more users enter, the average service time may stay constant, but waiting delays will ultimately rise to an intolerable level due to queue delays.

On the bright side, update to the data base can be handled relatively easily. What this implies is that a designer utilizing this method of file distribution can be relieved from considering expensive update synchronization algorithms since they are not required. The update algorithm is simple to perform. An update simply sends them all to the central site which will handle the serialization of updates to provide consistency of data. Another positive aspect is that query processing is simplified at the remote sites. No optimization is required because all requests are sent to a single site and processed there sequentially. The basic problem with this file allocation scheme is the congestion it will cause during the operation of the system. This approach is only feasible when the volume of updates far exceeds the volume of queries.

REPLICATED (FULLY DISTRIBUTED)

In a system that utilizes a fully distributed or replicated file distribution all sites in the distributed computer system store copies of the entire data base. What this means is that if N sites are part of the distributed computer system, then N collections of assets are required. Hardware and software to support data storage and management must also exist (Figure 6.19). This method of distribution possesses the highest cost associated with hardware due to the N copies.

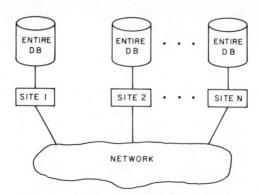

FIGURE 6.19   Example of a replicated data base.

With this type of system, the major benefit is to the end users in terms of increased reliability due to the multiple copies and reduced response time to queries. The reliability enhancement is caused due to a distributed system's ability to continue operations in face of failures and the fact that as long as a single copy of the data base is available, then the data base is available to service user requests. User query cost is minimized because no communications overhead is involved. This implies that all requests can be handled locally and that all the data bases are current and consistent. The problem associated with this mode of distribution of files becomes prevalent when updates are involved. Using this distribution scheme, updates are very expensive to perform. When a user updates his local copy all other copies must also be updated in some fashion to maintain currency of data. This will require specialized update synchronization algorithms to perform the update operation in a logical and correct fashion. The complexity of the update synchronization algorithms required and the attendant communications involved are directly related to the number of copies in the network and the consistency and currency requirements for the information. That is, if we have a tight requirement to keep all data current and consistent immediately, we may want to lock all copies of the data, update immediately, and then continue. This is expensive in messages required to do this and in delays caused by the inability of users to get at any piece of a locked record. On the other side, if we have a more lax requirement for all copies to be current, we may allow the update to be done at a later time by just downloading the new data base at a later time. The issues here will become more evident when we look at update synchronization algorithms later on in this chapter.

PARTITIONED

A partitioned or factored scheme of distributing a data base utilizes the notion of having only one copy of the data base as in the centralized case, but distributing pieces of it throughout the available sites in the network (Figure 6.20).

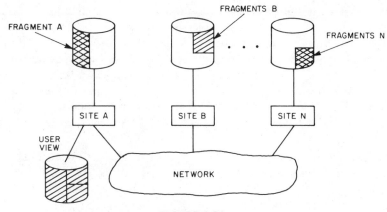

FIGURE 6.20

This method of file allocation is well-suited to distributed computer systems where most requests for data are from specific nodes only. That is, there exists a high locality of reference (local data is used mostly by local users and infrequently by remote users). This method, as in the centralized version, minimizes storage volume because only one copy exists, but it may have a higher hardware cost by driving up the need for secondary storage at all sites. With this type of distribution, reliability is higher than in the centralized version, but lower than the replicated. In this distribution mode the whole system will not be lost if one node fails. Only applications referencing data at the failed site need be affected.

In the design phase by requiring locality of reference as a partitioning criteria, the overall retrieval costs, as seen by users of the system, are reduced. Only users who request data from remote sites need suffer communications overhead. Another positive aspect is update. On the whole, updates will be cheaper and faster than both the centralized and distributed cases because all locks, processing, etc., must only be performed at a single site which is not generally overloaded as in the centralized case, and does not require sophisticated update synchronization as in the replicated case.

This type of distribution scheme will supply a higher degree of data available to users than that seen in the centralized case, but less than in the replicated.

HYBRID

The hybrid model of data base distribution has its basis in the previous three defined models. In this partitioning the data base is allowed to have any combination of the three previous models. This model also is the one referenced mostly in researchers' present studies. An example of a hybrid approach can be seen in Figure 6.21.

In Figure 6.21 a hybrid data base distribution is presented showing the centralized data at site D. This data would be stored in this fashion due to high percentage of updates versus queries. Also shown in this figure is factored or partitioned data, a little on each site. This data is distributed in this way because it is used mostly by one user for queries and updates or by a clustered group of users for a larger percentage of updates versus queries. A cluster refers to a closely (physically) located group of sites that utilized common data. The data is stored at one of the sites, say the middle one, and is accessed by all the other surrounding sites of the cluster. For example, site E could be turned into a cluster as seen in Figure 6.22.

The final type of data shown in Figure 6.21 is replicated data. This data is distributed in this fashion when the volume of queries is much greater than the volume of updates and the data is required by many sites. If it were required by a few it would be clustered.

In general, this approach represents the selection of the best features of the previous three while minimizing the effects of the expensive portions of each.

File Allocation Methods

As shown previously there are numerous methods upon which one can distribute an organization's data base. The question is, how does one go about doing this in an intelligent and methodical fashion. Many algorithms have been used to study this problem. For example:

File placement
  Add-drop algorithm
  Branch and bound algorithm
  Probabalistic branch and bound algorithm
  Integer programming technique
  Steepest ascent algorithm
  Dynamic programming methods

Warehouse location problem
  Hypher-cube technique
  Clustering technique
  Dynamic programming methods
  Max-flow min-cut network flow

The following paragraphs will discuss one method in detail that was an early attempt at deriving a method for allocation of files in a distributed network.

The method being presented was first presented by Wesley W. Chu in 1969 [51]. Other works in this area include [6], [40], [47], [78], [127], [189], [231]. Knuth's series on the art of computer programming presents many of the basic algorithms from which these works were derived and the interested reader is directed to the above references for further details of other methods and algorithmic techniques utilized.

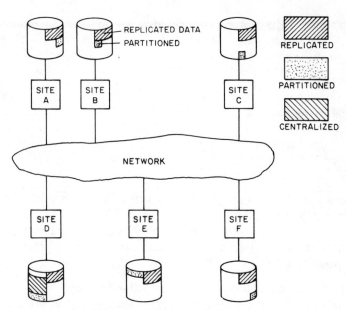

FIGURE 6.21   Hybrid data distribution.

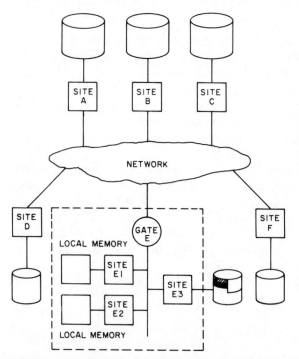

FIGURE 6.22   Hybrid distribution with cluster at site E.

In Chu's model, the problem considered is how to allocate files in a distributed computer system based on a set of constraints. Chu's model considers various system parameters such as:

Storage costs
Transmission costs
File lengths are fixed
Request rates—are fixed and give rate of use of file J from computer i
Update rates—are based on frequency of change per transmission
Maximum allowable access time for each file J at computer i
Storage capacity is fixed per computer

He views the file allocation problem as a (0,1) integer programming problem, (dynamic programming algorithms, Knuth) and looks to minimize storage and communications cost in allocating files in a distributed computing environment. In Chu's model he simplifies the optimization problem by levying some constraints on system attributes such as:

Fixed a priori is the number of allowable redundant copies
All computers can communicate directly point to point at a fixed cost per character transferred
All computers begin with fixed storage capacity
The routing of messages is static (point to point) and cannot change
Updates require only one message to perform (uniform cost)
Requests are shorter than messages in the network

Chu's algorithm looks at minimizing the following cost function (Equation 6.1) based on restrictions of storage cost, redundancy at copy levels, storage capacity, and access time constraints.

The algorithm allocates one file at a time based on placing files where they are mostly used first—until when not enough memory is left then they will be placed in the next highest user and so on.

The following example, taken from Chu's early paper, will further explain and exemplify the method.

The example utilizes a system with three computers (Figure 6.23) and five files. Computer 1 uses files 1, 3, and 5. Computer 2 uses files 1, 2, 4, and 5. Computer 3 uses files 2, 3, and 5. Table 6.1 outlines the file number, its size overall, the size involved in each transaction, the update percentage, and the utilizations of each file by each computer and its maximum allowable average retrieval time for each file. Initially, this model fixes the capacity at each computer at 110×10^3 characters.

Equation 6.1

Cost C = Storage cost and transmission cost

$$C = \sum_{i,j} C_{ij} L_J x_{iJ} + \sum_{i,j,K} \frac{1}{R_J} C_{iK} / l_J \, U_{iJ} \, X_{kJ} \, (1 - X_{iJ}) + \sum_{i,J,K} (iK/l_J \, U_{iJ} \, X_{Ky} \, P_{iJ}$$

Lj   = File length

X_{iJ} = File J stored at computer i
R_J = # of redundant copies of File
U_{iJ} = Utilization level of File J by computer i
P_{iJ} = Frequency of modification of File J
l_J = Transaction File Size

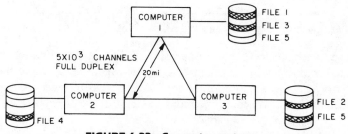

FIGURE 6.23 Computer system.

TABLE 6.1 Data of example for file allocation.

File j	L_j	l_j	P_j	Computer 1		Computer 2		Computer 3	
				u_{1j}	T_{1j}	u_{2j}	T_{2j}	U_{3j}	T_{3j}
1	100×10^2	500	0.5	5	30	2	10	0	0
2	10×10^2	500	0.5	0	0	2	30	5	1
3	10×10^2	500	0.5	3	10	0	0	4	1
4	10×10^2	500	0.5	0	0	4	0.1	0	0
5	100×10^2	500	0.5	1	1	1	1	5	1

P_j = the frequency of modification of the jth file after each transaction.

L_j = length of the jth file in characters.

l_j = file length (in characters) of each transaction for the jth file.

u_i = average hourly request rate of the entire or part of the jth file at the ith computer.
Request arrivals are assumed to be Poisson distributed.

T_{ij} = maximum allowable average retrieval time in seconds for the jth file to the ith computer.

C_{ij} = (storage cost) = $\$0.58 \times 10^{-8}$/char second.

C_{ik} = (transmission cost) = $\$1.4 \times 10^{-7}$/char.

b_i = (available storage capacity of the ith computer) = 110×10^2 char for $i = 1, 2, 3$.

$1/\mu$ = l/R (the time required to transmit the reply message) = 0.1 second.
optimal allocation.

Even for this simple example Chu's dynamic programming algorithm, which looks at all possible combinations, required 25 seconds of an IBM 360/05 CPU. It can readily be seen that such programs will blow up in processing time for large allocation problems.

In all the previously referenced type models, the prime goal is to determine the "best" way to spread out the data files over the available sites. In all cases this is weighted by the query and update rates. Later papers look at the problem along more dimensions and take into account topology design capacity of links, communications overhead, replication levels, reliability constraints, processing capacities, storage hierarchies, and capacities. Most interest in such models has been from an academic viewpoint and not much has been done to utilize these tools in actual production systems work.

Update Synchronization

The previous section looked at how to allocate files in a distributed computer system and looked at the pros and cons of each method. Some of the methods described included allocation of replicants of files to meet specific availability requirements. When replicated files exist in a distributed computer system they increase the availability of data to meet user queries, but spawn the problem of how to maintain these replicas in a consistent state. Following is a discussion of five techniques developed to perform this task, namely:

Unanimous agreement
Primary copy update
Moving primary update
Majority vote update
Majority read update

UNANIMOUS AGREEMENT

Unanimous agreement implies the operation of its title. That is, in order to perform an update to the data base, all sites must accept the proposed update before the modification is allowed. In order to do this the initiator site must ask all sites if they can perform the update it wants to perform. The sites individually determine whether they will or will not agree to the update. If all sites agree the initiator will signal them to perform the update and it is done. All individual sites at the point of saying they can complete the transaction have the information available to complete the transaction. If one site is not available or does not wish to perform the update, it fails. Figure 6.24 describes the operation of this protocol.

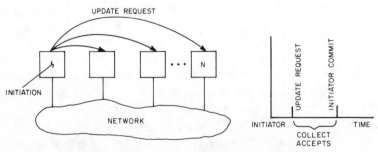

FIGURE 6.24 Unanimous agreement update.

The problem with this method of updating replicas is that if the probability of any site being available for update is P, then the probability of all N sites being available for update is P^N. If P = .9 and N is 10 the probability of doing an update is just .35. What this implies is that overall, the system will seldom be available for updates. This method of update synchronization is only good if the ratio of queries is extremely high.

PRIMARY COPY UPDATE

The primary copy update synchronization method utilizes the idea of designating a primary site where all update requests are sent. This central site acts as the mechanism to serialize updates, thereby preserving data consistency. The primary then, at some later time, updates all the secondaries. This "later time" is driven by user requirements for consistency/currency of data and could be immediately (becomes like unanimous agreement), at the end of transaction, in an hour, overnight, etc.

In this update method, if P is the probability of the master site being available for update or being up, the probability of the system being available is also P. The problem here is that if the system does not possess the ability to select a new master on failure, the system halts in terms of updates.

MOVING PRIMARY UPDATES

In this technique, there is an elected primary site and N-1 secondary sites. Updates are sent to any node. When updates are received, if the receiver site is the primary, it performs the update, then sends a cooperation request to a secondary telling it of the update. The secondary performs the update and acknowledges the update to the primary and to the original requestor. The secondary then passes the update on to the next secondary and so on. Thus, at this point two-host resiliency is achieved. If the host fails, the secondaries in the system select a new primary and continue on. If the original request was not sent to a primary, it will be forwarded on until it arrives at the primary. Figure 6.25 depicts the operation of the moving primary update.

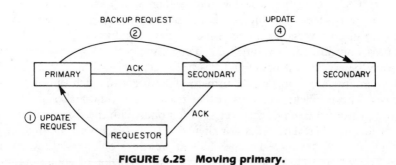

FIGURE 6.25 Moving primary.

This method will be more reliable than the single master version because it has the ability to continue in the face of primary failures.

MAJORITY VOTE UPDATE

The majority vote update synchronization protocol views all sites in the network, with replicas, as "peers" (equals). In this scheme updates originate at the requestor site and are coordinated from there. Updates succeed and are incorporated into the data base when a majority of the peers accept the update message, as in Figure 6.26. The majority is determined by the assignment or election of a majority and acquiring of a monotonically increasing version number. If a group of devices is not part of the majority (site failure) its updates will not succeed. It will request to be added to the majority or told to become a member by one of its peers, as at least one site is common to both majorities and is in the present ruling one. When a failure occurs, a new majority is determined (with a new increasing version number) which then continues updating under the new regime. When failed units return into the network they are sent catchup messages to bring them up to par with the majority. When using this method the probability of successful updates approaches 1 for large N. What this infers is, if a sufficient number of sites are available for updates then a majority can always be determined and the update can be accomplished.

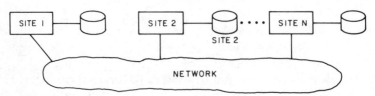

FIGURE 6.26   Majority vote—to succeed if N = 5, a majority of 3 would suffice to incorporate update.

MAJORITY READ UPDATE

The majority read update scheme performs the update at the local site of the request. The update performed locally is then broadcast to all online sites. The update is successful only if it is accepted by a majority of peers. All updates are given a version number which increases monotonically. Updates are accepted only in order, Figure 6.27. For example, if update i is received, it can only be accepted if update i-1 has been accepted for this item. This algorithm requires a catchup mechanism to allow users to catch up with missed updates. The problem with this is that read requests must also be sent to a majority of peers. Each of the peer sites responds with the data requested and its version number. The requestor then selects the data with the highest version number as the correct value. This approach is only feasible when messages are fast and cheap as this protocol requires a lot of communications.

For reads to be done and time delays to collect a majority of reads responses could be excessive in most systems and particularly so in a real-time distributed computer system.

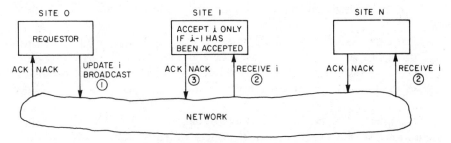

FIGURE 6.27   Majority read update.

The interested reader is directed to specific implementations of these algorithms. See references [8], [199], [204], [392], [393] for more specific information.

Concurrency Control and Recovery

The primary aim of concurrency control is to allow distributed execution of transactions while preserving the integrity of the data base. The most basic goal of concurrency control is to provide mechanisms to guarantee against simultaneous operations on the same data item. In order to realize this, the concurrency control mechanism must ensure that the concurrent execution of transactions constitutes some serial execution of the transactions. This notion is the same as described in the section on serializability. In distributed data bases two basic approaches to achieving the goal of serializability of transactions have been devised, namely: locking and time-stamp ordering. As shown in [395] there are many variations on these two basic methods and a discussion of all these approaches would be beyond the scope of this text. Instead we will examine two basic methods, namely: basic 2 phase-locking and basic time-stamp ordering.

BASIC 2 PHASE-LOCKING

The basic operation of the 2 phase-locking protocol is as follows:

1. If a transaction wishes to read or write from or to an object in the data base, it must first acquire either a read lock or a write lock on the item. A lock can be best viewed as a mutual exclusion primitive that allows only one entity to acquire an object and hold it at any time.

2. Once the lock is acquired, the transaction can use the item as it wishes to read it or update it, dependent on lock type.

3. Once completed, the transaction gives up the locks it possesses.

In basic 2 phase-locking, locks are defined by two rules, namely:
1. More than one transaction cannot concurrently hold conflicting locks.
2. Once a transaction surrenders a lock it cannot obtain additional locks.

What this implies is that 2 PL transactions go through two phases during execution, namely, a growing phase where all required locks are acquired and a shrinking phase where all completed operations will release held locks. 2 PL allows for the serialization of transactions based on mutual exclusion of data items.

To implement 2 PL in a distributed computer system would require the definition list of a 2 PL process (manager) which would receive the lock request from requestors, process them based on centralized 2 PL as previously defined, then release the locks. Once the lock release commands have been received from the initiator, it is required that a lock table of known data items (Figure 6.28) be present on each site so the lock manager can determine the status of any data item without searching the data base. The lock manager at each site will determine whether to grant a lock, refuse a lock, or rollback (undo) a transaction based on the status of its lock table.

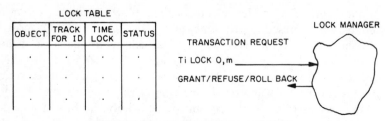

FIGURE 6.28   Lock manager and table.

The problem with global locking is the possibility of deadlock. In order to avoid this, locking must utilize a method of deadlock detection and avoidance such as resource allocation graph analysis which is extremely hard if not impossible in distributed systems, ordering of selections, or some time out or wait condition to get out of potential deadlock. Further information on deadlocks can be found in [60], [61] and references at the end of the text.

BASIC TIME-STAMP ORDERING

The other basic method of concurrency control is time-stamp ordering. This method serializes transaction operations based on system-wide time stamps which act to specifically serialize the data base reads/writes based on their time ordering in the system. This time ordering is typically derived in a distributed system from a system clock and the site's ID. If the global time clock is tightly synchronized, then conflicting transactions with the same time stamp can be differentiated and ordered based on the site ID values which are unique in a distributed computer system.

The algorithm to implement the time-stamp ordering will be the same as described earlier, but is now distributed to N sites. Each site will have a time-stamp ordering manager (Figure 6.29) which will act as the entity that performs the serialization of transactions based on the time stamp of the items.

Read requests: R_i [X]
   If time-stamp(i)< write - time stamp (X)
      Then "reject" read and abort transaction
      Else "accept" read and
         update read-time stamp(X) =
         max(read-time stamp(X), time stamp(i))
Write "request"W_i[X]

      If time stamp(i)< read-time stamp(X) or
                   write-time stamp(X)
      Then "reject"write and abort xaction
      Else "accept"write and update write time stamp =
         time stamp(i)

The scheduler can accept many and queue up the requests.

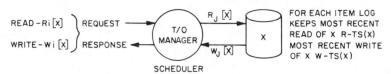

FIGURE 6.29   T/O management function.

This concurrency control technique will avoid deadlock and therefore does not require any extra deadlock detection or avoidance algorithms. The interested reader is directed again to [395] for additional details and variation on these two concurrency control methods.

Commit Protocols

The previous two sections discussed problems with distributed computers to maintain redundant copies of a data base and to provide mechanisms to guarantee the serialization (correctness of operations) on this data base. The question is how to implement these solutions on a distributed computer to guarantee that their actions will occur as defined. The problem here is what type protocols to use to make sure that the update will be done or that the transaction is done correctly and to be sure that if it cannot be done correctly not to do it at all.

2 PHASE COMMIT

The idea of the two phase commit protocol is to provide a means to guarantee that a transaction being performed on a distributed data base management system is either processed at all sites or at none at all. This protocol allows multiple sites to coordinate transaction commit (completion).

During phase I of the 2 phase commit, all sites involved in the transaction are queried as to whether they can commit (complete the transaction). Each site that determines that it can commit becomes recoverably prepared to go either way (commit, abort) and awaits the coordinator's decision.

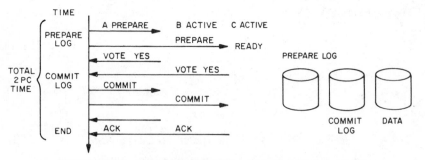

FIGURE 6.30   Centralized 2 phase commit with no errors.

During the second phase the coordinator makes its decision on which way to go and notifies all sites of this decision. At this point, the other sites have expressed their willingness to commit to the transaction and no longer can be allowed to unilaterally abandon the transaction.

An example of 2 phase commit protocol is the centralized 2 phase commit. In this example we will have three sites involved in the transaction, with site A being the originator site (Figure 6.30). Site A, as the originator, sends all prepares and commits. Each cohort (involved site) on receipt of the prepare message, if willing to commit, will force write a prepare log record (all data needed to do/undo the transaction). At this time the cohorts are in the prepared/ready state. A cohort who does not want to prepare, force writes the transaction in the log and sends a no vote.

If all the votes returned from the cohort were yes votes, the coordinator moves to the committing state by force-writing a commit-record to the log. The coordinator then sends commit messages to all cohorts who upon receipt will force-write a commit-record to their logs and send an ACK message to the coordinator. After all the ACKs have been received at the end of phase II, the coordinator writes an end of record and forgets about the transaction. If a cohort fails while the coordinator is waiting for yes/no messages to prepare, it aborts the transaction.

If the cohort fails while the coordinator is waiting for an ACK message, it hands over the transaction to recovery for redo or undo actions based on the conditions.

If the cohort is in the ready state and the coordinator fails then it waits until the coordinator is recovered.

Another method of 2 phase commit is the linear 2 phase commit. In this model, instead of having a central point coordinate all activity, the sites propagate, prepare, and commit operations from site to site involved and ACK back to predecessor. (See Figure 6.31). This method requires a list of cohorts for each transaction.

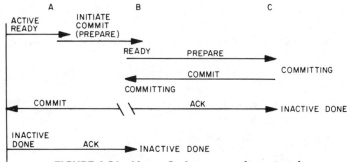

FIGURE 6.31   Linear 2 phase commit protocol.

Recovery in a Distributed Data Base

Recovery in a distributed data base system is used to handle failures. The recovery manager has the job of handling transaction failures, system failures, and media failures. It also coordinates system restart and shutdown when performed.

In distributed data bases there are two classes of failure: system site failure, that falls into the above category, and communications failures, which may cause network partitioning. The question is, where in the distributed data base software picture does the recovery manager fit.

Under normal operational conditions, maintaining the consistency in the data base is the task of the concurrency control mechanism being utilized, and transaction atomicity (serializability) is the task of the commit protocol used. The recovery manager has the function of preserving data base consistency and guaranteeing transaction atomicity and survival during system failures. This implies that the recovery manager is tightly woven with the concurrency control and commit protocols. The problem is well understood in centralized data bases and algorithms have been developed [60] to handle the problem. In distributed data bases the problem is much harder due to multiple site failures or communication failures, as shown in Figure 6.32.

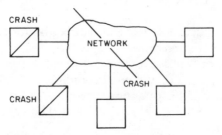

FIGURE 6.32   Failures in distributed data base.

Traditional methods of solution will not work in this environment due to extra variables which cause problems such as: What does a site do with transactions execution when—

1. Cohorts fail
2. Communications break down
3. Cohort recovers from failure
4. Communications is just established

Each one of the above may cause the site to take some different view of the other sites. To solve this and other problems, recovery management relies on some method of 2 phase protocol for guaranteeing operation and relies on communication retransmissions for lost message problems.

In order for recovery to work under the 2 phase protocol, if a message is lost the communications network must have the capability to remember it and continue to try until it gets through. This solves the problem of a lost message, number 2 above. If a site fails (cohort) during the first phase of 2 phase protocol, then all abort. If during phase 2 and after receiving commit the cohort fails, then local recovery manager must come in and recover to the committed state. The all or nothing condition holds here. If failure happens before the commit is received by the cohort, then the entire transaction must either wait or abort because the cohort is in a limbo state.

System R* at IBM research San Jose utilizes the 2 phase commit with a mechanism to detect communication failures. In R* if the commit procedure is interrupted, then a special recovery procedure is required. This process takes over responsibility of recovering the transactions. The recovery process utilizes "datagrams" (short messages) to determine parent site status and cohort status. This process will periodically come in until either it determines it cannot complete within some given time or it is received by another recovery manager who restores the transaction to its proper state using the local transaction manager. The recovery manager then sends ACKs to all involved parties. More information on this can be found in [357].

Query Processing/Optimization

Query processing and optimization is the method by which distributed data base management systems determine what is to be processed and how to do it in the most economical fashion. The driving factor for requiring query processing in distributed data base is efficiency due to the ability to decompose and process in parallel queries which otherwise would have had to be processed in a centralized location.

Much work has been done in the area of query processing since Wong's paper in 1977 [298]. Various algorithms based on different processing strategies have been developed since this early work. Other efforts in this area include the work done on SDD-1 for query optimization based on the idea of decomposition.

The following section will show why we need query optimization and describe some algorithms developed to date.

A very graphic example that has been used to emphasize the need for query processing is shown in Rothnie and Goodman's paper "A Survey of Research and Development in Distributed Data Base Management". This example was simplified in [60] and is shown here to make a point. In this example, three relations are shown: a supplier, parts, and supplier-parts relations of size 10,000, 100,000, and 1,000,000 tuples, respectively. The example simplifies the problem down to where the driving cost is the communications delay. There are two sites with relations S and SP stored at site A and relation P on site B. It is estimated that 10 parts of the required type and 100,000 shipments of the part will answer the queries. The example looks at what happens if—

1. You move the parts relation to A and process all of it there.
2. You move supplier and supplier-parts relations to site B.
3. For each supplier that meets (100,000) check if he supplies that part.
4. For each part of the proper type (xx) check if it is supplied by the proper supplier.
5. Move supplier shipment (100,000) to B and process it there.
6. Move the part type required to A.

The summary of estimated time to do this is shown in Figure 6.33.

STRATEGY	COMMUNICATIONS TIME
1	16.7
2	28 HR
3	2.3 DAY
4	20 SEC
5	16.7 MIN
6	1 SEC

FIGURE 6.33   Summary of results.

From this it can be seen that the proper selection of processing strategy is of utmost importance in the efficient operations of a distributed data base management system.

The following will present some algorithms developed to date for the efficient processing of queries in distributed data base systems and direct the reader to more extensive readings in this area.

Many publications have appeared describing new methods for query processing and optimization over the last few years. Most have dealt with the problem from a communications minimization point of view. Recent papers have begun addressing the other costs involved in query processing; namely I/O and processing cost of performing the queries as well as the communications cost involved.

Generally the techniques discussed perform optimization based on the following strategy:

1. Reduce the initial set of relations to work on via performance of selections and projections. The reduction typically shrinks the volume of information to be processed drastically.
2. If union, join, interest, difference, etc. are to be performed, then preprocess the files involved to supply the data in sorted order. This allows quick methods to access and compare data in the files for their class of operations.
3. Perform operations in order of greatest minimization effect on the total problem.

The first technique we will examine is one described by Chu and Hurley in reference [400]. This model describes a technique for determining the optimal policy for processing relational queries and looks at costs of communications and processing.

Their algorithm operates as follows:

1. Assume the set of operations on a query is initially represented as a query tree (Figure 6.34).
2. Proper placement of operations on the tree is performed to optimize volume of data transferred.
3. Local operation groups are formed with edges to other groups representing communications paths and costs. These are computed into processing graphs.
4. These new graphs are optimized by computation of costs and selection of the optimal graph for best processing strategy.

This algorithm requires that a technique for building the query trees and processing graphs exists.

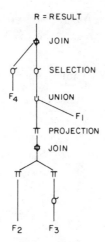

FIGURE 6.34   Query tree.

The query trees are constructed by using the decomposition capability of relational operations. That is, we try to break up the query into pieces that can be performed in parallel, then unite these where required to do combined operations and so on. For example, if given a query such as: generate a listing of part number, supplier name, quantity for all calculators produced in Los Angeles in a quantity greater than 1,000 by any one supplier.

Given

R1 = (part #, part name)
R2 = (supplier #, part #, quantity)
R3 = (supplier #, supplier name, city)

We can in parallel perform a selection on R1 of part names = 'calculator' and do a projection of the result to yield just the part numbers for this result and also be performing the selection of all tuples in R2 that have quantity >1,000; and finally R3 can also be processed partially in parallel by selecting all the city = Los Angeles and then projecting this across the supplied tuples to yield just supplier name and supplier number that meet the restriction wanted.

From this we must next perform a join on part number to the result of R1 and R2s operation. This join will yield the tuples in R2 that meet the part number restriction found through the selection and projection of 'calculator' done on R1. This yields some number of tuples less than the original cardinality of R2.

Once this is complete, the next job is to determine the suppliers who supply this part from Los Angeles. This is done by joining the result of the previous join with the projection and restriction done on R3.

This last operation will provide the wanted elements in a relational format as seen below.

R Result (part #, supplier name, quantity)

The resultant tree is seen in Figure 6.35.

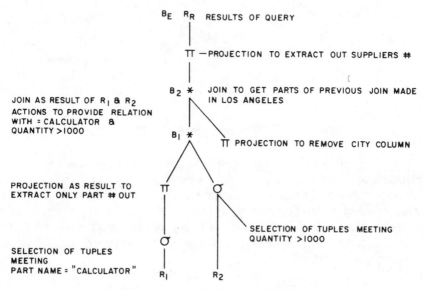

FIGURE 6.35   Query tree, for example.

This query tree is only one of many possible trees. Their algorithm will construct others in the same fashion and build cost models of each approach.

If this was a centralized computer system, then the operation would simply be performed as indicated. The problem is since we have introduced a distributed computer environment, the selection of which tree approach to use becomes more critical. This is a result of the added cost of interprocessor communications.

In their algorithm, they take the initial selection, projection reductions, determine the new volume of data found from these reductions, then build cost models of performing the remaining operation on various sites.

To see the example as on a network refer to Figure 6.36.

The problem becomes one of how to best do the joins and their restrictions in order to minimize overall cost. This is accomplished by building query graphs showing the possible ways of doing the operations. In this example, if the initial selections and projections on R 1, R 2, and R 3 yielded the following cardinalities:

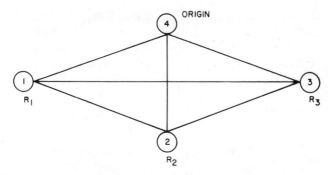

FIGURE 6.36   Network topology and relation locations, for example.

	% of Relation	Length
R 1 Part # = 'calculator'	.05	$.5 \times 10^4$
R 2 S#, P#, quantity >1,000	.10	$.1 \times 10^4$
R 3 S#, sup name city = Los Angeles	.30	$.3 \times 10^4$

The possible graphs which result from this can be seen in Figure 6.37.

The job is to compute the overall communications cost utilizing the volume of data transferred in each graph and the cost per byte transferred. This is then used to select the best graph to do the processing. The algorithm must then perform the job to determine the processing cost associated with each graph to determine if any of the choices is better due to the combination of processing and communications cost. From this an optimum processing strategy can be selected to perform the processing of the distributed query based on least cost comparisons.

Decomposition Method

Another optimization technique is one initially described in [391] and later in [327]. This algorithm looks to break up (decompose) the query job into separate pieces using a few simple heuristics. The overall objective in this model is to minimize communications delay and response time.

This model allows data to be fragmented about the network. Relations can be split along tuple lines for distribution in one node or another. Their algorithm will be described below. The site which originates a query is referred to as the master. This site coordinates the operation of the query. The first step in their algorithm is to break down the query into as many one-variable quera)

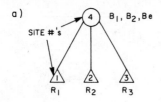

Reduce all initial relations to smallest point and ship to requesting node for processing.

Communications Cost = Σ Relation Sizes.
Unit Communication Delay = 1.8

b)

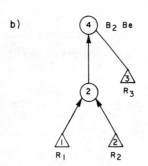

Reduce all initial relations as before but join R_1 and R_2 result at Node 2 then join this result with R_3 Result at Node 4.

Communications Cost = 8.5

c)

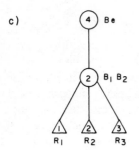

Reduce all initial relations as before, but do the 2 joins at Site 2. Then move final result to Site 4.

Communications Cost = 9

d)

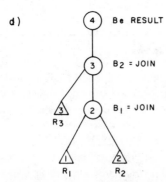

Reduce all initial relations as before, but now do first join on R_1 and R_2 Result of Site 2. Then ship result to Site 3 to join this result with R_3 Result, then ship final to Site 4.

FIGURE 6.37   Generated query trees.

ies as possible. These are then distributed to all slave sites to be performed at all sites in parallel.

The next phase of the algorithm performs the reduction on the remaining queries. This selection looks to break up queries into subqueries (like a divide and conquer type of algorithm), then execute these in parallel. The algorithm operates on these subqueries in some order that will preserve the result of the overall query. This section must decide where to process the subquery and how to distribute the data and/or commands to do this in an efficient manner.

This algorithm is classified as a "greedy" heuristic algorithm. This implies that it looks to optimize its result on each stop autonomously, not looking forward to the global consequences of the local decision. The algorithm will continue to subdivide subqueries until no gain in performance is determined. It will then process all the pieces and reunite them for the final result. As in the previous example, the cost of doing an operation is computed and used in determining if more decomposition is feasible based on cost heuristics. Cost in this model is viewed from two points, namely, communications cost and processing time. Additional details of this algorithm can be found in [281] and [400].

The two previous approaches look at each query and they try to determine an optimum plan for how to execute the query on a distributed system in order to meet some given performance constraints. Others have proposed techniques that look at minimizing multi queries at the same time [57].

In this work Cellary and Meyer look at optimization of queries based on mean response time as their criterion of optimality. They do this via the minimization of processing in all queries in the system at any period in time. Queries are provided to the system and are decomposed into query trees as shown previously. The main premise of their model is that each node has the ability to maximize its use of its resources based on preset loadings and priorities.

Their model distinguishes between three complementary levels of optimization, namely:

Optimization of tree structures
    The optimal subquery tree is determined.
Optimization of subtree processing
    For all subtrees the selection of optimum node to execute in is determined/dependent on transmission costs.
Optimization of process scheduling
    Try to optimize use of local resources.

Construction of trees is done similar to the way described earlier, namely to construct all possible trees for executing the given query. From this construction, the next algorithm looks to determine the best way to process the leaves of the tree and how to work to distribute the results for further execution.

Finally the algorithm looks at how best to utilize the resources available in minimizing the overall average response time for the N queries it is working on. It does this through intelligent scheduling and synchronization of processes in the nodes and in the network by utilizing information about the query processes of search, receiver, non-sender, and terminal receivers.

An example of this method is shown for clarity.

S 1 R 1 = P #,PNAME

S 2 R 2 = S#,P#,Q

R 3 = S#,S-CITY

Given two queries, i and j, with similar requirements for selection, projection, and joins. The problem is how best to perform the two queries to lower the overall mean response time.

Q i = generate list of part numbers + supplier names for all calculator producers in Los Angeles.

Q j = generate list of name and quantity for all calculator producers in Los Angeles.

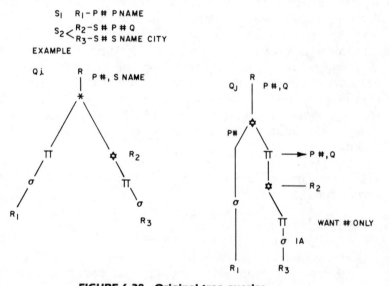

FIGURE 6.38 Original tree queries.

From this we can determine the nodes to execute are as follows:

do Q i R 1 + Q j R 1   Q i R 2, R 3 + Q j, R 2, R 3

on site 1   on site 2

site 1   site 2

From this we can determine the initial processing and communications graph as seen in Figure 6.39.

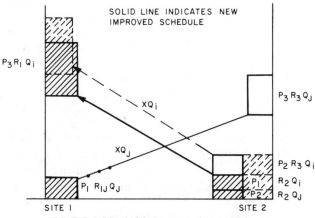

FIGURE 6.39   Initial processing graph.

This graph shows the initial cut at distributing this query out for execution. The cut shown indicates the best way to distribute the queries out for execution while minimizing communications. The next phase of the algorithm is to determine the optimum way to perform the overall set of processes to minimize overall response time. It does this by looking at how it could readjust the processing schedules to decrease the average execution time.

In this example the algorithm would determine that executing the two subparts of Qi on site 2 first will drop the overall execution time for all nodes. Figure 6.39 depicts this result. The results indicate a potential new avenue of research for distributed query optimization. The interested reader is directed to [57] for more details on this topic.

Summary

This chapter introduced the reader to basic concepts of data base management. Covered within this chapter were concepts of the major data base models, namely, hierarchical, network, relational, and entity relationship models. Introduced were concepts of serializability, concurrency control, update synchronization and query processing.

This chapter introduced many concepts which are developed at length in volumes of papers and books. The intention of this chapter was to introduce the reader to data base management and distributed data base management concepts and some work done to date in order to stimulate a deeper interest in work done in this area.

CHAPTER SEVEN

Performance Evaluation

This chapter will introduce and discuss concepts for performance evaluation of computer systems. As part of this discussion the reader will be introduced to techniques used for analytical modeling of computer systems, simulation techniques with emphasis on discrete, continuous, network and combined modeling, as well as coverage of operational analysis techniques for measurement of system performance.

Why do we need performance evaluation of computer systems? We have three periods of time when we should do performance assessment of systems. The first should be before building any hardware or coding any software. This is during system specification. Performance evaluation and prediction will aid us in determining what the performance of the system we want is. It shows how to meet our expected needs and through analysis how to adjust our initial specification to meet the realistic goals of our future designs.

The next period of time that performance evaluation and prediction should be used is during design. This allows us to evaluate our designs as to their performance before the designs become unchangeable and to find problems early in a design phase before too much effort has already been expended. This aids in more complete first level designs and lends itself to designs which require less changes once delivered.

The final period of time in the life of a computer system where performance evaluation is important is in the field. When systems have been delivered and are operating in the field environment, measurement can be made using hardware and/or software monitors and these results can be used to determine the operation and efficiency of the system.

The first section of this chapter will look at analytical modeling techniques used in performance analysis of computer systems. The review will not be in depth, but will be sufficient to get an understanding of the concepts. It will also lead interested readers to additional discussions in this field.

The next section will describe simulation techniques and how they can be utilized in performance assessment of computer systems. Covered in this section is an overview of simulation methodology, simulation techniques, and examples of simulation of simple queuing networks. The final section will delve into techniques used in performance assessment of operational systems. This will describe measurement and analysis techniques.

Analytical Modeling

Performance evaluation of computer systems has existed since the beginning of computers. People have recognized the need to determine the performance of computers based on work loads and to determine the effect of adding or deleting resources as well as the impact of new technology.

In order to be able to study the effects of verifying parameters we must introduce some basic concepts of analytical performance and evaluation techniques.

In computer systems the major metrics of interest come in two types, namely, system metrics and user-oriented metrics.

System metrics typically used are throughput and utilization. Throughput is the measure of jobs performed per unit of time and is dependent on the arrival rate and the service rate of a device or system.

The utilization of a system represents the percentage or fraction of time the resource being measured is busy. In computer system performance evaluation the most common devices measured in this way are the CPU and I/O devices. The other important measurement class is the user-oriented class. In this class are important measures such as job response time, which describes the length of time a request for service spends in a system until its completion (response).

The common way of viewing and analyzing these systems is with analytical queuing models. The classic model of a computer system is shown in Figure 7.1.

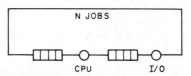

FIGURE 7.1   Queue model of batch computer systems.

The two major components shown in this figure are the CPU and its queue and the I/O device and its queue plus the number of jobs in service in the system. Using the concept of basic query theory or simulation techniques we can evaluate the performance of a wide class of designs.

The remainder of this chapter will introduce analytical queuing techniques and how they relate to computer system performance evaluation, followed by a look at simulation techniques and computing with system testing.

Analytical Queuing Analysis

Queuing theory has been well described in many texts such as Kleinrock's [358] definitive work on the subject, as well as Trivedi and Lavenburg [360], [359], who delved more into computer applications.

The basic premise of queuing theory is the mathematical study of queues. Queuing theory is a branch of probability theory related to service facilities. The basic structure of a queue is shown in Figure 7.2.

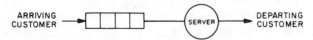

FIGURE 7.2   Basic structure of a queue.

The queue is comprised of a waiting line (the queue) and a service facility (the server). Customers arrive to the service facility at some rate (arrival rate) and find either the server is busy—therefore, the customer will join the waiting line (the queue)—or find it free, then get served at a server at some rate (service rate). Waiting customers are selected from the queue of customers based on some service rule known as service discipline. Examples of common disciplines utilized include first come first served, priority scheduling, and round robin. These three items describe the way in which one views the queue and its attributes for modeling purposes.

ARRIVAL PROCESS

Customers arrive at a service facility from a population of customers. Typically it is assumed that this population is infinite to simplify the analysis. Beyond this it is often assumed that the arrivals are independent random processes known as Poisson Process. Utilizing the properties of a poisson process [358], we can much easier describe the arrival pattern to any server in our system. The poisson process has the property of addition and decomposition. That is, any number of poisson input streams can be merged into one poisson input stream (see Figure 7.3), and any poisson stream can be split into any number of poisson streams (see Figure 7.4).

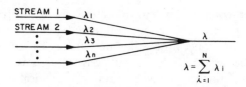

FIGURE 7.3   Addition of poisson processes.

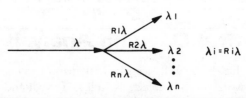

FIGURE 7.4   Decomposition of poisson processes.

SERVICE TIME DISTRIBUTION

Another component in our basic queuing system is the server. The server has a capacity, C, which is the amount of work it can do in a unit of time. This measure is referred to as the service time, S, and can take on many characteristics. Again, for ease in computation it is assumed that distributions are of a fixed number. Common distributions utilized include the exponential distribution, the Erlang, and the Hyper Exponential distribution.

The exponential distribution is the most commonly utilized and computationally the simplest. The exponential distribution used in queuing theory has the form

$$Fx(t) = 1 - e^{-\mu t}, \text{for } X \geqslant 0.$$

μ is referred to as the "Rate" of the distribution. The mean rate for this distribution referred to as the Expected Service Time, $E[X] = \frac{1}{\mu}$ and the variance from the mean is referred to as, $\sigma_x^2 = E[(x - \bar{x})^2] = \frac{1}{\mu^2}$

Servers that deliver this type of service are referred to as exponential servers with service rate u. The most important aspect of this distribution is that every arrival is independent and has the same arrival distribution given by

$$P[X \leqslant t] = 1 - e^{-\mu t}$$

This property is referred to as the memoryless property of the poisson process.

Another important distribution is the Erlang. The K-stage Erlang distribution is formed by the combination of K exponential stages with service rates = Kμ. What this means is that we can represent an Erlang server with rate μ by K exponential stage of rate Kμ, as in Figure 7.5.

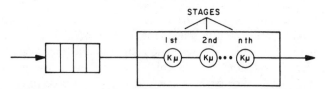

FIGURE 7.5   K-stage Erlang in terms of experientials.

The distribution of this function can be seen in Figure 7.6.

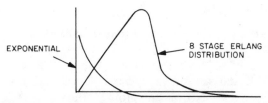

FIGURE 7.6   8-stage Erlang distribution function.

This distribution is also referred to in many texts as the hypo-exponential.

The last distribution introduced in this text is the hyper exponential distribution. This distribution becomes important in situations where multiple-different exponential distributions better represent the physical system under study. This distribution is represented by the sum of the contributions of each exponential server. This can be shown as the probability Π_i of each server being utilized times its service time $\frac{1}{\mu_i}$.

$$Fx(t) = \sum_{i=1}^{k} \Pi_i(1 - e^{-\mu_i t})$$

Pictorially, the hyper-exponental distribution can be constructed as shown in Figure 7.7.

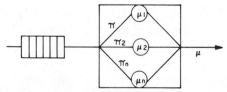

FIGURE 7.7 Hyper-exponential distribution represented with exponential server.

In this distribution, the mean service rate is found from

$$E[S] = \sum_{i=1}^{n} \Pi_i/\mu_i = \frac{1}{\mu}$$

Scheduling Algorithms

In order to determine the performance of a program's use of a resource, we must know information about scheduling algorithms. That is, we need to know the method by which the resource is allocated to the programs or jobs seeking service. In queuing systems this is referred to as the queuing discipline. There are four major types of queuing disciplines used in computer system performance modeling; namely:

First-come-first-served (FCFS)
Last-come-first-served-preemptive-resume (LCFSPR)
Round-robin (RR)
Processor-sharing (PS)

The two main criteria a scheduling algorithm must handle are given the present state of the server, which job should be serviced next and, second, should the present job be allowed to run to completion.

First-come-first-served scheduling operates by selecting the job sitting in the queue the longest. No preemption is allowed and a job runs to completion.

Another scheduling discipline is last-come-first-served-preemptive-resume. This scheduling operates by selecting the last item which came in for service, preempting the present service operating job and resuming it once this one completes.

A common scheduler seen in many computer designs is round-robin. Round-robin scheduling revolves around the notion of a time slice or "quantum." Jobs are serviced in first-come-first-served order until they exceed the quantum. At this time, the job is preempted and placed at the end of the queue and the first job in the queue is brought in for service. The problem is to select a quantum of large enough time to allow useful work in relation to switching time.

Processor sharing is a scheduling algorithm used in describing many analytical models of real systems. Processor sharing is the ultimate limit of round robin scheduling. That is, processor sharing is round-robin scheduling with a quantum size of zero. This relates to the view that under this scheduling algorithm all N jobs get 1/N of the service time for any period of time.

Before we go on to more detailed views of the example system analysis, we need a notation to describe what type of queue is being analyzed. The following is a list of symbols and definitions used frequently to define queues.

The notation is A/B/M where M denotes an M-server queuing system. A and B represent the inter arrival time and service time distributions, respectively.

A and B can take on one of the following distributions
   M   : Exponential
   En : n-stage Erlang
   Hn : n-stage Hyper exponential
   D   : Deterministic
   G   : General

M/M/1 QUEUING SYSTEM

To introduce the ideas of analytical queuing techniques and performance analysis we will look at a simple queue, the M/M/1 queue. This queue is a single-server system with poisson (exponential) arrivals and exponentially distributed service times; Figure 7.8.

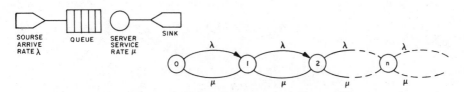

FIGURE 7.8   Markov state diagram of M/M/1 queue.

This system can be described as a birth/death process and can also be described by Markov state diagrams; Figure 7.9.

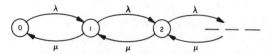

FIGURE 7.9   Birth/death process.

This shows that the number of customers in the system is a counting process with rate $= \lambda$, and is reduced by rate $= \mu$, Therefore, $\lambda(n) = \lambda$ n$=0,1,....$ and $\mu(n) = \mu$ n$=0,1,.....$

The idea of balance of flow [280], [361], [358] describes a method for determining the state probabilities from the state diagrams and flows.

The simple case is the balance equation for state O which is:

$$\lambda P(0) = \mu P(1)$$

From this we can see:

$$P(1) = \frac{\lambda}{\mu} P(0)$$

The same approach can be used for the other states in the system to determine their local balance equations.

For example, state 1 yields:

Flow Out $=$ Flow In
$(\lambda+\mu)P(1) = \lambda P(0) + \mu P(2)$
expanding $\lambda P(1)+\mu P(1) = \lambda P(0)+\mu P(2)$

and substituting in $^\mu P(1) = \frac{\mu\lambda}{\mu} P(0)$

yields
$\lambda P(1) + \lambda P(0) = \lambda P(0) + \mu P(2)$

which simplifies to

$$P(2) = \frac{\lambda}{\mu} P(1)$$

From this we can see that repeating this for states 2,3,4,....will yield the general form:

$$P(n) = \frac{\lambda}{\mu} P(n-1) \qquad n = 1,2,3, \ldots$$

Other work has shown that

$$P(n) = (\tfrac{\lambda}{\mu})^n P(0) \qquad n = 0,1,2,\ldots$$

And from the fact of probability that

$$\sum_{n=0}^{\infty} P(n) = 1$$

then

$$\sum_{n=0}^{\infty} (\tfrac{\lambda}{\mu})^n P(0) = 1$$

From series relationships

$$\sum_{i=0}^{\infty} a^i = \tfrac{1}{1-a} \quad 0<(a)<1$$

yields

$$\frac{1}{1 - \tfrac{\lambda}{\mu}} P(0) = 1$$

which tell us that

$$P(0) = \frac{1}{1-\tfrac{\lambda}{\mu}} = \frac{1}{1-\rho}$$

Substituting

$$\rho = \tfrac{\lambda}{\mu}$$

given that the utilization of a server is equivalent in this case to the throughput (arrival rate) divided by the service rate shown as

$$\rho = \tfrac{\lambda}{\mu}$$

and that

$$P(n) = \rho^n(1-\rho)$$

We can now determine the average queue length or number of customers in the system from the above results.

The average number of customers (N) in the system can be found by summing the results from states O to infinity of the number of customers in state i times the probability of being in state i as seen below.

$$\overline{N} = \sum_{n=0}^{\infty} nP_n = \tfrac{\rho}{1-\rho}$$

The average queue size can be found by summing the result of the number in state i -1 times the probability of being in state i from 1 to infinity, seen below.

$$\overline{Q} = \sum_{n=1}^{\infty} (n-1) P_n = \tfrac{\rho^2}{1-\rho}$$

In order to use these results to determine some other interesting results, we introduce Little's formula or rule. In his paper "A Proof of the Queuing Formula $L = \lambda W$" *Operations Research* 9, pp. 383-387, 1961, he proves that the mean queue length including those in service is equivalent to the arrival rate times the mean wait time in the queue.

Using this result, we can now show that the average wait time in the queue W is:

$$\overline{W} = \frac{\overline{Q}}{\lambda} = \frac{\rho}{\mu(1-\rho)}$$

And also using another form of Little's result, we can solve for the average or mean response time $\overline{T}$ which is:

$$\overline{T} = \frac{\overline{N}}{\lambda} = \frac{1}{\mu(1-\rho)}$$

Queuing Analysis and Modeling of Computer Systems

Now that we have introduced some basics of queuing analysis (for a more detailed presentation see [358], [361], [362], [359]), we wish to extend these simple principles to the analysis and performance assessment of models of computer systems.

The simplest form of a model of a computer system, yet one which is realistic, is the central server model; Figure 7.10.

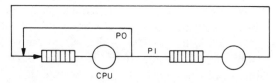

FIGURE 7.10   Central server model of a computer.

In this model the assumption is made that there is a fixed number of jobs in the system at all times (called the degree of multi-programming). That is, as a job finishes it is immediately replaced by another to maintain the level of jobs. It is assumed that the CPU service rate is given as xx jobs/sec and the I/O service rate is given as λ jobs/sec. Also at the end of a CPU service period a job requests an I/O operation with probability $0 \leq P_1 \leq 1$ and the job completes service with probability P o. Given that the degree of multi-programming is 3 we have the following states and Markov state diagram; Figure 7.11.

The states are represented as the 2 tuple (N 1, N 2) where N 1, is the number of jobs in the CPU queue and in service), and N 2 is the number of jobs in the I/O device (queue and in service).

State	(N 1 , N 2)
0	(3 , 0)
1	(2 , 1)
2	(1 , 2)
3	(0 , 3)

From the above list it can be seen that this is a complete and exhaustive representation of the states represented in the example.

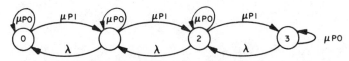

FIGURE 7.11   Markov state diagram from model of Figure 7.10.

From the Markov state diagram the local balance equations can be written and the solution of the state probabilities can be found. This is shown below:

State Equation (Flow In = Flow Out)

0 $\lambda P(1) + \mu P_0 P(0) = (\mu P_0 + \mu P_1)P(0)$
   $\lambda P(1) = \mu P_1 P(0)$
1 $\mu P_1 P(0) + \lambda P(2) = \mu P_1 P(1) + \lambda P(1)$
2 $\mu P_1 P(1) + \lambda P(3) = \mu P_1 P(2) + \lambda P(2)$
3 $\mu P_1 P(2) = \lambda P(3)$

Note:
Can ignore
flows out
and back into
same node
will cancel

Since

$$P(O) + P(1) + P(2) + P(3) = 1$$

having this information and by solving using simultaneous solution methods, we can obtain the state probabilities as follows:

$$P(0) = \frac{\lambda}{\mu P_1} P(1)$$

$$\mu P_1 P(0) + \lambda P(2) = (\mu P_1 + \lambda) P(1)$$

$$\lambda P(3) + \mu P_1 P(1) = (\mu P_1 + \lambda) P(2)$$

$$P(3) = \frac{\mu P_1}{\lambda} P(2)$$

$$P(2) = \frac{(\mu P_1 + \lambda) P(1) - \mu P_1 P(0)}{\lambda}$$

$$P(3) = 1 - (P_{(0)} + P_{(1)} + P_{(2)})$$

$$1 - (P(0)) + P(1) + P(2)) = \frac{\mu P_1}{\lambda} P(2)$$

$$1 - (P(0) + P(1)) = (1 + \frac{\mu P_1}{\lambda}) P(2)$$

$$1 - P(0) + P(1) = (1 + \frac{\mu P_1}{\lambda}) (\frac{\mu P_1}{\lambda} + 1) P(1)$$

$$- \frac{\mu P_1}{\lambda} P(0)$$

but $P(0) = \frac{\lambda}{\mu P_1} P(1)$ Therefore

$$1 - (\frac{\lambda}{\mu P_1} + 1) P(1) = (1 + \frac{\mu P_1}{\lambda})^2 P(1) - \frac{\mu P_1}{\lambda} \frac{\lambda}{\mu P_1} P(1)$$

$$1 - \frac{\lambda}{\mu P_1} P(1) - P(1) = (1 + \frac{\mu P_1}{\lambda})^2 P(1) - P(1)$$

$$1 = [\frac{\lambda}{\mu P_1} + (1 + \frac{\mu P_1}{\lambda})^2] P(1)$$

$$P(1) = \frac{1}{\frac{\lambda}{\mu P_1} + (1 + \frac{\mu P_1}{\lambda})^2}$$

$$P(0) = \frac{\lambda}{\mu P_1} P(1) = \frac{\lambda}{\mu P_1} / (\frac{\lambda}{\mu P_1} + (1 + \frac{\mu P_1}{\lambda})^2)$$

$$P(2) = (\frac{\mu P_1}{\lambda} + 1) P(1) - \frac{\mu P_1}{\lambda} P(0)$$

$$P(2) = \frac{(\frac{\mu P_1}{\lambda} + 1)}{\frac{\lambda}{\mu P_1} + (1 + \frac{\mu P_1}{\lambda})^2} - \frac{\mu P_1}{\lambda} \cdot (\frac{\lambda}{\mu P_1} / (\frac{\lambda}{\mu P_1} + (1 + \frac{\mu P_1}{\lambda})^2))$$

and

$$P_3 = 1 - (P(0) + P(1) + P(2))$$

But there is a simpler way, referred to as the product form solution. This method allows us to solve for the state probabilities utilizing a simpler form shown below:

$$P(N_1, N_2) = G \cdot (\frac{1}{\mu P_1})^{N_1} (\frac{1}{\lambda})^{N_2}$$

G is the normalization constant and is found by putting all the state probabilities in the form $P(0) = X\ P(1) = \ldots$ then summing these elements n from the previous section.

$$G = \frac{1}{\Sigma P(0) + P(1) + P(2) + P(3)}$$

Where P(0) . . .
= P(N₁, N₂) . . .

This normalization is done to guarantee that the sum of the probabilities will yield unity as per definition.

Once these state probabilities have been determined, we can then go about determining various performance measures of interests for evaluation purposes.

From the above example we can determine the CPU utilization by looking at the probability of being in a state where the CPU is utilized and summing these up. For this example CPU utilization is determined by:

CPU Utilization = $P(3,0) + P(2,1) + P(1,2)$

which is the sum of the probabilities that the CPU is busy.

Next we can determine the CPU's throughput by taking the utilization and multiplying it by the service rate. This will yield a number in jobs per second based on the probability of being busy.

CPU Throughput = $u (P(3,0) + P(2,1) + P(1,2))$

Another measure of interest is the queue length at the device here, the CPU. This is determined by taking the probability of being in a state that jobs are either in service or waiting for the CPU times the number of jobs in the CPU and its queue.

CPU Mean Queue Length with job in CPU service)
= $3P(3,0) + 2P(2,1) + P(1,2)$

From the above measure we can derive one more, namely the CPU average queue time (with service included):

= the CPU mean queue length/CPU throughput = $\frac{3P(3,0) + 2P(2,1) + P(1,2)}{\mu (P(3,0) + P(2,1) + P(1,2))}$

The same type of analysis can be supplied to the I/O device to yield measurements for its performance.

Many variations and extensions to this basic model have been performed to model the performance of computer systems. Models for multiple CPUs and/or I/O devices as seen in Figure 7.12 have been widely studied in existing literature.

Other variations include cases with multiple CPUs and single memory (multiprocessor, multiple I/O devices, faster CPUs, various processor schedulinmg algorithms, various job types, etc.).

For more details and specific examples and for a more complete coverage of analytical queuing models and how they relate to computer performance evaluation, see the following list of texts on the subject: [358], [359], [360], [361], [362].

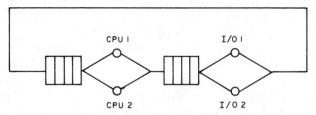

FIGURE 7.12   Cyclic queue model with multiple CPU and I/O servers.

These texts cover various aspects of computer systems performance analysis in great detail and it would be hard to add to what these texts have provided in this area.

Simulation

The use of simulation in modeling of systems is undertaken when the system of interest is too complicated for analytical modeling or requires more detailed analysis than the analytical model can provide. A simulation model can be as detailed or as simple as the modeler requires. That is, we can model a computer down to the bit level, or model it as a black box, or as something in between. The level of modeling utilized depends on the level of detail required for analysis purposes.

In order to construct a simulation, one needs to determine a model for the real system to be simulated. That is, we require an abstraction of the real system that includes all the points of interest and their associated attributes or descriptive qualities. Before this is done, first a determination that the problem requires simulation must be done based on factors of cost feasibility of doing the test on a real system, or the feasibility of analytical models. Once the determination to build the model has been made, then the task of determining the structure for the simulation can begin.

At this point, one may ask, what does a simulation gain for the analyst? One of the primary gains is the ability to analyze a system which otherwise would have been nearly impossible to approach using analytical or operation research techniques.

Simulation allows one to analyze complex and intractable mathematical models as well as models that lack a firm mathematical foundation or possess complex interactions amongst the system variables.

Advantages of simulation which make it desirable even when other techniques are available include:

1. The ability to control the experiment. This implies that the simulator has the capacity to control the environment the system under study will exist in, can drive the model with the same stimulus for multiple tests with conditions held constant when wanted, can determine what aspects of the system are important and need emphasis during experimentation,

and can control the execution and monitoring of the model at points relevant to the experiment.

2. The ability to do analysis plus testing without disturbing the real system. This implies that the modeler can test conditions on the model which in the real world may cause harmful or dangerous consequences, such as the examination of stress conditions, or limiting parameters.

3. The ability to analyze the effect of varying input variables. This capability allows the experimenter the chance to be able to study the effect or sensitivity of parameters of interest based on variable stimuli. This is an important feature of simulation modeling. This type of capability is unattainable by analytical modeling techniques.

4. It allows time compression to be used. This feature allows experimenters to study the effect of a phenomenon in real-time, compressed time, or expanded time. That is, one can view a system's events as if they were occurring naturally, or speed them up, if the real-time event is extremely slow. This would be done in order to study more cases of a particular study element in a given time period, or allow the study plus interaction of events that otherwise would be impossible or extremely time-consuming. It also allows one to study an experiment on elements in expanded time. This allows us to slow down events that are too fast to study in real-time and allows us to get a better view of each event as it occurs.

5. The simulation provides an effective vehicle for training. The construction of a simulation model provides the designer with much insight into the real-world entity being studied, which may lead to ideas for changes in the system being modeled. The simulation now allows you to go in, change the particular areas and see how it affects the overall system. The running simulation can be used to train individuals as to the operation of the simulated system and will aid in greater understanding of the user's real-world system.

Simulation is not all pluses though. There are disadvantages to using simulation for analysis of real-world problems. Simulation of real systems requires in-depth knowledge of the system under study in order to accurately represent the system. This in-depth knowledge requires extensive research time to acquire, and once acquired, the knowledge must be transposed into a simulation model of the real-world system. This transposition of knowledge of the system and simulation model is also prone to errors. Hidden or misunderstood entities could cause the model to diverge from the reality under study. The model entities or parameters may be very difficult to initialize. That is, to properly start the simulation in motion at some period of time the modeler must collect, analyze, and interpret the collected data in order to put together the proper initial values for parameters to set the model in motion at the proper instant and in syschronization. If a parameter is off, then the results would also be erroneous due to the inaccurate initial conditions.

Another problem encountered in many simulation projects is the cost associated with developing the model, running tests, and maintaining the model. Another associated problem is the developer's zeal. In my experience, modelers always will find "just one more improvement." Simulation models can become very expensive in terms of manpower and computer time due to the size and nature of simulation programs. Even with these shortfalls, simulation has been used very successfully to aid in the performance evaluation of various classes of systems.

Simulation has been used for training, such as flight trainers for airline pilots, and trainers for police departments for training of policemen. They have been used in analysis of manufacturing systems to study effects of changes to the facility or processes or plant efficiency and productivity. Simulation has been applied to studies of the economics, long-range financial planning, modeling of medical conditions, space transportation, systems, air pollution projects, railroad transportation, oil transportation and digital computer systems to name a few. Much literature exists as to specific simulations constructed and used in the performance modeling of these systems and interested users are directed to them in the references. Most models developed were built for use on a specific problem and have little use beyond that of the initial design.

Modeling

A simulation model is a mathematical and logical representation of a real system and can be operated to study changing phenomenon of that system or to acquire a better understanding of its operation. That is, the simulation is a usable, testable, laboratory facsimile of the real system.

In order to build the simulation of the real system, we need to represent the real system by a concepted model as shown in Figure 7.13.

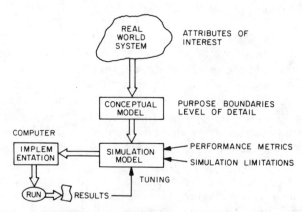

FIGURE 7.13   Simulation methodology.

The conceptual model provides the vehicle by which we represent and extract the important aspects of the real system by analytical or descriptive event techniques. The development of this abstract model still is viewed as an art. The modeler must acquire an in-depth understanding of the system to be modeled in order to derive the essence of the system, and he must also avoid being dragged into unwanted or unnecessary details. The problem here is to know how much detail is adequate. The proper level of detail can be determined only by reviewing the purpose of the model and leaving out all details not relevant to the items of interest or that do not impact these items.

Once a conceptual model is constructed, the next phase is to formulate a simulation model of the conceptualized system. What this means is we now take the conceptual elements of interest and transform them into a simulation model with emphasis on control of sequences and interaction of the elements of the model. This simulation model can then be transformed into an executable simulation program by utilizing a suitable computer language. The simulation model can be transformed using a general purpose language such as FORTRAN, PASCAL, etc., but doing this will require the modeler to construct his own methods for keeping track of time in the model, of all variables, and state transitions. This implies a large additional effort in coding of support routines to provide required timing, data collection and services, and event management services.

Another alternative to the above is to utilize one of the many available simulation languages to implement the simulation model developed. The problem here is to choose a language suited to the problem at hand. We must decide what is to be modeled such as continuous events like aircraft dynamics or discrete events like a transfer loading and unloading facility. Another type of simulation model is the queuing or network model which allows queuing analysis without the work involved in constructing and analyzing the analytical form.

Languages available for use in continuous change simulation include Dynamo, Gasp IV, Slam II, Midas, and BHSL to name a few. For event-driven modeling, the number of languages is much larger. For example: Forsim IV, Gasp II, Slam II, Simula, POD, SOL GPSS, Simpac, and Simscript. For network simulation the author is only familiar with Slam II though I am sure others exist.

Once we have coded a simulation model into an executable language, we must go about the task of verification and validation. Verification refers to the determination of whether the computer model operates as the modeler intended. Validation is the act of determining if the model's results are accurate for experimentation purposes. Validation can be done by comparing simulated results with those generated analytically or by measurement with the actual system.

Once the model is verified and validated, we can now use it to experiment with the system of interest. The outputs of these experiments are then used to analyze and predict the effect of tested conditions and changes on the real system.

The following example will be developed and discussed to illustrate the overall simulation methodology.

An often-used example for showing the use of simulation modeling is the bank teller system. This system represents a basic queuing model with independently arriving customers and 1 to n servers. This model can be analyzed by two methods rather easily, the event model and the network model.

The important aspect or entities of this model which describe it are the customers and tellers. Customers arriving at the system may be required to wait in a line, are selected for service, are provided service by the teller entity, and once service is completed, exit the system, as shown in Figure 7.14.

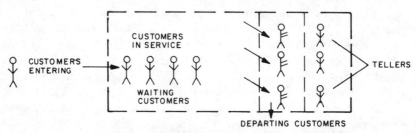

FIGURE 7.14   Bank teller simulation system.

The state of this system is determined by the status of the tellers (busy, idle) and the number of customers waiting for service. The state of the system remains unchanged except when a customer arrives or departs from the system implying that we need to analyze what happens on departures and arrivals to describe such a system.

THE EVENT MODEL

The first method we will examine to model this system is the event model. In this model we look at the execution of activities associated with each event based on adherence to a time-ordered sequence of these events. What this means is that each activity (event) in the system is created or scheduled with a time tag. This time tag describes the ordering of events in the event queue of the simulation. This ordering determines the sequence of execution for the events and therefore describes the operation of the model.

In the bank teller example, the events would be the arrival of a customer, the starting of service for a customer, and the departure of a customer from the network. To describe the events that would occur, let us translate the above event points to pseudo code. The first event describes the action of customers arriving into the queue and is comprised of code which schedules customers' random arrivals. The second event is caused by the actions of tellers and arrivals. This event looks at the tellers' status. If busy, the customer waits; otherwise the customer is serviced.

The first two events are shown below:

Event arrival
      Schedule another arrival event
      call service event—tag this event at present time
End event arrival

The second event is really a subset of the first because it is only triggered by the occurrence of the first.

Service event
      Tcustomers = Tcustomers + 1;
         If all tellers are busy
            Then number in waiting = number in waiting + 1;
               take stats on queue length
            Else
            If any teller is free
               then set count of busy tellers to busy + 1
Set time of begin service for customer at present time, take stats for single user and total aggregate queue waiting time and schedule an end of service event for the present time plus the service time at this teller;
end;
End of service event

The next event of importance is the end of service event. This event is where we remove the customer from the system and determine statistics for this customer and all customers in the system to date.

End of service event
/remove a customer/
      If number in waiting >0 then
         Number in waiting = number in waiting -1;
         Schedule a service event for Tnow;
         Take stats on time in system;
         Return
      Else
         Since number in waiting is 0 then
            Set teller to free;
            Count of busy tellers = busy -1;
            Return

It can be seen from the simple example shown above that one can quickly put together a simulation of simple systems such as this. The requirement to allow this though is a simulation language which supports gathering and computation of statistics, time management, and priority scheduling management based on event times and much automated file management and manipulation to allow the above actions to occur.

This author is familar with languages such as Gasp IV, Simscript, and Slam II which supports such a modeling capability. Without such a language a simple simulation of the above system would require extensive time and design to implement the requisite support software totally separate from the goal of the simulation exercise.

The other method of simulating this problem is the network model. In this method of modeling we look at the problem as if it were queuing systems, as in the analytical modeling technique described earlier. The difference is that in this method we do not have to solve the local balance equations or the product form solution. The simulation will perform this tedious job for us in a simple fashion. The only thing the modeler must do is describe the network of queues, its branching probabilities, arrival rates, and service rates for all the queues. This will then be used by the simulation to solve for the collection variables set up by the modeler.

Using Slam [229] as the vehicle to illustrate this, we can first show the queuing model for the bank teller as seen in Figure 7.15.

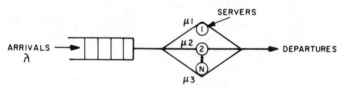

FIGURE 7.15 Queuing model of bank teller.

This queue representation of the system shows the arriving customers, the waiting queue, the teller servers, and the departing customers.

In the Slam II language, the arriving process is represented graphically by a symbol called the Create Node, as is Figure 7.16. This symbol allows a modeler to describe the arriving process for modeling purposes.

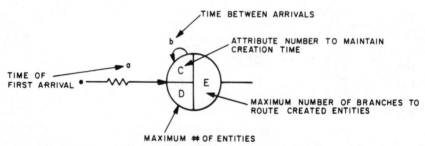

FIGURE 7.16 Create node symbol.

The queue node is used to describe the queuing process for the waiting line in the bank teller problem. The queue node is shown in Figure 7.17. This symbol allows the modeler to describe the attributes of the queue for the simulation.

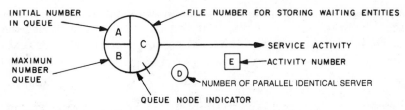

FIGURE 7.17   Model of queue node.

The activity on the server in the Slam II language is represented by the arrow, circle, and box emanating from the queue on the selection symbol. The activity or service time is described using the symbol shown in Figure 7.18.

FIGURE 7.18   Activity symbol.

In the bank teller problem, if the tellers are all viewed as having the same qualities, then we can model them as a parallel set of activities. This can be shown by using the activity symbol as above, but set N = to the number of tellers.

The final piece required to describe the bank teller system is the terminate node; Figure 7.19.

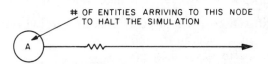

FIGURE 7.19   Terminate node symbol.

This node describes the point at which the simulation run will end.

Other important symbols are the assign node to assign quantities to attributes and the collect nodes which allow us to collect statistics for performance analysis use.

Using the above described symbols we can describe the bank teller problem in two steps. The first step is to describe the problem using traditional queuing model symbols as shown in Figure 7.20.

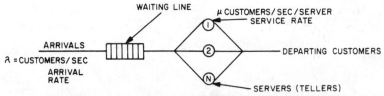

FIGURE 7.20   Queuing model for bank teller problem.

Once we have this model we can directly write out the symbols for the Slam II network model by replacing the arrival process, queuing, and service process and departure by Slam nodes as previously described. This is shown in Figure 7.21.

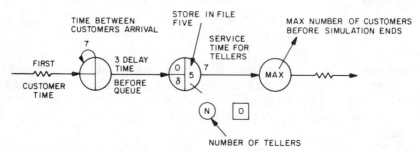

FIGURE 7.21   Slam II representation of bank teller system.

This model can then be easily expressed in Slam II code as shown below:

; Slam II Bank Teller Network Mode

Create,7.,0.;	Interarrival time for customers
Activity,3.;	Time for users to do bank business
Queue (5);	Use file 5 for queue
Activity (N)/0,7;	Service time for tellers
Terminate, max;	Run model for max entities
End network;	End of simulation statements

To enhance the effectiveness of performance evaluation, we can insert collect nodes at various points in the model to extract pertinent statistics to allow for analysis of activities at these points.

This simple model only describes some of the basic capabilities of this language. In order to more fully appreciate the breadth and abilities of such modeling languages, the reader is directed to the many texts and articles referenced at the end of this text.

THE CONTINUOUS MODELING TECHNIQUE

Another class of simulation modeling is the continuous modeling technique. This technique allows modelers to study dynamic systems where we cannot determine specific events, but can characterize the operation by rate equations (differentials).

This type of modeling approach is used to study systems where flow rates, such as fluid flows, heat transfer, energy losses, cyclic phenomenon, etc., are involved.

An example of such a system could be the modeling of an oil loading and unloading facility where we are only interested in modeling the efficiency of the loading and unloading process. The dynamics of the fluid flow into the refinery and out of the refinery can be modeled as a collection of state equations of the form dx/dt which describes the flows in and out of the refinery controlled by the arriving tankers and flow-controlling devices involved. Detailed examples of this type of modeling approach can be found in Pritsker's book *Introduction to Simulation and Slam*.

The above-described three methods, Event, Continuous and Network Simulations, describe the three basic methods used in simulation programming. Beyond this, as models of real systems become more complex and involve interaction between many subsystems and components, we will be required to use hybrid techniques in order to provide us with clean and implementable methods to model these systems. Many simulation languages have been developed which allow us to utilize the best features of each modeling technique to construct our analysis tools of the systems under study. Notable among these is the Slam II simulation language which provides methods to integrate all three basic techniques into one program in support of user requirements.

It is hoped that this discussion of this important aspect of computer performance evaluation will stimulate readers to look into this subject for more details and specifics. Chapters 8 and 9 will describe how simulation modeling has been used to enhance our ability to design better computers and systems.

Operational Analysis

This method of performance analysis is done on operational systems. The main emphasis here is to determine the operating characteristics of a computer system and its components by taking measurements of important points and events in the system. This can be done by inserting hardware monitors that collect data continuously or that collect data at specific points in time via triggering mechanisms. Another method of collecting data is to imbed collection calls into the system code which, when encountered, cause a trap to service routines which take a snapshot of system status at the time of the trap. Data collected include register status and contents, device status, computation status, and system status.

Operational analysis utilizes many of the same techniques as other descriptions in collecting and determining the statistical nature of the entities of interest. In this type of performance assessment real data is collected, then used in determining the performance and operational characteristics of the system under study. Details of this technique can be found in references at the end of the text.

Summary

This chapter introduced the basics for performance evaluation of computer systems using analytical simulation and operational analysis techniques.

Analytical modeling techniques were described, introducing the reader to basic nomenclature and techniques to evaluate systems utilizing analytical queuing techniques.

The next section described methods for utilizing simulation programming in the performance evaluation of systems. This section described some of the basic methods available for simulation programming.

Finally a very brief introduction to outline the use of operational analysis in computer performance evaluation was described.

CHAPTER EIGHT

Computer-Aided Design

In recent years, computer-aided design has become more common due to the increased complexity of the designs being attempted. As the size of these systems increases, the need for assistance at all levels rises proportionately. Designers are faced with more tradeoffs and decisions at all phases of the design process and they need assistance in making the optimal decisions based on the requirements being levied on them. Computer-aided design in the traditional sense generates the image of a hardware hacker sitting at his trusty system developing some new, exotic piece of hardware. This view is still accurate though the present thrust is to utilize the knowledge gained in building chip CAD systems to help provide the basis for total system specification and design. Once tools such as this have been developed, designers of large real-time distributed systems can utilize these tools to help them track designs and aid in the tradeoff analysis that must accompany any fair-sized system. Without tools such as those described above, the plight of the systems designer will not improve in the future.

CAD Technology

To introduce the notion of a total design tool, let us first digress to a description of present VHSIC/VLSI CAD tools and their basic structure.

The need for computer-aided design first gained support in the late 1950s when large corporations such as aerospace firms saw the potential power in using computers to assist in error-prone design tasks such as backplane wiring and logic diagrams. By the 1960s the industry began to truly realize the significance of this technology to aid in handling more complex designs, such as circuit board layout.

During the 1970s CAD systems grew in complexity to handle the advent of SSI (small-scale integrated circuit) design. These tools helped designers to control the documentation of a design, its layout, and the bounds checking on technology limitations and provided a means to evaluate simple tradeoffs such as power versus delay.

Present LSI/VLSI systems handle thousands of gates and assist in the design process from specification to fabrication.

A typical LSI/VLSI CAD system is comprised of four major sections (Figure 8.1), namely, design definition and entry, design verification, phsyical layout and design, and design test profile. These sections work together to provide a tool which assists the designer during initial specification, in design test, actual design implementation, and on to product testing to assist in testing and integration of final products.

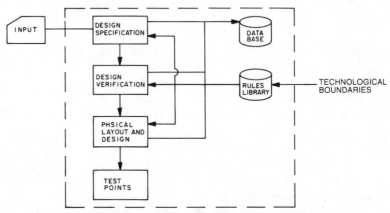

FIGURE 8.1   Typical LSI/VLSI CAD system.

Design definition and entry allow a designer to use either a graphical input to specify the design or a language interface. These techniques allow for the specification of what a design will do and the logic required to perform the specific function.

These interfaces allow designers the ability to describe their design structurally in terms of library elements available, Figure 8.2. These blocks are then connected together by the designer to provide the wanted effect. Designers also can develop and design their own discrete designs for a component or interface if the library is deficient in the description of a component using low level library entities.

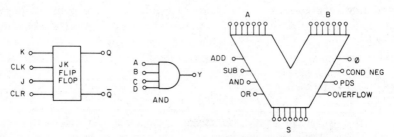

FIGURE 8.2   Example of library logic elements.

The design defined by using the interactive input is stored in a data base and can be recalled later for performing more work or can be printed out either graphically or gramatically in a language for reviewing by the architects.

The next phase a designer would be performing once he feels his design is mature enough is to take the inputted and refined design and put it through a design verification process in the CAD systems. At present this is either done while the designer is defining his design so as to not allow errors to creep in or is done once the design is complete. In this discussion we assume it is done after the specification stage of design is completed.

Design verification in traditional hardware CAD systems is done by simulation. The hardware chip design is stimulated with simulated logic signals. The CAD system then simulates the actions caused in the circuits of the design and delivers the proper outputs as called for in the design. This process is done for specific clock periods and for each input sequence provided. This method of analysis allows the designer to check his design for the specified characteristics of the total design for correctness to a priori required outputs based on the state of the chip's stimuli.

These simulations of the circuits could be performed at varying levels. One could simulate logic at the gate level or up to chip levels. The designer could use this approach to iterativly build more complex designs by the designing of lower level logic into chip designs and then utilizing these chips to design larger systems.

Once design definition and design verification have been performed, the next step is to perform a physical layout for the design. This process must now take into account physical limitations and technology parameters in performing the layout. Physical parameters include elements such as: how much logic can be put on a specified chip area and maintain a specific yield of good chips. Or they may require the system to determine how to lay out a chip within a fixed area and with a fixed number of I/O pins with the overall objective to construct the total design in the least number of chips and interconnects.

Techniques utilized in physical layout are either intended to maximize the use of chip area to put the most possible devices on a chip with a given set of I/O connections, or are based on functional boundaries. In the case of maximal use of the chip, the system will look at all possible layouts with the goal of minimizing the amount of wasted space to maximize the volume of devices that can be put on the chip. This type of solution requires an optimization algorithm which analyzes all the options.

The other technique is more natural to human and organizational boundaries. That is, ordinarily if a device is being designed it is usually broken up into sections based on functional boundaries such as an ALU, memory, I/O device, controller, etc. These functional units are typically designed by one designer who must interface to other designs with a given set of links and protocols. This method will not, on the average, result in the maximum utilization of chip area. The problem is caused by the nature of functional vice total design. The functional design is a piece of the whole and as such will not require as much logic to perform the requisite task.

In either case, the CAD system must now go through the task of allocating pins and space to the chip. The first job is to estimate constructability of the design. That is, to check and see if the design is not exceeding the technology limits in terms of packages to be used, power dissipation, and cooling ability of material to name a few parameters.

Once the preliminary checks have been performed, the typical CAD system will then go about the job of allocating physical pins to the initial design inputs and outputs while providing the required power and ground pins. This process requires the CAD system to estimate the location of major chip functions to keep logic close to its inputs and outputs, thereby minimizing wire runs. Once the pins are assigned to the package, the CAD system must run through the design and place all components into the chip.

The placement can be done totally automatically, if the system uses a fixed grid approach known as masterslice. In this approach a fixed grid of cells is provided with wiring channels available between them (Figure 8.3). The cells are then used by the system to place the various circuits of the design. Using this method the system has a fixed number of possible ways it can place the circuits in a design, thereby providing a bounded number of potential configurations limiting the complexity that the placement algorithm must handle.

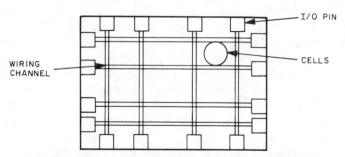

FIGURE 8.3   Masterslice chip before placement.

A more common approach to design of integrated circuits is the custom design approach. This concept provides much more flexibility to the designer at the expense of the placement program in the CAD system. The designer will develop and integrate many small component designs, then integrate them into a system design. The difference here is that cells need not be regular. This allows the designer the room for complex design without the need to partition the cells. The problem is that the placement algorithm now has a more difficult job in determining the optimal placement of circuits in meeting the total design. The placement problem is much harder in custom design due to the nonregular shapes possible, whereas in masterslice all the cells are the same size. Therefore, the placement problem here is one of ordering which cells need to be adjacent to each other due to wiring connections and how to best structure a path to traverse the smallest distance in doing an operation. Custom design must additionally look at how to use the area of the chip optimally without wasting space. This job is complicated by the varying size of components and shapes. The placement algorithm must now balance both ordering and space utilization based on area available and requirements specified.

The next significant problem in designing circuits using VLSI CAD systems is the wiring problem. Wiring involves the connection of subcircuits into a total circuit or card design. Wiring programs have been studied for over 20 years with first cuts looking at a maze running technique [396] to algorithms such as that of [120] who viewed the problem more from a system view. He looked at total runs versus a run at a time, thus being able to make more optimal system decisions. The wiring problem is compounded by the fact that some circuits feed many others and that present technology, e.g., number of layers available for wiring runs, is limited in its ability to provide the requisite volume of paths required by such intricate and intertwined designs. Future designs will require more intricate algorithms to minimize wire delays and volume as circuit densities rise and component volume shrinks. These combined effects will cause great disparity in the ability to construct effective VHSIC (Very High Scale Integrated Circuits) circuits in a timely and cost effective manner.

The final phase in hardware CAD design is to generate tests. This process determines a sequence of inputs which, when driven into the hardware, will force specific patterns at the package's output pins.

This portion of the CAD system ensures that a design is testable and determines how to test such a device to ensure faults will be detected. Test generation is very important so that designs can be examined for quality off the assembly line and that problems in the field can be traced to the proper device generating an error condition. Fault detection and recovery represents a massive subculture of computers. In order for distributed computer systems to survive under harsh and error-prone conditons, built-in testing and detection is required. This whole area is beyond the scope of this test, but is covered in depth in [397].

CAD of Software

Technology of the past has shown that we can utilize computers to aid us in the design of computer hardware. The next step is to ask if this same technology can be applied to software development.

In the past, software design has always been viewed as an art not a science. There have been some gurus and hackers, but there did not exist a stringent set of rules and techniques for good software designers to follow. Software was designed on the fly and debugged until it worked. Changes were and still are expensive due to the inability of people to assess the impact so-called minor changes will have on a running software system.

The objective of recent work is to close these holes in the software world.

Researchers have been looking at ways to make software design easier, more productive, and survivable. Efforts towards these goals came in many forms. An effort viewed as having much merit was to develop high-order languages. That is, languages that would be better suited to human understanding and that would have better and simpler control structures, variable and name types, etc., which, when taken together, would yield easier code to write, use, and maintain.

High-order languages, though, only supplied one point in the line of necessary tools to provide an overall environment for better software design. High-order languages such as PASCAL and more recently ADA have provided a rich variety of structures and techniques which aid in the ability of programmers to develop and implement better code. But without structured programming practices, these coders could risk developing unreadable and unsupportable code, as was the case in the days of assembly coding.

Structured programming represented the movement of programming from an art toward a science. In structured programming the goal is to develop code in a structured fashion. That is, coders now were expected to develop the entire program from a higher view and fill in the lower level details as required. This is the notion of top down design; Figure 8.4.

The philosophy of top down design is to code and debug programs from a total system view. The overall task (program) being developed is specified at a high level. The designer develops data flow specifications for the program, then control flow diagrams which together specify the control and information flow necessary to realize the given level of the design. This level is then coded with all underlying levels left stubbed. This allows the designer to design code and debug the design in an iterative method, first allowing the overall design to be tested for content structure, completeness, and operation at a very high level. Then it provides a basis to design, code, and test the lower, more detailed stubs in an environment which has been tested and verified a priori. Theoretically, if this methodology is rigorously adhered to, programs should require less debug time during coding and should be easier to maintain due to the modular design.

Structured programming saw much growth in acceptance and use during the 1970s, though it was not the panacea as originally thought. It did provide a means for better code development if utilized properly and as such was successful. Structured programming was the impetus that began the drive toward a more methodical, structured, and logical approach to software development. Designers realized the benefits of structured programming, but saw its limitations. They needed a more automated technique to support the ever increasing complexity of software projects.

The other problem with structured programming was the coder's perception of productivity and project goals. Programmers had and still have a view

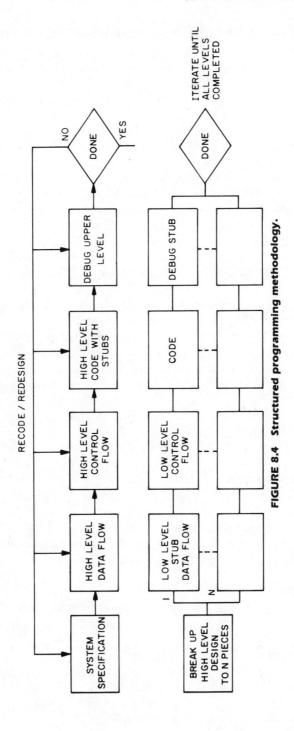

FIGURE 8.4 Structured programming methodology.

that coding should commence immediately in order to leave time to debug, etc. But, by coding only when appropriate as in structured programming, then the need for debugging would lessen or be nonexistent near the end of projects.

The next phase in the development of software engineering, the development of structured, methodical, and logical methods for software such as that which exists for hardware, came with the advent of structured design techniques and tools. As software projects grew in size, beyond the ability of individuals to easily manage their complexity, corporations realized the need for computer assistance in managing this complexity.

The first attempts to more fully structure the software development cycle came about due to this need. Early endeavors such as structured design and analysis met with success when utilized properly, but designers' acceptance was slow. Early techniques of structured design such as Yeordon's technique revolved around early specification and refinement of designs before coding would begin. The goal of the techniques was to be better able to determine when a design was complete—when it had presented all the essential parts and all these parts were sufficiently defined. Another important aspect of early manually structured design techniques was the notion of consistency. Consistency deals with the determination of interfaces between parts of a design. To be consistent, a total design must not have conflicts among its components nor should it have inconsistencies or missing interfaces.

Structured program design for major and minor software products have four major steps:

Requirements specification
What is being designed and what is it to do.

Product design specification
Defines the overall product architecture and its parts.

Detailed design specification
Defines the specific parts in detail as to data flow, control flow, algorithms, and data structures utilized.

Code and documentation
Taking the detailed design specification and converting it into actual code.

In large systems, all of these specifications are required and each must be verified and validated before the next specification or step in the design process can occur, if a correct design without flaws is to be produced. The process involved in each step is tedious but extremely important if a consistent, complete, and correct product is to be realized.

Once an idea for a product has been formulated, the process of building the product begins. The first element is the requirements specification. In government programs this is known as the A specification. This constitutes the basis upon which the product must perform.

Requirement specifications deal with defining the problem the product is being designed to solve, and the bounds on performance required to achieve the wanted operation. This implies that the computer program to be developed is specified as to what it must be capable of doing within the bounds that exist on that capability. For example, in a requirements specification one might specify that the data base management program shall be capable of processing 30 transactions per second of benchmark load 1 in appendix A, or we may specify more explicitly that the data base manager must respond to type 1 queries in 1 second or less, to type 2 queries in 3 seconds or less to type 3 queries in 10 seconds or less and so on. Type 1 to N queries are defined in appendix B. In both cases in order to make the specification complete, the requirement specification must have the exact bounds specified in the appendices. In this case, either the transaction benchmark load or the definition of query type must be provided in the appendix. Doing this leaves no ambiguity in the eyes of the designers who will take the requirements specification and develop the product design specification from it. The requirements specification represents the yardstick upon which the system's functionality and performance are measured throughout the design and life of the product. Due to the reliance of all other portions of the design process and also its effect on the final product's ability to perform as wanted, this portion of the design process must be precise, free of errors, and have no missing pieces. If any of these flaws exist, they will find their way into the final product as designer errors, reducing functionality or creating a loss in accuracy of computer operations.

In order to see that such conditions do not arise, verification and validation of the requirements specification needs to be performed. Earlier studies have shown that if errors are cheaper and easier to find during the early phases of a design, and if these flaws are corrected early on in the project, the overall project time can be cut or at least be directed more towards the job at hand.

The verification and validation process is best performed by an organization other than the specification designers. This allows the specification to be reviewed by someone not closely attached to a particular design. Usually in most designs, flaws and errors are best found through the interaction of a knowledgable designer and an impartial second party who together uncover hidden errors. Verification and validation as shown before refers to the correctness and completeness of a specification or design.

The process for achieving this goal varies from totally manual means to computer automated techniques. Manual methods for verification and validation of specification deal with reviewing and analyzing the document via reading, interface checking, discussion, modeling, and operations analysis.

Reading refers to the process of the verification and validation organization reading the specification for holes or misrepresented facets. The readers bring a different perspective to bear on the specification. They may represent a wide range of people from diverse disciplines such as management, testing, software coders, architectural designers, system engineers, etc. Their varying skills and views will put the specification through the magnifying glass from different slants, thereby providing a broader coverage. Another form of reading is the inspection or walkthrough. In this type of approach the specification is presented to a group of individuals of varying disciplines and is scrutinized as to its correctness and completeness to the specified intentions.

Interface checking is a more complete analysis of the document's consistency and correctness. This stage of verification and validation involves analysis of the state transition of the system, the data flow, and control flow between major components, as well as verification of data structures and contents. This phase in the verification and validation requires the use of diagrams and cross referencing tables and data base to analyze the interaction amongst the major components specified in the requirements document. This type of checking is invaluable in ascertaining the completeness of a design. It allows for the detection of missing components like dangling references in programming language data structures, for example. Cross referencing and interface checking become even more important and more difficult as the design progresses, so it is of the utmost importance to correct deficiencies early on to not impede future efforts in this area. This technique will be further discussed when we progress into the more automated vehicles for design specification, verification, and validation later in this chapter.

Another method used in verification/validation at all phases is meeting with and discussing of the specification or design with the originator. As most experienced designers can attest, discussions with interested colleagues and with outside individuals usually are beneficial to both parties. The outside interaction brings in a new view which often reveals weak or missing points in a design or specification that otherwise may have gone undiscovered until later in a design or during service time. This approach tends to reveal blatant errors and missing components, leaving small errors and hidden errors for interface check, modeling, and operations analysis to uncover. But it still represents a valuable tool to aid in the correct and complete design of software systems.

The next phase in ascertaining the correctness and completeness of the requirements specification—even more so in further layers—is modeling and operations analysis or structured scenario walkthrough.

Modeling, from the view of manual analysis, takes the form of mathematical representations and manual manipulations. These mathematical representations of system structure and interaction may take the form of formulas which represent the dynamic behavior or queuing models which provide a means to study many forms of interaction, as shown in previous chapters. As an example of such modeling, we may wish to see if the performance levels we specified in the requirements specification are realistic. That is, are they correct and sound based on available or projected technology? We could construct a queuing model of the data base manager at a very high level, i.e., in terms of average achievable service time based on either measured quantities or projected quantities and analyze if the given DBM can handle the mix of transactions provided to it from a theoretical viewpoint. Such modeling will help the originator of a requirement specification to be reasonable in the selection of boundaries for components' operation. The problem, though, is that such models cannot look at and analyze the dynamic effect of changing conditions and parameters on the software system's behavior.

A final manual tool available to organizations doing verification and validation for requirements specifications and for other levels of the design, is what is referred to as operations analysis or scenario testing. This type of analysis requires the specification team to walk through the operation of the particular specified product based on some given scenario (fixed set of input stimuli and conditions). This will give all parties visibility into the total systems operations as viewed from the eyes of the designers. This scenario approach will force originators of the specification to look at the document from yet another and different view, thereby possibly providing for another chance to discover holes in the specification.

If all these techniques are utilized, the requirement specification produced should provide a firm, complete, concise, and feasible basis upon which further, more detailed, design can ensue—while also providing a sound yardstick for measuring success of the ultimate product.

Product Design Specification

Once a verified and validated requirement specification has been completed, there is the task of performing a more detailed product design specification. This phase of the design process deals with defining the software architecture, the components of this architecture, and their interactions. At this level, knowledgeable software architects are required in order to provide the level of expertise required to produce a complete architectural specification from the provided requirements specification.

The architecture for the product is derived from the previous requirements specification. As noted previously, the requirements specification tells us what we are building and the constraints to build to. The architectural portion of the product design specification extracts the major components of the product's specification and refines these down though an iterative process to a total product design.

This level of design introduces the concept of data flow and control flow in a more meaningful context. The components of the software architecture are defined at the upper levels utilizing some modeling technique such as (PDL) Program Design Language, (SADT) Structured Analysis and Design Technique, or possibly data flow diagrams.

For example, if we were designing a data base manager for a distributed architecture we would start by defining the major components (Figure 8.5).

FIGURE 8.5   High-level architectural description for a DBMS software subsystem.

These components are then described as to their operation and functionality within the system. Once this is accomplished a high-level vista of the information flow between these components is produced to more clearly define their architecture and interaction. The major goal of this phase of design is to describe all the components from the highest to the lowest in terms of their functionality and informational requirements. The process in most techniques is fairly uniform. Upper-level system components are defined, their lower levels are then described as stubs or unknown entities. Once the entire system is clearly defined at one level, the designer then reiterates the entire process to the next level and so on until a complete specification of all components and subcomponents is accomplished. In all levels the design is again put through the same rigorous verification and validation process described in the previous pages.

There are manual methods that have been developed to assist designers with this tedious and error-prone iterative design process. One such technique was described in [346]. In this paper the authors describe a methodology of structured systems design based on decomposition. SADT provides means to structure the task of software design, to allow decomposition of large projects into meaningful and controllable parts. It provides a uniform way to represent and communicate analysis and design results. It allows for a means to document the overall design process and provides a means to control the level of detail, accuracy, completeness, and quality while supplying a management tool to assess results of the design team's efforts.

SADT syntax is simple, thereby allowing very complex structures to be developed with the simple constructs of boxes representing components of the whole with arrows showing the interface between them. Using these boxes and arrows, diagrams can be constructed. These diagrams can then be connected to form more complex structures up to the total system.

The SADT model represents a structured way to view a system. Designers can begin to form the major blocks of a system, and describe the blocks and their interfaces. Once these are completely specified the designer goes to the next level of detail to take the upper level boxes (diagrams) and break them down to their components and so on until the entire system is specified (Figure 8.6).

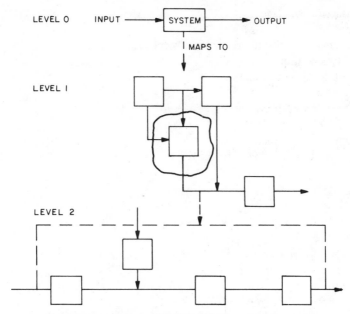

LEVEL O   INPUT ⟶ SYSTEM ⟶ OUTPUT

LEVEL I

LEVEL 2

FIGURE 8.6   Example of SADT hierarchy of graph.

The low-level blocks and interface arrows will represent the total specification of the product system being designed. The use of SADT diagrams in a design totally specifies the relationship of the boxes (components) of a design among each other.

SADT represented a step in the right direction, but it still was only a manual tool to aid in the design process. It still relied on the human in the loop to do the crosschecking and other verification and validation required to ensure correctness. It did supply a more natural and structured way to view and think about such complex systems and interactions.

The next phase in the software design process is the detailed design specification. In this phase of the design the goal is to completely specify all components of the system in terms of data flow, control flow, data structures, and operations. Once this specification is complete it will leave just a simple coding phase to complete the design. This is the core design phase in the software products life cycle.

The upper level blocks and interfaces specified above in the product design phase must now be converted to actual required data flows to realize the above architectural design and its requirements. Given an architectural design to start with, the detailed design specification writer must take the blocks and allocate them to specific designs for detailed development. For example, if given an architectural component describing a distributed data base management system, we could have details of the transaction manager look like the following:

```
Transaction Manager
Inputs are
      Transaction synchronization commands
      Query requests
        local and global
Outputs are
    Query requests/responses
      Local and global
    Optimization plan
    Transaction synchronization responses/commands
Parts are
    Query processor
      Input queries
      Output plans
    Update sync algorithm
      Inputs update req
      Outputs update resp
    Trans sync
      Input sync commands
      Output sync response/commands
    End

    Subparts are
      Query processor
        Input queries
        Output plans
      Parts are
        Query parser
        Query optimizor
    End
```

The example shows only a very high level portion of the architectural design specification in pseudo language. If we focus on query optimizor, then in the detailed design phase the job would be to specify completely an implementation description, not code. That would represent the design of the optimizor that meets the requirements levied on it from the two previous design steps.

We begin this step again by taking the upper level blocks and breaking them into the subparts and defining them iteratively until a complete definition exists.

This process of interative design will bring us to a point where we have very low level blocks remaining that now need to be designed. In the example above, the query optimizor would possess components that examine directories, examine remote dictionaries, perform cost estimates, iterate all possible ways to perform query, make recommendations, and build plan. These represent a partial list of the components required by a query optimizor to perform its specified task. This task is to take a request for information and find the fastest method to produce the requisite result.

The detailed designers would take each of these components and describe their lower blocks and interfaces, if possible. Once they get to the level where this decomposition does not gain much more insight into the design, the designer will then switch to detailed data structure specification to describe the requisite data structures for his portion of the product. Then he will describe the data flow between all the functional blocks in the design beginning at the highest view and working down to the lowest required data flow to completely specify the architectural informational interactions. The next phase is to take each functional block and describe its control flow utilizing control flow diagrams. These diagrams taken with the data flow diagrams, the data structure, and the upper level specification diagrams totally describe the product. The designer must perform verification and validation of the design as was done in the other phases. Such verification and validation should be more encompassing, as it will have more data to act on, but should be easier to perform if the upper level's verification and validation was properly and completely executed.

Once the detailed design specification has been completed and the verification and validation process has been completed, the only remaining task is code generation, test, and integration. If a thorough job in developing the three specifications was performed, then the coding job should represent a small portion of the actual software development cycle. What this means is that code should easily be generated from the detailed data structure diagrams, data flow diagrams, control flow diagrams and block annotation describing operations. This author's experience with this approach has proven out this fact. Projects I have been involved in that used this technique were easier to code, debug, and integrate due to the strict adherence to the structured design philosophies described in this section.

Automated Techniques

The manual process constitutes a very difficult job if a large amount of code is to be developed. Due to this, engineers realized a need for automated means to aid in the software development process. Two early tools still in wide use are PSL/PSA and SREM. PSL/PSA [349] is useful in many environments, and SREM is applicable for large missile defense systems.

PSL/PSA is a tool which provides for the description and analysis of system specifications. PSL (Problem Statement Language) is the language which provides designers the ability to express specifications using a very structured function and information flow technique like SADT. PSL represents an automated version of earlier described structured design techniques. PSL provides the means for designers to specify the system structure, data structure, data flow, and control flow as well as the behavioral aspects of the target system.

PSA (Problem Statement Analyzer) acts on the PSL data base to analyze the specified design. This analysis consists of various reports which can best be classified by the type of output provided. Four major classes of reports are available. The modification report stores and controls the change process to the data base, the reference report, various summary reports, and analysis reports.

The modification report represents a trace of the data base being acted on, the actions performed on it as well as possible error flags based on actions performed on the data base. Reference reports represent various views of the data base based on user preference. For example, we may wish to examine all the objects in the data base and view their type as well as who changed it last and when. These can be found using a reference analysis report.

The next class of reports is the summary report. This report supplies what its name suggests; that is, a summary of collections of data base information from a particular user's viewpoint. For example, one may wish to look at all objects associated with a particular set of inputs/outputs and see how much has been specified about the objects. Using the summary class of reports one could examine the data flow in the specification in graphical form or study the heirarchy of structuring present in the system. The final type of report available from PSL/PSA is the analysis report. This is by far the largest contribution of PSL/PSA to the ultimate objective of aiding designers in the correct, consistent, and timely design of large software systems. The analysis report provides output of analysis performed on the PSL data base. Reports generated include the content comparison report which analyzes the various objects in the PSL data base to check the correctness of the inputs and outputs in order to bring out areas of weak definition, etc. The data process interaction report is used to find dangling objects or gaps in specifications due to missing or ill-defined inputs/outputs or objects. Another analysis report available is the process chain report. This report allows designers to view the dynamic behavior of their design. The designer can trace an events flow through the design and see the effect of one object's action on others. We can use this report to study the flow of control/data in a system in the PSL data base. This tool represents a trend towards a more automated means to manage large software projects.

Another such endeavor was the SREM (Software Requirements Engineering Methodology); see Figure 8.7. This methodology represents another level in the software-aided design time line of developments. SREM represents a total system design approach. It provides a means to specify a software system to determine its completeness and correctness as in PSL/PSA and additionally provides a means to model the design to study its dynamic operational characteristics, thereby allowing for a complete analysis and assessment of the software system's design.

SREM uses a language similar to PSL to input specifications and it is referred to as RSL (Requirements Statement Language). This language provides

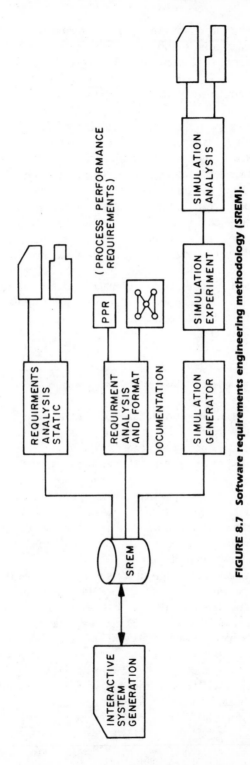

FIGURE 8.7 Software requirements engineering methodology (SREM).

a flexible means to specify a software design utilizing primitives such as elements, attributes, relationships, and structures. Using these features, designers can specify a wide range of designs. SREM has been used by BMDATC (Ballistic Missile Defense Advanced Technology Center) to aid in the design of large real-time software systems. More information on this can be found in [347].

These two examples represent some preliminary attempts at constructing computer-aided tools to assist in the software development cycle. A hole in the integration of the previous technologies still exists. The combination of hardware and software constitutes a total system as one tends to drive the capabilities realizable from the other. This tells us that it would be desirable to have a means to specify the "what we want" without specifying the "how." Leave the how up to later designs to better make the best choice to meet the requirements. Present approaches have a baseline of either hardware or required software and they must develop from the base, not from a clean slate. The goal of a total design tool is to supply a methodology of design which aids the designer of the total system to make the optimal design decisions from a system view which aids the underlying hardware and software designers while meeting the specified requirement. The next section will discuss this philosophy of system design.

CAD for the Total Systems

Earlier in this chapter it was shown how computers have been used to aid in the design of hardware as well as software for computers. The next logical question is: Can they also be used to assist in the total system design. That is, can computers be used to assist in the developing of a total system's architecture and can they be used to realize the various tradeoffs required at the total system level to aid designers in selecting the optimal mix of hardware and software to meet system requirements. In order to develop such tools, one needs to assess the framework upon which to perform the design process. One must determine the hierarchy of tasks to be performed in order to deliver a sound system and component design.

As was seen previously, the design process is an iterative one in which each level is iterated until a wanted response or capability is realized.

The notion of computer-aided design of systems has seen much growth in acceptance over the past few years. Various universities, corporations, and government agencies have conceived and developed early tools aimed at this ultimate goal.

These early efforts at computer-aided design of systems have looked at the problem from a high level. These early tools were aimed at aiding designers in the selection of a class of technologies in meeting a particular class of problems. Present efforts are leaning more toward a total system design approach which encompasses the system specification and analysis, machine design, and software design.

The process performed in all these total system design approaches is basically as follows:

1. The determination of need is derived.
2. The requirements based on the need are developed.
3. The system's architecture is developed to support the requirements from a system's hardware and software view.
4. The architecture is evaluated from a requirements view and iterated until the system meets the requirements.
5. The system architecture is broken into hardware and software blocks.
6. Hardware design and software design are performed using present state of the art CAD tools.
7. The total design is delivered once all iterations on the design are complete.

In order to realize such an automated tool in the future, early work looked at defining what each level truly needed to perform in meeting the total design goal. This definitional phase will aid designers in developing criteria for automated tools which can perform the given task in less time and more accurately than the manual methods.

The following section will describe the function of each of the previously defined phases to clarify the methodology of the total design approach.

DETERMINATION OF NEED

In order for any undertaking to be successful one must determine the need for the product. That is, does this item meet a need? If it does, then the product is worth producing.

In terms of computer system development, this state represents the specification of the performance requirements that this system needs to be built against. System specification during this phase is comprised of identification and solidification of requirements for the total system. The identification process is comprised of defining the problem at hand, the constraints on performance of the device to address the problem, interfaces from the device to the outside world, and device responsibilities in terms of functionality. This phase represents a very important aspect of the total design because this is the phase where user requirements are initially formulated into a conceptual model of reality. This phase develops a model of the final system from the eyes of the user and his applications. The system developers use this phase to firm up all the user's perspectives of what the system is supposed to do. Representative of this phase would be a specification of the concept of operation for the system. A document would be developed which captures the user's views of how the system is to be operated, what is required for operation, what performance the user should see from the system, and what the user sees and views the sysytem to consist of. The output of this phase can be viewed as a total system requirement specification of performance. This output will then be used as a yardstick to measure the conformance of all phases of the design to the actual user requirements.

ARCHITECTURE DEVELOPMENT

Once a solid foundation of system requirements has been developed, the job becomes one of how to design a system level architecture which will provide the requisite performance. This level in the total system design process has many tradeoffs involved. The system architect must look at the myriad combinations of technologies and techniques to provide the optimal system for the given requirements. In traditional design the architect relies on experience to weed out bad alternatives, and uses brute force analysis and intuition to select the final choice of hardware and software components to meet the design requirements.

Using manual design methodologies, the architect would be limited to a small number of actual options with which he can perform detailed tradeoff analysis. This hinders the architect's ability to select the best of all combinations of components for the system. If automated means of performance assessment were available, then tradeoffs of many combinations of hardware versus software configurations could be tried, and various techniques to implement the many hardware and software components could also be investigated. This would allow the architects the ability to fine tune and optimize designs before too much effort is expended to design the final system.

An example of an architectural design at this level in the design process is as follows: Given that we have a distributed computer system that must supply a certain level of responsiveness to users of the system in terms of response to queries, the system architect can look at the requirements and determine how many system parameters such as:

Number of nodes required
Data distribution
Replication factor
Update synchronization scheme
Potential concurrency control schemes
Level of query optimization required
Data model to use

are required to support the user requirements.

The architect has the choice of using classical analysis techniques, such as queuing models and simulation, to study various options for each of these items dependent on the requirements. Let us look at a few of the options and study how decisions could be made.

For the aforementioned data base specification problem, the architect must look at how many user stations are required, what kind of query load is expected, and what type and volume of data is required to support these queries as well as the underlying background applications and systems processing data requirements. Keeping these requirements in mind the architect must look at all options for number of nodes required to support the data base, the resident data at each, the replication level present as well as the update rate and mechanism for the system to meet the user requirements. For example, to determine where to place the data items the architect must first look at how the data should be split. He must determine if the data will be split by location or by function. For example, should he split the R&D files based on what computer is connected, or distribute to a computer data base specifically set up for project A, or another set up for B, etc. Once we have acquired this organizational information the architect must determine how many computers are required to support the requisite load and what files to put on what machine in order to perform this allocation. The designers can begin by the assumption to put all data files closest to the user who requires them. The problem arises when more than one user needs a particular file. The architect must then either allow replication with its illities for performance reasons or regroup processors into clusters or spheres of view to bound the options.

The better way to solve this problem is to utilize some modeling capability to study the various options available, with their pros and cons as weights. The architect, given that he has available an automated tool, can study the options of having 1 to n computers available with either centralized, replicated, factored, or hybrid data file distribution. This analysis would allow the architect to determine the optimal number of nodes to supply for the data base subsystem to provide the specified user response time and availability requirements.

In order to make this selection the architect could take one of n file allocation algorithms which have been developed which will optimally place the given files based on specified user requirements and constraints. These algorithms all basically operate in the same way. They all assume that there is a good knowledge of user queries that use the data and that the data files are all defined as to size, aggregate contents, and update rates. The job then becomes one of how to weigh the various cost functions based on the given constraints, such as a given number of nodes, capacity of storage, communications paths, and update versus retreival processing requirements. The system architect can study the effect of varying the number of nodes, the update rate, the capacity of nodes, the topology of connectivity for the network, the capacity of the links, the redundancy level (number of copies), and the availability requirement in determining the optimal allocation of files to nodes in providing the requisite user responsiveness.

Once the architect has determined the baseline for the number of copies of the files and the number of nodes through either manual or computer-assisted means, the next job is to determine the system architectural components which will maintain the data base's integrity, correctness, and currency in the face of various loads and failures if fault tolerance is also a requirement. For example, if we have determined that we require a distributed architecture with n nodes each having a portion of the entire data base with high use pieces redundantly stored, then we must determine how we will maintain the data base at all sites in a consistent and up-to-date state with updates occurring from many sites into many copies. To accomplish this we need to address the issue of update synchronization and concurrency control. Specifically, we need to determine what method of file updates is to be used and how concurrent reads and writes are to be handled to multiple copies while still supplying the requisite transaction throughput to the user application and online process.

In order to do this the architect must look at the processing resources required or present at each site. He must look at the volume of updates versus queries being levied on the system's data base nodes and perform a tradeoff analysis of various techniques versus payoff in relation to the requirements. For example, if we have a high level of reads versus updates we may be able to tolerate a primary copy update scheme with its large volume of internodal traffic, while on the other hand if we have much more updates than reads we may wish to look more at a moving primary type updater where updates are initiated from the source site and propagated to other nodes.

Once the architect has studied all the options for the various system level components and determined their qualities, he next must take the total system architecture, hardware and software and perform final verification and validation assessment for the total system's design. Once this final tradeoff analysis and performance assessment phase has been completed, a total systems specification can be developed which describes the system from a user requirements and system architectural view.

At this point the design specification is mature enough to place the design into two categories: a hardware and software specification and design phase. The system specification is passed on to the hardware and software architects who will now use traditional manual or computer-aided techniques to determine the detailed architecture for the hardware and software for the system.

Hardware design will be comprised of two levels, namely, selection of off-the-shelf hardware, where applicable, and high-level specification for any custom components required. The custom components can then be developed using off-the-shelf CAD tools as previously described. In each case the design levels must go through design verification and validation as was previously shown. This ensures a correct and complete design from start to finish.

The system design approach presented is more a collection of techniques than an integrated design tool. The optimal goal would be to convert the total system design approach into a computer-aided system design tool, thereby providing an environment for assisting designers of large computer systems from start of design to completion.

Viewing the design approach from the front end, that is, from the view of the specifier and system architect, we can find that some work has ensued on developing tools to aid these people in their jobs. Early work in this area was aimed at developing performance evaluation and comparative analysis tools specific to subproblems of the total system design problem. Tools developed at this time dealt with comparative analysis of various computer network topology and protocols to allow study of various topologies and protocols based on particular system workloads. Additional work has looked at comparative analysis of various computer architectures within the distributed architecture to assess the cost versus performance of one machine over another, again for set workload constraints. More recent work has begun to address the system software tradeoffs in terms of distributed data base management systems, distributed operating system approaches, reconfiguration capability, as well as when and where to utilize performance monitoring in hardware and software to address the reliability and availability problems.

One example of work in this area is the University of Texas in Austin dealing with development of tools to aid in the total system performance analysis and tradeoff analysis of computer networks for distributed computer systems. These efforts were geared at addressing the problem of network selection. They developed tools which allow the systems architect to determine the optimal topology, link capacities, and protocols based on a given set of user requirements. Their work represented a start towards the development of generic modeling tools to allow for tradeoff analysis of various technologies and configurations for total systems design. Other work that followed dealt with various other components of the design process, such as data base management. Tools of that type dealt with selection of data base models for best fit to user requirements. For example, do we use a hierarchical, network, or relational model of data. They also look at how to distribute the data for optimal performance, as well as providing the basis for selection of data update schemes and concurrency control schemes based on the user performance and system constraints. The real goal, this author believes, is to develop a specification and analysis tool which provides designers with the capability to specify a product system, verify and validate the system, develop an architecture, and provide the means to assess how the architecture meets or falls short of design specifications in a unified environment.

Early work falls short of this, but by utilizing knowledge gained at each level, a total system design tool can be built which will supply these characteristics. Chapter 9 will address this issue and introduce an example of an advanced development tool which will provide such a capability.

Summary

This chapter introduced the notion of computer-aided design for hardware, software, and total systems. Also we discussed the basics for computer-aided design of digital circuits using CAD design tools. These discussions introduced the problems of VLSI design and directed the reader to more works which deal with this technology in much greater detail. The second section of this chapter looked at the problem of software development and how this has become a large problem in present system designs. The reader was introduced to techniques such as structured software design with its data flow diagrams, control flow diagrams, and top down development, to name a few. Additionally, advanced techniques for structured design such as SADT were addressed along with automated techniques such as PSL/PSA. These showed how software design is being elevated more to a science than an art and emphasized the goals of correct and consistent designs up front to eliminate or mitigate problems during the design and life cycle of software systems.

Finally, the notion of a total system design philosophy was introduced. This discussion dealt with development of a philosophy of total system design which encompassed the intital system need specification, the development of requirements, the development and tradeoff analysis for systems architecture, and the design of the final hardware and software for the specified system. Stressed in this section was the need for automated means to assist in this system specification and design process.

CHAPTER NINE

Total System Design

The previous chapters presented the technologies involved in distributed and real-time computer systems. This presentation was derived to provide a basis for readers to understand the characteristics and assess the performance for such systems. This presentation stressed the high-level technologies involved and strived to provide a wide view of the alternatives at each phase. As part of this presentation the reader was also introduced to methods of performance assessment and computer-aided design for such systems.

This chapter will strive to bring all these elements together and provide an example of a total systems design philosophy spanning all the material previously presented. The computer-aided design and analysis tool being presented was developed as a prototype and represents just one such effort. Many others have embarked on similar projects aimed at simplifying the design of large real-time and distributed computer systems.

Systems Design Methodology

The notion of a methodology for total system design was presented in the previous chapter. In this presentation the philosophy was to provide a means to simplify and make more correct and complete the problem definition, the product specification, the architectural specification, the system hardware and software specifications, and the actual design of the final product. This goal is to be met through the use of manual and automated techniques as previously discussed. The manual techniques include structured design augmented by specification walkthroughs and interface completeness matrices to check for the completeness, accuracy, and correctness of the specification.

The tool to be discussed here is no different than the previous total design structure. What is meant by this statement is that the automated design aid being presented strives to aid the system developer at all stages of development. This is done by providing aids for simplifying the specification process and guaranteeing its correctness, by providing a simpler means to document and retrieve information on the design, and by providing a means from a system's view to analyze the performance of a design before it is constructed. Finally, once a solid architecture has been developed and analyzed, the system

211

designer can turn over the detailed subdesigns to traditional CAD tools, if it is required. Utilizing a total system design tool will aid designers in selecting off-the-shelf components which will work optimally together in a final product. Using this approach to design can save much design effort and time in delivering an operable system. For example, if it is desired to construct an information management system to provide a product for inventory control in a large corporation, traditional design would indicated that we either build it from scratch or take off-the-shelf components and integrate them for the final product. The problem here is how one goes about determining the best of the two alternatives, each with their own merits and flaws. Traditional techniques would rely on the architect's experience to know which fits best in the particular situation. Using an automated tool, we would look at both alternatives from a cost versus performance tradeoff and select the best based on actual measurable quantities, not on intuition or simple hand analysis.

The automated total system design philosophy lends itself to providing highly optimized yet cost effective architectures for given requirements. In order to realize such a goal, the tool must possess a knowledge base of design to draw on, as well as a wealth of design, use, and technology rules to use in assessing a design and selecting alternatives based on the analysis.

A truly automated system design aid, therefore, must possess the following:

1. A means to document a design in a structured and clear fashion.
2. The ability to determine the completeness of a specification or design.
3. The ability to examine the data base of system structure information from any angle.
4. The ability to draw on previous design work or components in constructing a product.
5. The capability (on any level) to assess the ability of the architecture or component to meet its specification.
6. The ability to assess performance from low-level components to the total system structure based on a priori knowledge or user provided data.
7. Once the system structure is complete, the ability to provide a total system specification upon which detailed design can ensue.

The above list represents a fairly aggressive view of a capability for automated design spanning artificial intelligence, data base management, automated structural analysis, and performance analysis ending in traditonal CAD environments being utilized to realize the conceptualized system. If produced, such a tool would enable the design of a total system from realization of need to actual design implementation of the hardware and software—all within a unified environment which enables more optimally correct and complete designs to be developed.

But one may ask, "Why is such a capability necessary?" To answer this we must look at the increase in complexity seen in recent VHSIC designs as well as that in large centralized and distributed systems. As can be readily seen, such systems have grown, not shrunk, in complexity. With this increase in complexity comes an equal increase in information that must be managed in order to specify and design such systems. The problem becomes one of tractability and completeness. As the physical complexity rises, designers become very hard-pressed to manage and utilize all the pertinent information to make sound engineering judgments utilizing manual means. Manual techniques are prone to errors and have a great time factor involved in them. On the other hand, automated techniques possess the capacity to handle much more information with few or no errors and in much less time. This alone provides a driving reason to pursue advance system CAD techniques. Such tools will enhance the productivity of all the design, implementation, and user communities.

A classical example of this notion can be found in VHSIC CAD systems. Without the aid of a VHSIC CAD system design, engineers would be required to design their systems using discrete logic. Then they would be forced to either perform laborious analytical walkthroughs to assess performance or require new simulation programs to be developed and written for each version of a design. Not only would such a method be prohibitive in time, but it would also drastically increase the cost of components due to the designer's lessened productivity. This simple example points out an important feature of CAD systems of any type: Such systems, if utilized properly, can save both money and time while increasing overall productivity through faster turnaround time and more optimally validated components and systems.

Goal of the Total System Design Aid

The notion of an automated aid for total system design is relatively new. Therefore, the major goal of attempting such a product is to prove the feasibility of the approach as well as defining and pointing out its potential value to the systems engineer. Such a major research and development effort requires, as shown previously, much effort to determine the proper level of support required to realize the tool. And with such efforts, first time products tend to be experimental and help bring out the strengths and weaknesses of the product. Usually such efforts end in a redesign or added design to correct early deficiencies or missed capabilities.

The design aid to be described in the remainder of this chapter is of this type and it represents a current effort at defining, developing, and evaluating a capability to assist designers, architects, managers, etc., in their respective jobs in relation to real-time distributed computer systems.

The Tool

The tool referred to as the Design Aid for Real-Time Systems (DARS) is comprised of three major pieces, namely, the documentation aid, the specification aid, and the performance evaluation aid. Coupled with this are standard hardware and software aids to assist in detailed design for the subcomponents; i.e., the low-level hardware and software which comprise the system. These system components are united together, as depicted in Figure 9.1.

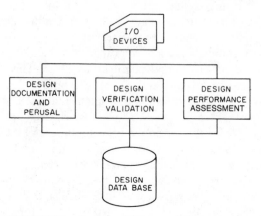

FIGURE 9.1   Design aid for real-time systems.

When taken together with other aids, these components supply an implementation of a total design philosophy [93], [94].

The design documentation component provides an interface for users to input designs manually or select components from predefined categories and link them up into a system design. This section of code also allows the designer or system engineer or architect to query the design data base for statistics, performance results, and design parameters as used as management data about the design in question. This provides a powerful vehicle for management as well as designers to control and bring to a manageable level very complex designs.

The design specification component is provided to allow a means to determine the completeness and correctness of a design based on its flows of control and data. It also supplies another level of documentation and analysis support by providing the means to tabulate and correlate many aspects of the hardware and software design in various ways.

The last piece of the tool is the performance assessment component. This component was derived to provide the means to evaluate various aspects of a system as well as the total system. This allows designers and architects the ability to analyze many alternative structures before a final structure is selected. Such a capability allows for more complete and optimal designs to be realized.

This chapter will examine and present these components in more detail, and ends with an example of use for the various sections.

DOCUMENTATION AID

This piece of the tool represents the user interface. It allows the user to define a design, to modify a design, and to examine a design in a highly interactive and user-friendly fashion. It does this by providing front end components to interface to underlying relational data bases and analysis components. The front end consists of software which allows users to input their designs either via canned skeletal component blocks or via discrete and detailed free-flow definitions based on the system's syntax.

For example, if a user wishes to define a software entity for a system such as a data base management system, he would proceed by indicating that he wishes to define a software component. Then he would assign a name to it. If new, it would require a version number; if old, it must be updated. The designer would then input the design starting at the highest level by defining the objective of the module, its expected code size, expected average execution time, what outputs are derived, what inputs are required, and the subparts of the module. This would be followed by definitions of the interfacing components at the same level until all the design exists at that level. From this would follow the interactive definition for the subparts and their subparts until the entire design is deemed complete and accurate by the designer. If during the design definition the designer wishes to stop he can save the state of his design and return to it later. Also provided is a means to allow many to work on the same major design and upon completion link them up into a unified design (Figure 9.2).

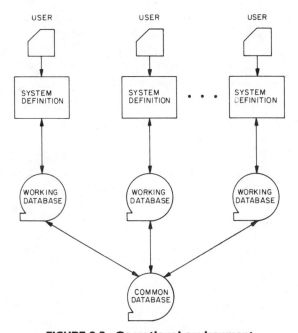

FIGURE 9.2 Operational environment.

The documentation and design aid allows the designer to view the final design as a collection of subdesigns, namely, specification, hardware, software, and performance design. The designer uses the tool to first specify the goals of the product to be constructed. This is done through the use of automated structured design techniques. These techniques consist of high-level data flow and control flow definition tools to allow designers to provide names to components with annotation to intent. These in turn are utilized to more fully define the specification as it matures, allowing designers to close gaps in their specification and verify the completeness utilizing the specification aids provided. Once a high-level specification of intent exists, the architects can be brought in to determine a high-level structural design based on the performance specification derived previously.

You may ask what is different from this approach versus the previously described manual approaches. Essentially, the major difference in this method is that it is automated. What this provides is a means of ensuring design integrity. This is accomplished by providing automated means to check designs of one person compared to another to ensure no conflicts exist in the two subparts. Another advantage is the ability to maintain an entire design in a readily recallable data base. This allows the user the ability to recall part of a design to modify its contents or just to examine it for information recall. Also, by having such an automated vehicle, it provides management with the ability to more closely monitor and control a large design. Later in this chapter we will look at an example to understand more fully the operation of this component of the tool.

To provide a tool for aiding in design and documentation we used off-the-shelf design aids and data bases to provide the low-level capability and then built on these the additionally required capabilities. The documentation aid rests on top of a relational data base management system and an automated structural definition and analysis tool; see Figure 9.3.

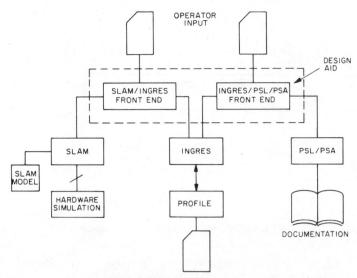

FIGURE 9.3 Design aid configuration.

The problem becomes one of how to provide the same information to two entities expecting different formats. This was accomplished by providing designers with templates to use in defining their products. These templates exist as skeletal structures which span the range of potential computer designs; see Figure 9.4.

1. MODULE NAME	2. MODULE ID
3. MODULE VERSION	4. MODULE PRIORITY
5. MODULE CODE SIZE	6. MINIMUM EXECUTION TIME
7. AVERAGE EXECUTION TIME	8. MAXIMUM EXEXUTION TIME
9. RESULTS UTILIZED BY ⁝⁝⁝	10. MODULE PART OF ⁝⁝⁝
11. MODULE PERFORMED BY ⁝⁝⁝	12. ETC ⁝⁝⁝

FIGURE 9.4   Example of template.

For example, Figure 9.4 represents a high-level template for specifying software modules. In order to make such templates useful, they needed to be quite general and offer many options—including a user-definable version. As in any design process, the templates come in a hierarchy of levels. These provide designers the view of the design wanted based on the status of the design. Figure 9.5 provides a subset view of the collection of templates provided by the design aid for the users of the tool.

These templates can be selected for use in a user's design either in skeletal form, providing structure only, or as a complete design component, if a completed, totally filled in template is used. This provides users the ability to construct a total system using off-the-shelf hardware and software components. It also allows for the selection of wanted pieces from the library of completed templates augmented by user-defined or filled templates.

The types of templates that exist in the library include those that would be found in a CAD system for VLSI design as well as templates of higher-level hardware components such as memories (CCD, magnetic, semiconductor, cache) of varying speeds, types, and characteristics; various processor types such as microprocessors (68,000 Z8000, 286, VAX, UYK-44, MV 8,000, etc.) with varying clocks and hardware technology; I/O devices such as terminals, disks, (hard and floppy of differing capacity and technology such as magnetic and optical); sensors; I/O processors; I/O concentrations; and bus interface units for a variety of protocol types. Beyond the hardware templates there exists a wide range of software templates that also can be used by the architects. Software templates would include a variety of distributed communications protocol code such as required to implement CSMA (Carrier Sense Multiple Access techniques) contention-based, daisy-chain, and token-passed type protocols, to name a few. Additionally, templates for various network operating systems and distributed operating systems code and performance are

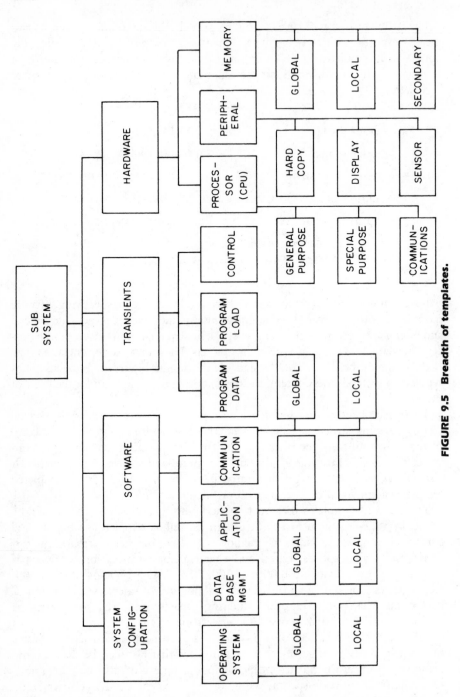

FIGURE 9.5   Breadth of templates.

provided. Beyond this, templates exist for distributed data base management systems of the relational, network, and hierarchical form, as well as various templates for data base update synchronization, concurrency control, and query processing.

These represent a selection of the hardware and software templates that are available for designer's use. Additional templates are provided to aid the designer in developing test cases and procedures to aid in the verification and validation of the design. These templates are of the form of scenario generators. They allow the designer to construct test cases of system workloads based on applications software loads over a particular time period of interest. For example, if we wished to observe how a group of computers configured into a distributed computer system would operate and perform, we would do the following:

1. The system would be developed utilizing the design aid to configure the hardware. Utilizing templates one could choose off-the-shelf computers, I/O devices, memories, and a communications environment to build the hardware system. Then the designer could select either templates for an operating system, data base system, and reconfiguration environment or utilize the ability to specify a unique design for any of the objects.

2. Once the designer or architect has specified what they wish to develop, the next job is to determine how to test it and analyze its performance. What is needed is a way to characterize the environment the product will operate under. The aid allows the designer to construct a scenario of actions that will allow the architect to stress and examine the system using the structural verification aid (PSL/PSA) and the simulation modeling aid.

The scenario generator takes many forms. One could model the above example at varying levels by splitting the loading into a hierarchy of loads. For example, one could generate loadings for the processors in terms of processing only as depicted in Figure 9.6.

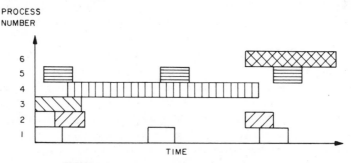

PROCESS
NUMBER

TIME

FIGURE 9.6 Processing load versus time.

This processing load would require that the processing structure of each process is known (Figure 9.7). This processing structure would exist as a collection of processing steps with generated messages to other processes as part of the structure. Each process would then exist as n steps with each step requiring either local input or remote input to operate and initiate the various steps. This would allow a designer to study, utilizing a simulation model, the activity of his design under given loading conditions compared to analytically derived or distribution provided load.

PROCESS I

AVERAGE PROCESSING TIME PER STEP= Nmsec

PROCESSING STEP		DESCRIPTION
I	0	REQUIRE MESSAGE FROM PROCESS 3 SENDS MESSAGE TO PROCESS 3
2	0	REQUIRES NO EXTERNAL DATA SENDS MESSAGE TO PROCESS 3
3	0	REQUIRES MESSAGE FROM PROCESS 2 SENDS MESSAGE TO SELF
4	0	REQUIRES NO EXTERNAL DATA SENDS MESSAGE TO PROCESS 2
5	0	RECEIVES MESSAGE FROM PROCESS 2 END OF PROCESS I

FIGURE 9.7 Processing load example.

The scenario generator can be used to construct various levels of loads to stress and analyze the design at any level. It allows analysis of specific components or collections of components at differing levels. The level of detail for the scenario is left up to the user's analysis needs and does not force any level on the designer.

The use of these templates allows architects and designers the ease of use of utilizing a library of system components, as in a hardware CAD system, while providing the additional flexibility of allowing for ad hoc user-defined objects. The documentation aid will accept these new component objects and insert them into the data base of objects to be used later by the same designer or by others. This feature allows the system to grow with technology advances. The documentation aid utilizes a relational data base to create relations describing the object with its associated attributes while at the same time uses a structured analysis tool to take these same objects and configure them into a collection of objects and associations in order to allow for analysis for structure and content of the design.

SPECIFICATION ANALYSIS AND INTERROGATION AID

The previous section outlined that portion of the tool which allows users to specify and construct systems. This section will describe the portion of the tool which allows users to utilize the data stored in the design data base.

The design data retrieval entity allows the user (designer, manager, architect, etc.) to query the design data base and retrieve records dealing with information about the design of interest.

The retrieval tool allows users to easily extract information from the design data base for use in design management and perusal.

This data base of system components reveals a hierarchical structure in all areas. Architecturally, the hardware is decomposed from a system to major components (such as data base processing, etc.) to devices and then to components. Physically, this hardware goes from major boxes or components to subcomponents to chassis and power supplies, to printed circuit cards and interconnections, and finally to low-level card and circuit designs. Software, on the other hand, is comprised of code, messages, and data tables. Software code is decomposed from system to functions (accounting), program (piece of a function such as accounts receivable), subprogram (account editing), process or function, and finally tasks. Messages are comprised of source and sink(s) along with amplifying information such as size of message, priority, periodicity, composition, and conditions. Data tables are accessed by code, whether system or applications, and represent either control-related status tables, computationally generated information, or static information.

Through the use of the specification and interrogation tool, the user may access and use the above classes of data to:

Query to hardware and software design data.
Analyze system properties.
Generate reports for the above two activities.
Drive existing simulations.

QUERY

The query capability allows the user to access the design data base to browse through the design data via a hierarchical structured method or to provide relational queries to the relational data base to extract combinations of information about collections of entities or cross sections of designs or any other combination of entities of interest.

For example, if a user wishes to examine the major hardware pieces that make up the system being designed he would use the query capability to browse through the data base, viewing it from various viewpoints. The query could be constructed as follows:

Provide all major system hardware units from design data base "identifier."

The query system would then provide a list of all major components that meet the qualities of major with amplifying information, as shown in Figure 9.8.

Unit ID	Desc.	Weight	Power	Cost
T2106	CPU			
T1620	DISK			
T1212	TAPE			
T1820	PRINTER			
T1916	TERMINAL			
X2111	I/O CHASIS			

FIGURE 9.8   Example query output.

ANALYZE/GENERATE REPORTS

This portion of the tool allows a user to query the data base of information and collect it into usable statistics. For example, if the manager of a project wishes to determine how much code has been developed for a particular project, he may ask the system for statistics on the sum of generated code for all pieces of project X, or he may wish to view only the volume of code for the data base manager, etc. The method for extracting the information is to embed a query in an analysis structure such as:

Sum all data base management = code size for project #X.

This represents the selection from the information bank of all entries which have the major designator of "data base manager" and the restriction of "code size" and "project #X".

This type of capability allows designers, architects, managers, etc., to extract useful statistics about the status of various pieces of a design, thus enabling the user to have more visibility into the design process and its status. This capability could be used by a designer to sum all the messages generated from or to a component to assess the throughput for the device for engineering studies. As another example, one could choose to view the application running on a system as a load. We wish to see what level of resources are utilized under a given scenario or selection of application. The user would select the scenario or construct it using other tools, then use the analysis capability to generate the statistics of resources utilized by this collection of applications software.

Another analysis tool available to users under this heading is the specification analyzer. Basically, this is the PSL/PSA (Problem Statement Language/ Problem Statement Analyzer) developed in the Department of Industrial and Operations Engineering at the University of Michigan. The previous tool extracted user inputs and translated them into PSL statements as well as relational data base table entries. This data base of entities can now be extracted and analyzed using PSA's capabilities. Using this feature the user can generate many levels of reports describing various pieces of the specification/design.

The analysis tool provides a menu of available PSA commands which allows the user to utilize the power of PSA without knowing all the intricacies of the language.

The reports and analysis available using this feature are:

Data base modification report.
   This output provides a record of changes that have been made along with diagnostics and warnings based on changes made to the PSL/PSA data base during the present session. Analysts/designers can use these reports to aid in the definition of deficiencies and the correction of errors in a design or specification. Such a report can also be used as a time map of changes to a design or specification allowing for trackability back into a design.
Formatted problem statement.
   This output provides a list of all objects defined in the system along with a complete listing of all relationships the object is involved in.
Object dictionaries and directories.
   This output lists various objects based on qualifiers such as name-list which produces a list of objects in order and with synonyms. This type of report could be used to review consistency of naming in a design. This capability allows users to annotate object names and provides a means to recover them easily for future reference.
Structure report.
   This output allows users to graphically view the hierarchies and connectivities of all the objects in the data base. The report provides features which allow for various formats showing, for example, how one could look at the contents of an object such as its ouput with all its intervening data structures.
Data Derivation report.
   This report provides the view from flow of data from one object to another. This report is often used to detect gaps in logic or missing or dangling references. This report can be produced graphically or in list structure, at the user's preference.
Dynamics report.
   This report allows for the graphical representation of the dynamics of the system such as periods of processing events and conditions of activity. This is the means to view the scenario-type information previously described.

This list represents a fraction of the outputs and analysis possible with this tool. Many papers have been written which describe this tool in much more detail [275], [274], [349]. The interested reader is urged to acquire these references and read them for a fuller definition of this tool.

Appendix I to this chapter has an example PSL/PSA output done by the University of Michigan in June 1981. This is a subset of the output provided by the tool.

Simulators

The documentation tool provides the capability to extract data from the data base and insert it into a simulation configuration data base to initialize and configure a simulation of the system or components of interest.

The documentation provides a presimulation report which allows the user to verify the design and point out possible or blatant inconsistencies that exist in the definition of the system under study. Also generated is a cross reference map of the system which will indicate the interconnections between system components. This aids in the user's ability to detect flaws and inconsistencies in the simulation setup.

The documentor works on a copy of the original working system data base, and, in setting up the simulator, it keeps a log of any changes made during a simulation run. This allows the user to examine the log after the simulation run and edit out the original system specification/design based on approved changes which were tested during the simulation operation. Using this copy of the data base allows the user the option of returning to the original system design or to update the design depending on the outcome of studies performed.

The simulator also provides much documentation as to system design and statistics. Before the run time statistics are provided. The simulator provides a summary of all inputted parameters and their set values along with any internal default values. This gives the user a comprehensive view of what is being modeled and what the results will mean.

The following section will describe a modeling capability for use in such a dynamic design aid as previously described.

PERFORMANCE ASSESSMENT AID

This portion of the design aid has the job of providing a means to assess the performance of postulated architectures provided to it. This provides a means of assessing the system's performance before the expense of actually building the hardware and software components and expending additional time and effort on integration and performance testing.

The analysis tool is comprised of five major sections (Figure 9.9) that can be operated separately or as a unified system model.

The five sections include models for data communications simulation, data base management simulation, operating system simulation, applications simulation, resource simulation, and driving routines and data collection analysis

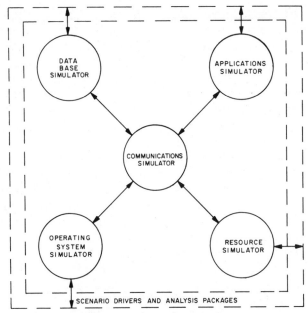

FIGURE 9.9   System modeling tool.

routines. This collection of routines represent the major modeling capacity at the systems level.

The structure of the systems simulation, if viewed on the highest level, is very similar to the structure of any distributed computer system. The basic hardware component is the computer or processor with its associated resources. Within a distributed computer system there are a number of processors each charged with a portion of the job required of the system. Embedded in each processor are three major software entities: the operating system, the data base manager, and the applications programs or processes. Using this software along with network hardware and protocols, these processors and processes are able to communicate information through a communications network—herein referred to as simply the "network"—in performing their requisite function or task. The role of the simulator is to model these components in as accurate and general a fashion as possible in order to provide the capability of evaluating a wide range of components in any distributed computer systems configuration.

The network simulator is responsible for modeling the transmission and control of messages among the simulated processes. This model consists of two parts: the physical link and the logical interface. The physical link models the hardware components involved in the transport of messages between discrete processors in a distributed system. The physical link includes those activities which manage network access, error checking, transmitting and receiving signals onto or off the network, as well as the cabling mechanism used to carry electronic signals between the processors.

The logical interface provides for process-to-process communication via a logical connection such as an address, name, or route. The logical interface consists of message communications software which handles message routing and supplies the interprocess communications (data-link-protocol) necessary to complete data transmission accurately and in a timely fashion.

The operating system simulator consists of those simulated mechanisms necessary to support the allocation of system resources among multiple processes executing concurrently within a single or multiple processor, as well as the capacity to model various levels of system services such as error detection and recovery and performance monitoring.

The CAD environment, via the use of templates, provides the tools for specifying these mechanisms as a set of primitive functions and incorporation of these into a model of an operating system. Each function represents a system policy decision about the sharing of a system resource. The resources include processor time, memory space, and peripheral devices. These primitives define the kernel of an operating system; that is, the basic rules used to synchronize access and allocation of resources among concurrent processes as well as the mechanisms required to realize this.

The functions provided by the kernel are:

1. To provide facilities to initiate, halt, restart, and terminate all processes.
2. To intercept messages from I/O devices on the behalf of applications/ systems processes. This includes the fielding of interrupts.
3. To provide facilities for processes to communicate via messages in order to permit signalling and exchange of information between processes.
4. To maintain status information on processes. This includes descriptor information as to the progress or "state" of each process in the simulator. The operating system simulator must also maintain queues of processes waiting for various events or state changes before they can proceed; e.g., I/O to secondary storage, block condition, waiting, ready, resume, etc.
5. To implement mechanisms for scheduling protection and memory management.
6. To provide mechanisms to support distributed operating systems; e.g., process communications mechanisms such as open, close, initiate transaction, etc., and object synchronization in object-based systems.

The operating system simulation can be viewed as having a dual role in the system simulator. In a passive role, it utilizes information about each of the processes' resource utilization in order to simulate processing time and delays incurred as resources are consumed. In an active role, it maintains process status and provides dynamic information used to synchronize other simulation activities.

The data base simulator provides the mechanisms to allow users the capacity to model various structures of data models and control implementation. This simulator also provides users the means to study various data organizational models such as the relational, network, hierarchical, or entity relationship models. Beyond this the user can specify various other aspects of a distributed data base management system such as:

1. Data manipulation language such as Icon, query, natural language, forms, etc.
2. Methods of concurrency control such as basic time-stamp ordering or a branch from it, 2 phase locking, or 3 phase locking, for example.
3. Methods for update synchronization such as primary copy, moving primary, majority vote, majority read, etc.
4. Security. This supplies the capacity to provide a mechanism to describe and model the techniques for data access.
5. Protection and recovery. This allows the user to specify and model the mechanisms for data protection and recovery from failures.
6. Query processing. This portion provides the means to model many algorithms for query processing and optimization in distributed data base systems.

The resource model provides the mechanisms to simulate the operation and use of resources in a computer system. The resource model provides templates to model a wide range of devices and performance ranges. The resources modeled include microprocessors, minicomputers, mainframe computers, I/O devices, such as tapes, disks, and display devices. The level of simulation describes low-level operation of the device. For example, a tape unit would be modeled by simulating the time a controlling device requests service, then continues through by modeling the tape control program time, the setup time, and read/write time along with an interrupt returned to the original requesting device signalling the end of the operation.

The last level of modeling is the applications processes. This component provides a mechanism to describe and simulate the characteristics and activity of a piece of applications code. The other components of the system simulator like the operating systems simulator, data base manager simulator, or processing device simulator use the information in the process description to simulate the execution of the applications in a real system. The process description block can be viewed as in Figure 9.10.

This block describes the attributes of the application which will be used in the performance evaluation of the systems architecture. Beyond this level of applications testing, the designer would use detailed code simulators to more fully test the applications of the system.

In order to more fully provide the reader with an understanding of the scope of such modeling, the following in-depth view of one component is provided.

| ENTRANCE SELECTION CRITERIA |
| ENTRANCE DESCRIPTORS |
| PRIORITY |
| SIZE OF CODE |
| UPDATED OPERANDS |
| DEFINED OPERANDS |
| EMPLOY OPERANDS |
| UTILIZED PROCESSES / COPROCESS / TASK |
| DATA REQUIREMENTS |
| PERIPHERAL DEVICE REQUIREMENTS |

FIGURE 9.10   Application process descriptor.

THE NETWORK MODEL—NEXT EVENT SIMULATION

The modeling technique used in this computer network simulation is called "next event simulation." Next event simulation views the world as a sequence of events rather than a continuum. If a department store checkout line is simulated in next event simulation, the process of checking out would be viewed as the following sequence: 1. a customer enters the checkout line, 2. the customer starts checkout, 3. the customer completes checkout. Between these events the customer is performing other activities, but these are unimportant if we are simply interested in the length of the waiting time.

The view of time taken by next event simulation is important in understanding the design and implementation of the system simulation. Time in next event simulation is viewed as a means of sequencing events and calculating time-related statistics. Events one hour or one second in the future are treated identically. Simulation is achieved by creating a file which contains future events along with the time of their occurrence. A simple loop program scans this file and selects the event with the lowest time. At that time, an internal memory location, which contains the simulated time, is updated to the occurrence time of the event. After the event occurs, mathematical calculations or logical operations can be performed to schedule other dependent events. In the checkout line example, this means that when checkout begins, the end of the checkout event is scheduled. In this way, the simulation proceeds from event to event and time constantly progresses.

The random or stochastic nature of scheduled events gives the simulation the characteristics of a real system. In the checkout line example, the time taken to service a customer is not a constant; it may be a minute or ten minutes. The service time is also randomly distributed. That is to say, the service time of previous customers doesn't have any effect on future customers. This means that the present customer may be followed by a customer whose service time is selected from a range of possible service times. The service times usually fall into a pattern, that is, it may be highly likely that a service time is 5 minutes, but relatively unlikely to be 20 minutes. The likelihood of certain service times can be described by theoretical patterns called distributions. These distributions can be used to generate service times or arrival patterns which resemble those which occur in real systems.

In a very simplistic view, a distributed computer system resembles the previous example. Messages are generated by the components of the system according to some distribution. They line up waiting for service. Messages are serviced by the communications network and arrive at the destination processor.

NETWORK GENERAL MODEL IMPLEMENTATION

The general model implementation is shown in the data flow diagram in Figure 9.11. The data flow diagram shows the flow of information in the system. In Figure 9.11 we see a user control file, random variates, and optional real-systems control data supplying information to the simulation and the output of information in the form of a final report. As shown previously, the user control data file supplies all the information which is required to configure the model into a unique distributed processing system, as well as the test data which will drive a simulation run. The random variates or random numbers supply the stochastic or random nature of the events which occur in a distributed processing system.

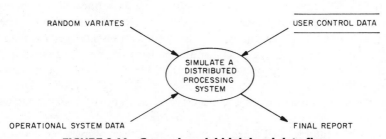

FIGURE 9.11   General model high-level data flow.

COMMUNICATIONS MODEL IMPLEMENTAITON

The simulation model has been made to resemble the generalized conceptual model of a distributed communications system shown in Figure 9.12.

The processing element in Figure 9.12 initiates and receives information. The information to be communicated is shown formatted into discrete packets or messages. Messages M1 and M2 are waiting in line or queue for service

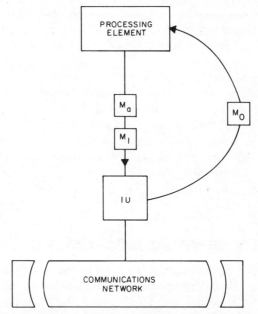

FIGURE 9.12   General model of a distributed processing node.

from the interface unit (IU). The IU acts as the intermediary between the processing elements and the vehicle of communication, the communications network. The IU removes messages from the queue, transforms them into a form suitable for transmission, acquires the use of the communications network, and transmits the message. In reality, distributed processing systems are composed of a number of these processing/IU units connected to a network. Thus, another IU in the system is prepared to receive the message. The receiving IU draws the message off the communications network, formats the message for the processing element and completes the process by making the message available to the processing element. The received message is shown as message MO.

The software simulation of the generalized conceptual model is shown in Figure 9.13.

Each of the bubbles in Figure 9.13 describes a major functional component of any distributed communications system. In general terms, each distributed processing system requires: 1. processing elements as a source of arrivals and the ultimate consumers of communication, 2. a queuing mechanism which stores messages waiting for transmission, 3. a method for arbitrating or allocating the limited resources of the communications system, 4. a communication network which physically transmits the message, 5. a system which routes messages through the system. For simulation purposes, a sixth component is required. The Analysis Module performs the analysis required to evaluate the performance of the system and issue a final report.

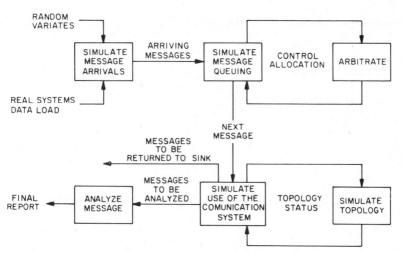

FIGURE 9.13 Software implementation of generalized DPS communications model.

Each of the process bubbles shown in Figure 9.13 has a subsequent section which contains more detailed descriptions of its function. In this introductory section, each will be described in general terms along with its interaction with other processes.

MESSAGE ARRIVALS

This process replaces the processing element in the generalized conceptual model. The function of this process is to take random variates or scenario/external message data and produce message arrivals. These message arrivals are essentially small buffers of computer memory which can be passed around the system, mimicking the movement of real messages. These simulated messages contain information which characterizes the message as to its origin, size, etc. During the passage of the message through the system, historical information will be attached to the message. It is this information which will be used to characterize the passage of the message from source to sink processor.

MESSAGE QUEUING

This process accepts the message arrivals and places them in a waiting line or queue corresponding to the processor of origin. Allowances are made for the fact that queue memory may be limited and overflow is possible.

ARBITRATE

It is not obvious from the general conceptual model, but the communication network is generally a limited resource. In order to use the communication network, this resource must be allocated. This function is performed by the Arbitor Module.

TOPOLOGY

The general conceptual model depicts the communication network as essentially a black box. Actually, it may consist of one or many interconnections between IUs. To guide messages around this network, a position keeper and "road map" are necessary. This routing and position-keeping is the function of the Topology Module.

SIMULATE USE OF THE COMMUNICATIONS SYSTEM

This process is responsible for all the delays and other procedures which are part of the physical communication process. This module takes the message selected by the arbitor and simulates its transmission. The module also changes the historical information contained the message for future reference.

ANALYZE MESSAGE

It is the function of this process to take the historical data from each of the messages moving through the simulation and accumulate statistical data. At the end of a simulation run, these accumulated data are formatted into a final report which analyzes the outcome of the simulation run.

INTERACTIVE SIMULATION INTERFACE

The User Control Data File supplies all the information which is required to configure the system simulation model to represent a unique distributed processing system. The User Control Data File will also supply test data which will be used during a simulation run. To reduce the labor required to use the system for experimentation and testing of distributed processing systems, a more "friendly" interactive user interface was built and described previously.

ARRIVAL MODULE

In a general sense, the mandate of the Arrival Module is to simulate the generation, if required, and queuing of messages within a distributed computer system. The function of the Arrival Module can be further broken down into two subfunctions: simulate message arrival and simulate message queuing.

SIMULATE MESSAGE ARRIVALS

Simulating message arrivals requires a source of message interarrival times. An interarrival time is defined as the period between two adjacent arrivals: tn, tn + 1, where tn is the time of the nth occurrence and tn + 1 is the time of the n + 1st occurrence. The generation of interarrival times will be discussed in subsequent paragraphs; for the time being, interarrival time can be defined as simply the time between message arrivals.

In order to understand how interarrival times are used to simulate message arrivals, a description of how the simulation starts and how messages flow through the system will be given. To start the simulation, an arrival event will be scheduled for each Interface Unit (IU). Scheduling consists of adding the present simulated time to the interarrival time to yield the event time or the time of actual message entry into the system (see Figure 9.14). In order to simulate the occurrence of the arrival event, the event time is entered into a file of all future events. During the simulation, this future event file is scanned and events such as arrivals are made to occur in their correct temporal sequence.

An arrival event occurs when the event time of a particular arrival in the file of future events matches the present simulated time. Simulated time is maintained by a software clock which is incremented to ensure the proper temporal sequence of events.

The occurrence of an arrival event is a signal to the system that a message generated by the simulated system is ready to enter the system and attempt transmission. At the time of a message arrival, another message is scheduled for the receiving IU by again invoking the interarrival time generator. This practice of triggering subsequent arrivals from the latest arrivals ensures a constant chain of messages entering the system. This is used only if a statistical load rather than a realistic load is used.

There are several ways to generate interarrival times for simulations of this type. The first method would be to measure interarrival times of messages generated by an actual running computer system. Properly generated data of this type can be used to answer the question: How would the present system function on a distributed network of type X?" As the system is running, interarrival times would be stored on some input media such as magnetic tape. As the simulation progressed, the values would be read from tape and arrivals would be scheduled appropriately. Another, perhaps more flexible, method would be to generate the interarrival times by a theoretical distribution. Theoretical distributions are mathematical relationships which are designed to closely approximate the distribution generated by the real system. Additional flexibility is afforded by an ability to change the theoretical distribution slightly in order to test some worst-case situations or some distribution that might exist in a future system.

The simple arrival of a message is not sufficient to simulate the generating of a real message. Real messages have several additional features: 1. they have a specific size, 2. they have a specific destination or destinations. The system needs this information to determine the path and the delays a message will encounter when passing through the system. For example, a large message will require longer transmission times and may be more susceptible to error.

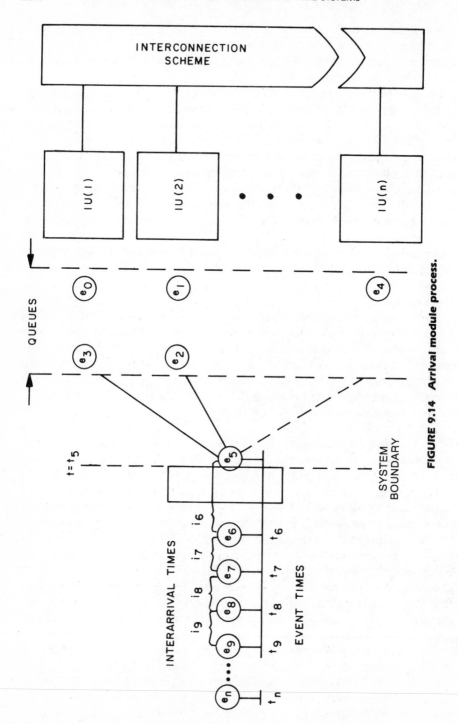

FIGURE 9.14 Arrival module process.

Also, messages bound for one IU may be required to take more intermediate transmission than another. To facilitate these characteristics, a message shall consist of a buffer of information which represents a specific message type. That is to say, computer memory has been allocated for each message and information is placed in this memory in specific places to allow easy data retrieval. Within the message type there are data which identify the origin, destination, and size of a message. The message type also contains information regarding the passage of the message through the system. The Analysis Module is concerned with these attributes, since they are used to yield the final statistical results.

At this point, a discussion of some of the parameters which form the message type is appropriate (see Table 9.1). Each of the items in Table 9.1 are called attributes. Attribute No. 1 is called event time; the event time contains the time at which the message will arrive. Attribute No.2 is the event type; the event type distinguishes this event as an arrival, since there are other

TABLE 9.1   Message data types.

Attribute Name	Data Name
1	Event Time
2	Event Type
3	Source Interface Unit (IU) Number
4	Destination Interface Unit (IU) Number
5	Present Interface Unit (IU) Number
6	Generation Time
7	Message Size (Words)
8	Message Overhead Length (Bits)
9	Message Wait Time ΔT 1 (In processor queue)
10	Message Wait Time ΔT 2 (Transit from queue to IU)
11	Message Wait Time ΔT 3 (Within IU)
12	Message Transmit Time
13	Message Transfer Time
14	Number of Stops
15	Number of Retransmits
16	Messages Lost
17	Sequence Number of Multi-packeted Messages
18	Number of Parts to a Packetized Message
19	Message Time to Complete
20	Message Priority
21	Message Identification (ID) Number
22	Database / Status
23	Operating System
24	Application #
25	Message Status

events which occur in the system. These other events will be discussed in subsequent sections. Attribute No. 3 is the source IU number or the designated IU which generated the message. Attribute No. 4 is the destination IU number and describes the ultimate destination of the message. Attribute No. 7 is the message size expressed in words. Attributes No. 17 and No. 18 are used when a message is too large to be sent in one packet. In this case, the message must be divided into a number of smaller messages each with the same source, destination, and generation time. Attribute No. 17 is used to identify the sequence number of any multi-packeted message. Attribute No. 18 is used to identify the total number of packets in the entire message. With attributes No. 17 and No. 18, it can be determined when the complete message is received.

Like interarrival times, message size and message destination must be generated by the system. Here again, the data could be generated by measurements within the real system or by using theoretical distributions. Thus, part of the Arrival Module is devoted to drawing from distributions of message size and message destination and initializing the appropriate attributes. The only remaining function performed by this submode is to divide messages which exceed the maximum message size into a sequence of smaller messages. The total number of messages generated is placed in attribute No. 18 of each message. Each message receives a sequence number, attribute No. 17. Attributes No. 22-24 describe the type of message. That is, which systems or applications module requires this message or what type of message this is. At this point, all attributes which define a simulated distributed system message have been defined.

Once messages enter the system, they must be held in a waiting line or queue until the IU can transmit them. To facilitate this, a FIFO queue is formed to contain the waiting messages. In a real system, this queue would consume some real memory, which normally would be limited. In the simulated system, this limit must be taken into consideration. When queue memory is exceeded, appropriate action should be taken. Appropriate action consists of: 1. waiting until sufficient memory is free to accommodate the message, 2. throwing away the message, 3. overwriting an older message.

Also, part of this module contains the logic which allows the rest of the system to access messages in the queue. In the real system, messages are read from the IU queue and transmitted through the system. A similar function is provided by program logic within the simulation. The major interfacing functions are copy, remove, scan, retrieve, and restore.

Copy allows the first message in the queue to be made available to other components of the system, presumably to transmit it through the system. Copy frees the memory occupied by the message, but retains a copy of message in an interim file. This copy simulates a holding area which exists in many IUs. This copy will remain until removed, presumably when successful transmission is completed. When a copy is performed while a message is in this interim file, the interim message will be made available. A status indicator is also available which supplies information such as: the status of the interim file, the presence or absence of a message or the contention block condition which will be discussed in subsequent paragraphs.

Remove serves the same function as copy, but removes the message from the queue or interim file. Status information is also supplied.

Scan simply supplies status information. No messages are removed or made available. Scan is destined to allow the queues to be tested for available messages based on supplied search conditions.

Retrieve and **restore** are provided to allow the interim message to be manipulated and restored to the interim file. This program logic might be used to alter statistics related to attempted transmission through the system.

There is one other feature to the queuing submode; that is the contention block feature. A contention situation may occur in some communication systems which allow several IUs to contend for the communications network during some specified period. If two IUs attempt to assume the communication network simultaneously, then a so-called collision occurs. Since both IUs cannot use the system simultaneously, some distinction must be made. The solution which is imposed on the system is to turn off each of the colliding IUs for an interval of time determined by a random number. At the end of this period, an IU would again contend for the communication network. During the contention period, the queuing submodule marks the IU unavailable, thus preventing any messages from leaving the queue, essentially turning it off. The blocks are removed when the contention period is lapsed.

Arbitor Module

The general purpose of the Arbitor Module is to simulate the control and allocation of the simulated systems communications resources; i.e., the Data Communications Bus. The functions of the Arbitor Module can be further broken down into subfunctions such as protocol, control, and allocation as all will occur within the module in some manner. Their descriptions follow:

SIMULATING RESOURCE ARBITRATION

Simulating control actions in a distributed system requires scheduling control arbitration, control mechanisms, and transmissions to occur. In this simulation, the following actions must occur or be present in order to perform the Arbitor's function.

To start simulation for arbitration of resources, an arbitrator event must be scheduled to occur at either time-now or some future time, dependent on simulated system states such as message arrivals or network timeouts, etc. Once the initial arbitration event has commenced, future arbitrations will be scheduled for a future time dependent upon the mechanisms being simulated; i.e., polling, daisy chain, contention, centralized or distributed, etc. Events are then filed away in the event file to be called upon for action in their correct temporal sequence. When the simulation controller recalls the arbitrator event to occur, the following sequence of subevents occurs to properly simulate the functioning of this module.

Control of the simulation is passed over to the Arbitor Module. It then determines the mode of control; i.e., centralized or distributed, by checking the user file space. Next, the method of resource allocation and control passage is sought through a second interrogation of the user file. Control types include polling, daisy chain, and request/grant. From this point, the Arbitor will request the location and status of the last controlling user element in the network from the Topology Module. Once the Arbitor has a reference point, it enters one of the control mode routines and performs the actions to simulate that mode's requisite scheme. If the control mode type is polling, the Arbitor must run through the possible polling schemes in order to determine which unit will receive control next. The possible methods include round robin, where it is passed from one logical unit to the next in a circular fashion (logical implies that units are not necessarily physically located next to each other); prioritized, where control is always started at the controlling node and physically branches out to the farthest unit one at a time, thus giving priority to the units closest to the controlling node; update counters, a method by which control is determined through the updating of internal counters in each unit and when matched to a predefined value gives control to that unit; or poll codes, a method through which the unit that last had control will calculate the code for the next user unit through a self-contained algorithm. A unit in the system will recognize this identifying code and take control of the communication subnetwork. If the control type is daisy chaining, the Arbitor Module will scan the possible schemes available, choose the proper user-defined subtype, and compute the next controlling unit in the following manner. If a unit is requesting service, the control will pass from one unit to the next until the requestor gets control. This always starts at the controlling node. If token passing is used, control will pass in a round-robin fashion from one unit to its physical neighbor, thereby allocating resources in a circular fashion.

If control is based on a request/grant or contention scheme, the Arbitor has many more functions to perform. It interrogates the active node file to determine if any unit(s) are requesting service. It next determines if the communication resource is free and responds accordingly. The Arbitor must next determine centralized or distributed submodes and perform the allocation based on this method. Centralized request/grant systems allocate distribution resources much as today's large time-sharing systems would in allocating CPU time. Distributed request/grant or contention has multiple types of control mechanisms and the Arbitor must determine the subtype; i.e., pure contention, p-persistent, persistent, nonpersistent, and multiple servers, then act accordingly to choose the next controller. Once this controlling unit has been determined, each method alluded to above will calculate its specific time to complete the arbitration cycle and check to see if there is a message to send by the new controller. If required, it reschedules the Arbitor and schedules the Use module to simulate message transmission and error conditions as required by the particular state of the system and sending unit. Once the Arbitor has completed its required processing, it will once again return control to the simulation controller and wait for the next scheduled call.

Use Module

The Use Module is a group of subroutines and functions which work collectively as that component of the simulation process which models the communications process in local computer networks.

FUNCTION OF THE USE MODULE

As distinguished from the two other major system modeling components, the Arrival Module and the Arbitor Module which provide for the generation of messages and the resolution of nodal competition, the Use Module is responsible for simulating all activity related to the actual transmission, propagation, and receipt of messages in accordance with system-dependent communication protocols. This includes:

The activity of a source node during its allocation period.
The activity of nodes receiving and processing messages or responses, which may occur at any time.
Background processing performed by nodes while they are waiting for control.
The passage of messages over the interconnection channels and the possible degradation of these messages.
Intentional and unintentional changes in the operational status of the nodes.

Proper statistics are maintained during all phases of the utilization process. When the simulation of the passage of a particular message through a system has been completed, the message is "unfiled" via the simulation's Analysis Module.

Viewed as a simulation entity, the Use Module integrates and coordinates all structures and activities which constitute the simulated communications process in the framework of simulation events which are independent with respect to each other as well as to the events of all other modules of the simulation. Events are independent if they can affect only future events. No two events whose duration overlap can have any affect on each other. For example, message arrivals in the system using selection channel access techniques can be scheduled to occur at any time. Arrivals which happen to have been scheduled to occur during a utilization event are queued by the simulators event-filing system and are run upon the completion of the particular Use Module component event being executed. In random access (contention) systems, message arrivals do affect utilization and, therefore, the overlapping of arrival and use events is precluded in the modeling of such systems. (Note: In all cases events are never executed simultaneously. It is the time frame of events which may overlap and only then if the events are independent).

ORGANIZATION OF THE USE MODULE

As with the simulation as a whole, the Use Module is general enough to efficiently support the faithful modeling of a wide variety of systems while simultaneously being capable of simulating the particular system to the requisite degree of accuracy.

The Use Module represents the communications process in terms of independent message transactions originating at the network nodes. A transaction is defined, for the purposes of the simulation, as the protocol-governed activity of the source and all receivers with respect to a particular message. Each transaction is subject to various delays and errors as it is being carried out.

Each transaction is modeled using an arbitrator-initiated sequence composed of three basic events which represent the three distinct phases of any message transfer; namely, 1. message preprocessing and transmission, 2. reception and response, and 3. response processing and retransmission. The exact sequence that is followed in any given case is dependent on system architecture, protocols, and the circumstances existing during the transaction. For example, the absence of a message for transmission will result in nothing more than a slight source delay and a return of control to the arbitrator, with no scheduling of any further events. A cyclic repetition of reception and retransmission may occur if a message repeatedly fails to arrive without error at its destination. Delays and errors are introduced into the transaction when and where appropriate.

As a software structure, the Use Module consists of three main event subroutines: 1. USEINIT, 2. RECEPT, and 3. RESPRO corresponding to the aforementioned major transaction phases.

USE—Scheduled by the Arbitrator, is the initial event in each utilization sequence. It consists of three main parts: the imminent collision processor, the preprocessor and the transmitter.

IMCLPR—the imminent collision processor provides for the modeling of the activity of multiple nodes that are given control during the same allocation period.

PREPRO—the preprocessor models all activity, excluding that related to message reception, that has taken place at the selected node from the end of its last allocation period until the transmission of a message or the relinquishing of control.

XMIT—this is the initial transmission of the message. The primary function of this routine is to schedule the reception event(s) at the destination node(s).

RECPT—the reception event models the reception and processing of a message by the destination interface unit. When mandated by conditions and protocol, a simulated response is formulated and a response event is scheduled.

RESPRO—the response models the processing of the response by the source. This includes the possible retransmission of an unreceived or unsuccessfully received message.

A collection of delay and error functions provides a pool from which the delays and errors, appropriate to the modeling of a particular system, are chosen.

EXTERNAL EVENT LINKS

The scheduling relationship of the Use Module to other simulation events is illustrated in Figure 9.15. As can be seen, the Use Module is scheduled only by the Arbitor, and schedules, in turn, the Arbitor. In some cases, e.g., in those systems in which arbitration is occasioned only by a message arrival, the Use Module schedules nothing at all, simply passing control via the simulation controller to the next scheduled event, whatever that may be.

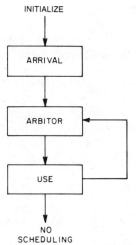

FIGURE 9.15   External event links.

EXTERNAL DATA LINKS

The Use Module requires data from and supplies data to other system modules. This data may be in the form of global variables or passed parameters.

Data exchange may be uni- or bidirectional depending on the module involved.

The Arrival Module furnishes information concerning message availability, size, destination(s), and other message characteristics. The Arrival Module receives no information from the Use Module.

The Topology Module provides information about internodal distances, propagation speeds and data rates, and node status. The System Status Change component of the Use Module schedules and randomly causes changes in certain Topology data.

When the Use Module has determined the final resolution or outcome of a particular transaction; i.e., the disposition of a message, it notifies the Analysis Module of the resolution category (success, lost message, etc.) and provides current message attributes which are used for the updating of system statistics.

INTERNAL EVENT LINKS

Internally, the USEINT event schedules the RECEPT event unless there is no message to be transmitted, a collision is predicated, or a reception node is found to be nonoperational. If any of these fault conditions exists, the Use Module will immediately relinquish control.

The RECEPT event schedules either RESPRO, the response processing event, or no event at all.

RESPRO either reschedules RECEPT or, if protocol allows no further retransmissions, relinquishes control.

Topology Module Description

The Topology Module consists mainly of a group of subroutines which facilitate the retrieval and modification of the data that physically describe the Local Computer Network. These routines will reside within the body of the Simulation Program with the exception of the Initialization Program which is a separate entity (see Figure 9.16). The following discussion will briefly describe the operation of each routine followed by a cursory view of the module as a whole.

Presently, there are eight call types which may be made to the Topology Module as listed in Figure 9.17. A brief description of each, along with the associated support routines, follows.

CDST—The call to the Topology Module for control distance is made by the Arbitor to obtain the actual distance Control must pass in a Control Transfer Operation. The routine CDST obtains its input information from the global variables representing the Present Controlling Processor (PP) and the Next Controlling Processor (NP). Using these two inputs as source and destination, the variables SRC and DST become initialized.

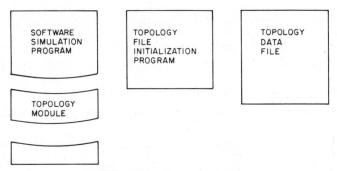

FIGURE 9.16   Model file areas.

Name	Function
COST	Continue distance request
COLIDE	Collision query request
CNVERT	Convert logical to physical address
RMVND	Remove node from system
ADDND	Add node to system
DIST	Distance request
DVAL	Destination validity request
BUSTO	Bus time-out routine

FIGURE 9.17   Topology module components.

A procedure called Route is then invoked by the CDST routine. The Route routine utilizes the Node Status Array (NSTA) along with the Link Table (LINK) to construct the Current Links Table (CLINKS). This operation involves the fill-in of an array with all active node links, thus creating an up-to-date representation of the system. Now with the actual system structure known, the shortest route algorithm (SHRTE) is invoked and it calculates the various possible routes that control may follow from point A to point B. This is done by manipulating the entries contained in the CLINKS array and replacing them with cumulative distance values. Upon completion of the SHRTE task, the Total routine is called to read the completed system map. Total returns the control distance in the variable Internodal Distance (IND). Program control is then passed back to the Arbitor.

COLIDE—The COLIDE portion of the Topology Module is called by the Delay Module when preparing to transmit a message. Input to COLIDE is provided by the variable Present Controling Processor (PP). Response is sent via the Variable Collision (CLSN using the Node Status Array (NSTA)). COLIDE checks the collision indicator flag of the transmitting node. If the flag indicates a collision, the appropriate response is returned to the Delay Module and the involved nodes are taken off the bus and placed in an ON-pending state. If no collision occurs, the appropriate response is returned via CLSN.

CNVRT—The Convert Routine is used by the Arbitor to find the corresponding physical node number when given a logical address. The input for this routine is contained in the variable Logical Processor Number (LPNO) and the corresponding physical node number is returned via the variable Physical Processor Number (PPNO). Correlation is accomplished using the Node Status Array (NSTA) attribute called Logical Address. The present model assumes that any one physical node will have only one corresponding logical address.

RMVND—Removal of a node from the system is accomplished by using this Topology call. The number of the node to be removed is passed via the variable Process Number (PRONO). The Node Status Table active flag for that particular node is reset.

ADDND—Addition of a node to the system is accomplished using this routine and the node number passed via Processor Number. The addition involves the assignment of a random number to the particular node and resets the bus timeout counter or the Node Status Array.

DIST—This routine, which returns internodal distance for the transmission of a message, is called by the Delay Module. Its operation is functionally identical to the Control Distance Routine (CDST) except that the destination of the message is found in the message attributes instead of Next Controlling Processor (NP). All of the same routines are used here (ROUTE, SHRTE, TOTAL).

DVAL—Destination Validity is checked by this routine which is called by the Delay Module. It uses the destination found in the message attributes and checks the Node Status Array (NSTA) for an active condition for that particular processor. It returns the result of the check via the Variable Valid Destination (VALD).

BUSTO—The Bus Time Out Processor provides a mechanism for updating sequence number and assigning new ones. It is called every time a Bus Time Out (BTO) appears in the system. The incrementing and checking of the Node Status Array (NSTA) quantities CCNT and RANU are done in this module. Also, upon assignment of a new sequence number, all others are checked for collision and the collision indicators are set.

As an overview, the Topology Module provides two major functions: 1. source to destination distance and routing statistics, and 2. constantly updates the system topology model. Grouping the subroutines into these two functional categories yields Figure 9.18.

Data Base Manager

The Data Base Manager simulation simulates the activities associated with a wide range of distributed and centralized data base management systems. The

Routine Statistics	System Topology Updates
CDST	RMVND
COLIDE	ADDND
CNVRT	BUSTO
DIST	•TOPINIT
DVAL	

•TOPINIT NOT PHYSICALLY CONTAINED
IN THE TOPOLOGY MODULE

FIGURE 9.18   Topology subroutines functional classification.

simulator provides tools to configure a wide range of data models and support software allowing for a wide variety of configurations to be studied.

The general model of a data base system, as shown in Chapter 6, fits nicely into the general levels of modeling in the simulator (Figure 9.19).

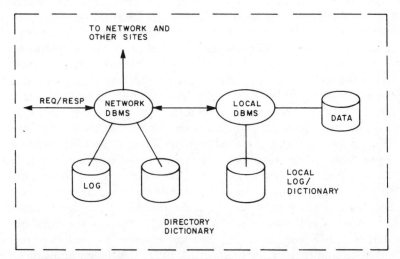

FIGURE 9.19   General model of a data base site in the simulator.

The role of the simulator is to faithfully simulate the components of a given specification to allow for evaluation of its operation in the specified environment.

The data base management simulator is comprised of three major components: 1. the Data Manipulation Language model, 2. the Network Data Manager model, and 3. the Local Data Manager model.

The Data Manipulation Language model provides the mechanisms to model a wide range of manipulation languages such as forms languages, Icon or pictorial languages, query languages, natural languages, etc. The role of this piece of the simulator is to provide a means to simulate the responses to a user request from many differing type sources. It must simulate the generation of a query, the action required to begin information retreval, and the response to the user after the information is recovered.

The Network Data Manager provides the simulation many aspects of control and coordination in a distributed data base management system. The major areas that it must model include query processing in terms of update synchronization, concurrency control, and optimization.

The simulator, again using the provided templates specified previously, provides the means to model various update synchronization schemes such as majority voting, majority read, master, moving primary, etc. The model accomplishes this by simulating the protocol's passage of messages, consequence of reception at the sinks, and outcome of transaction from the coordinator. The simulator maintains status on all updates in terms of number of messages to coordinate the updates and the average time to perform an update.

Another job of the simulator is to model the activity of coordination of reads and writes referred to as serializability of transactions. This requires the modeling of concurrency control algorithms as described in Chapter 6. The modeling of these techniques is performed by coordinating the activity of all the simulated nodes dependent on the concurrency control technique. For example, if we wish to model a basic time-stamp ordering technique, then each transaction in the simulated system is given a time stamp as to when it was generated. Then when the update or read is received at the local site where the actual operation is to occur, the simulator will serialize the update or read based on the basic principal and the current time stamp for the item of interest. (See Chapter 6 for an overview of Basic Time Stamp Ordering). One of the major functions of this module is to simulate the optimal processing of queries in a distributed data base. The Query Optimizor is a piece of code whose job it is to determine the best and least expensive method of performing the given transaction. It does this by processing the given transaction based on a set of cost functions which may include processing costs, communications cost, I/O costs, and fixed time for response. The simulator provides the means to model these activities, using either actual algorithms or canned "types" of algorithms. Once the simulator has acted on a given transaction at this level, it will then pass it on to the local data manager for processing. The local data management simulator will model the acceptance of requests for update or query by simulating the activity of performing translation of requests to low-level commands for the I/O unit and acting on requests based on the local query and update constraints in place at the network and local levels. This level of the model must be cognizant of data storage ordering and access mechanisms. Performance at this level is assessed by the determination of time delays for acceptance, processing, and response to supplied queries. The overall model is shown in Figure 9.20.

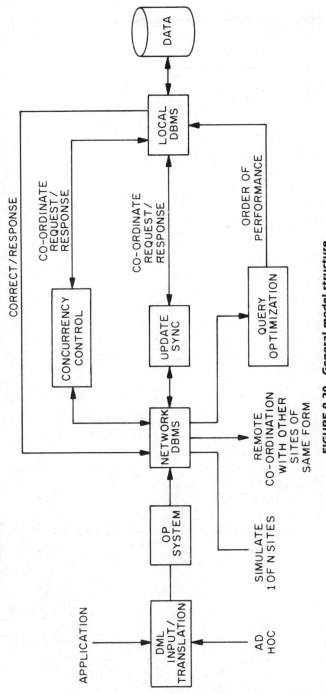

FIGURE 9.20 General model structure.

Performance Evaluation

Computer performance evaluation can be functionally divided in much the same way as the simulation is divided:

Node Level Performance
  Node Processor Performance
  Node Process Performance
  Node Operating System Performance
  Node Data Base Manager Performance

System Level Performance
  Processor Performance
  Process Performance
  Operating System Performance
  Data Base Manager Performance
  Network Performance

Processor performance is designed to show the effectiveness of the processor to perform the processing required of it. The main statistic which can illustrate this is processor idle time, or the time the processor is idle.

Process performance is designed to show if an individual process is performing its function in a timely manner (real time), and to show the performance of the system relative to the process function. Statistics such as the amount of time to complete execution of the process once it is started and the percentage of execution time used by the process are representative samples.

Operating system performance attempts to evaluate the management of resources by the operating system. The amount of time processes remain in a wait state is an example of such a statistic.

Data base manager performance is designed to show the speed and simultaneity of the data base. Such statistics as the average time between data requests and data returned and the age of the data returned relative to the update of the information would be computed.

Network performance is designed to show the speed and reliability of the distributed network. Such quantities as information throughput and message errors are important statistical quantities.

The goal of analysis is to: 1. provide quantitive measures which establish the effectiveness of distributed processing systems, 2. provide statistical measures which can be used to compare distributed processing systems having divergent design philosophies. To meet these goals, it is necessary to identify constant factors which unify distributed processing systems and derive statistical measures by which these factors can be compared. That is to say, a "common language" of analysis must be established by which a wide range of distributed systems can be described.

Establishing Analysis Criteria

In order to develop wide-ranging analysis criteria, it is necessary to identify those characteristics which are common among distributed processing systems. These common characteristics will be developed into statistical measures which analyze the relative merits of the underlying system. In developing common characteristics, three areas will be explored: 1. the basic physical structure of distributed processing networks, 2. the basic sequence of events, and 3. the overall function of distributed processing networks.

To provide flexibility and simplicity, most distributed processing systems have adopted a modular design philosophy. Modularity has resulted in a common physical structure. This physical structure allows the distributed processing systems to be divided into several functional components. These component parts can be examined and evaluated separately. The ability to divide the evaluation of a system into functional components allows more accurate analysis of the intermediate factors which contribute to the strengths and weaknesses of a system.

The basic functional components which form the physical structure of a typical distributed processing system is shown in Figure 9.21.

This diagram describes each distributed processing system in terms of the following components: 1. a number of processors which generate and consume messages, 2. a waiting line or queue containing messages which cannot be serviced immediately, 3. an interface unit (IU) which prepares messages for transmission, and 4. a communications network which performs the actual physical transmission of data and software routines which perform system functions such as control, information management, and applications processing. The physical implementation of these component parts differs widely from system to system. The outline presented in Figure 9.21 represents an accurate, generalized picture of distributed processing systems. The physical mapping presented in Figure 9.21 allows the identification of certain common features and checkpoints, which will be discussed in subsequent paragraphs.

The primary structural feature of quantitative interest in Figure 9.21 is the queue or waiting line. The length of these queues gives some quantitative information concerning the effectiveness of the underlying communication system. Exceptionally long or unbalanced queues could indicate the presence of system bottlenecks. Queues which grow and retreat wildly could suggest poor responsiveness to peak loads.

The basic components, which form the functional event structure in the typical distributed processing network, is shown in Figure 9.22. This figure reproduces the same general physical layout presented in Figure 9.21, but divides the passage of messages through the physical system into specific steps or phases. The major events of interest along the message path, shown in Figure 9.21, are: 1. the message arriving, 2. the message entering the queue,

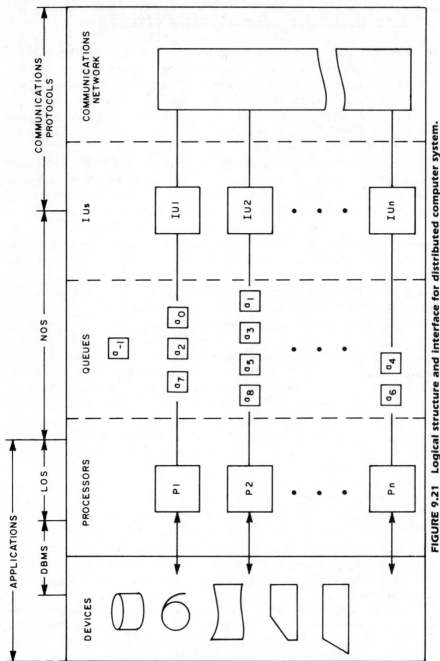

FIGURE 9.21 Logical structure and interface for distributed computer system.

3. the message leaving the queue, 4. the message becoming available to the interface unit, 5. the message starting transmission, 6. the message ending transmission, and 7. the message becoming available to the receiving processor.

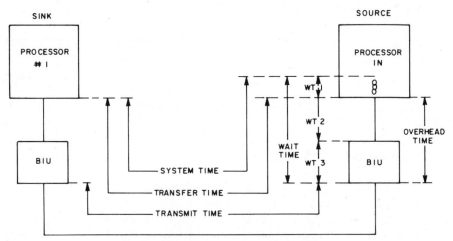

FIGURE 9.22 Communications metrics.

These common checkpoints are significant because they allow time measurements which chart the passage of the message through the system. As long as a particular system accurately implements communication, timing becomes a most critical factor. That is, the speed at which accurately transmitted messages are completed is of primary interest. This series of checkpoints allows analysis of overall as well as intermediate delays imposed on the communication process.

The time between basic checkpoints and combinations of checkpoints gives rise to specific descriptive quantities, shown by the arrows in Figure 9.22. These quantities will be compiled for each simulation run on specific distributed processing networks.

For upper level software, the same type of measurements are applied. In the data base model measurements, for transaction throughput and average delay, time spent in data manipulation language intrepetation, query processing and optimization, update synchronization, concurrency control, and local data manager time are extracted. At the operating system level statistics are taken for overhead timing for control transfer, scheduling delays, etc. These are also brought down to the level shown previously.

The structure of the software for collecting statistics and formatting the final report is shown in Figure 9.23. During a simulation run, information from a large number of completed applications transactions will be accumulated and stored, and the memory occupied by these transactions will be released. At the end of a simulation run, these accumulated data will be used in statistical calculations. These statistical calculations will be formatted and presented in the form of a final report.

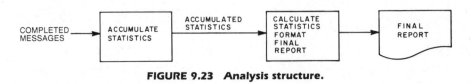

FIGURE 9.23   Analysis structure.

Statistical Output

The statistics generated by the system can be divided into three main groups: 1. time independent, 2. time persistent, and 3. periodic.

The time independent group are statistics which arise from independent observations. The traditional mean and standard deviation can be calculated for this group. These data, which are accumulated during the simulation run, are as follows: 1. the sum of each observed piece of data, 2. the sum of each piece of data squared, 3. the number of observations, and 4. the maximum value observed. From the accumulated data, the following statistics will be calculated and formatted for the final report: the mean, standard deviation, and maximum observed value. These statistics will be provided for all the time independent data points.

Time persistent is important when the time over which a parameter retains its value becomes critical. An example of this is a waiting line. If the waiting line has 10 members in it for 20 minutes and 1 member for 1 minute, the average is not $(1+10)/2n$ or 5.5. This quantity would indicate that there were approximately 5 members present in the line for the 21 minute period. The true average is more like $20/21*10 + 1/20*1$ or 9.57 or approximately 10. This is the time persistent average. As can be seen in this case, the average is weighted by the time period over which the value persisted. There is a similar argument which can be made for the time persistent standard deviation. These data which are accumulated during a simulation for the time persistent case are as follows: 1. the sum of the observed value times the period over which it retained that value, 2. the sum of the observed value squared times the period over which it retained its value, 3. the maximum observed value, and 4. total period of observation. From these accumulated data, the following statistics will be calculated and formatted for the final report: the time persistent mean, the time persistent standard deviation, and the maximum observed value. These statistics will be provided for all the time persistent data points.

Periodic statistics are designed to yield a plot of observations as a function of time. This group of statistics affords a view of the system as it operates in time. Data are accumulated as in the previous two examples except, rather than sums of statistics, an individual data point graph of time versus the value of the data points will be plotted. These plots will be produced for all groups of periodic statistics.

The preceding sections have described the workings of the Analysis Module and given general details on the analysis criterion and statistics which are drawn from this criterion.

Usage Example

As an example of such a systems capability, we will examine how we could configure the system to examine a communications network.

The network we will examine is comprised of a physical global bus with nodes connected on the bus. Control is passed via internal counters that are updated when a previous user of the bus sends out a token or scan signal code. The communications link is comprised of a coxial cable with taps off it for the interface unit. The distance between any adjacent pair of interface units is the same throughout the network. This will simplify the analysis. The bus timing is dependent on the sending of the token. If the token or a message is not sent in some period of packet times, then the count will be reinitialized at the first count token.

To specify this network, we would use the capacity of the specification tool to input the characteristics of the communications link, the interface unit, the protocol, the workload, number of processors, interface unit queue capacities, etc. Through the use of this tool and finally using the analysis tool, we will initiate the simulation of the above network.

The data base of filled templates and the system specification is used to build the file of simulation initialization parameters. The provided parameters include:

processor parameters
network control protocol setup
packet/message size
workload distribution
interface unit parameters
topology parameters
error statistics and setup
delay parameters (such as line delays, etc.)

These are used to set up the input stream for the simulator as shown below:

IR&D TEST #11
SIMULATION DATA

ARRIVAL RATE = 1.OE-5/MICRO-SECOND

MESSAGE SIZE = 100 BITS

MESSAGE OVERHEAD = 42 BITS

NUMBER OF PROCESSORS = 16

GEN,FORTIER,1,r1,15,1981*
STA,25,17,24,6*
LIM,22,12,1000,25,7,80000*
COL,1,T-PKS-SY*
COL,2,PK-XFER*
COL,3,PK-XMIT*
COL,4,PK-WAIT*
COL,5,PK-SZ-SY*
COL,6,PK-OVERHEAD*
COL,7,TIM-M-SY*
COL,8,MS-XFER*
COL,9,MS-XMIT*
COL,10,MS-WAIT*
COL,11,MS-SZ-SY*
COL,12,MS-OV(%)*
COL,13,MS-LATE*
COL,14,MS-SZ-P1*
COL,15,MS-SZ-P2*
COL,16,MS-SZ-P3*
COL,17,MS-SZ-P4*
COL,18,MS-SZ-P5*
COL,19,MS-SZ-P6*
COL,20,MS-SZ-P7*
COL,21,MS-SZ-P8*
COL,22,MS-SZ-P9*
COL,23,MS-SZ-PX*
COL,24,STEPS8
COL,25,SCAN*
TIM,1,P1-Q-LEN*
TIM,2,P2-Q-LEN*
TIM,3,P3-Q-LEN*
TIM,4,P4-Q-LEN*
TIM,5,P5-Q-LEN*
TIM,6,P6-Q-LEN*
TIM,7,P7-Q-LEN*
TIM,8,PE-Q-LEN*
TIM,9,P9-Q-LEN*
TIM,10,PX-Q-LEN*
TIM,11,SY-Q-LEN*

TIM,12,QS-BLOCK*
TIM,13,CONT-BLK*
TIM,14,MS-SY*
TIM,15,PKS-SY*
TIM,16,I-THROU*
TIM,17,SY-THROU*
TIM,18,CB1-BUSY*
TIM,19,CB2-BUSY*
TIM,20,CB3-BUSY*
TIM,21,CB4-BUSY*
TIM,22,DB1-BUSY*
TIM,23,DB2-BUSY*
TIM,24,DB3-BUSY*
TIM,25,DB4-BUSY*
HIS,1,A-TIM-P1,40,0,2E4*
HIS,2,A-TIM-P2,40,0,2E4*
HIS,3,A-TIM-P3,40,0,2E4*
HIS,4,A-TIM-P4,40,0,2E4*
HIS,5,A-TIM-P5,40,0,2E4*
HIS,6,A-TIM-P6,40,0,2E4*
HIS,7,A-TIM-P7,40,0,2E4*
HIS,8,A-TIM-P8,40,0,2E4*
HIS,9,A-TIM-P9,40,0,2E4*
HIS,10,A-TIM-P10,40,0,2E4*
HIS,11,MS-SZ-1,40,10,100*
HIS,12,MS-SZ-2,40,10,100*
HIS,13,MS-SZ-3,40,10,100*
HIS,14,MS-SZ-4,40,10,100*
HIS,15,MS-SZ-5,40,10,100*
HIS,16,MS-SZ-6,40.10,100*
HIS,17,MS-SZ-7,40,10,100*
HIS,18,MS-SZ-8,40,10,100*
HIS,19,MS-SZ-9,40,10,100*
HIS,20,MS-SZ-10,40,10,100*
HIS,21,DESTINAT,30,1.5,1*
HIS,22,MS-SZ-SY,40,10,50*
HIS,23,A-TIM-SY,40,0,2E4*
HIS,24,PRIOR-SY,12,0.5,1*
HIS,25,DUMMY*
PLO,1,TIM,8,1,0,1E5*
VAR,1,1,T,SY-THROU,0,0*
PLO,2,TIM,9,1,0,1E5*
VAR,2,1,Q,SY-Q-LEN,0,0*
PLO,3,TIM,10,1,0,1E5*

VAR,3,1,M,MSS-SY,0,0*
PLO,4,TIM,11,1,0,1E5*
VAR,4,1,R,REXMITS,0,0*
PLO,5,ARBIT,12,10,0,1*
VAR,5,1,A,CRT-PRO1,1,0*
VAR,5,2,B,CTR-PRO2,1,0*
VAR,5,3,C,CTR-PRO3,1,0*
VAR,5,4,D,CTR,PRO4,1,0*
VAR,5,5,E,CRT-PRO5,1,0*
VAR,5,6,F,CRT-PRO6,1,0*
VAR,5,7,G,CRT-PRO7,1,0*
VAR,5,8,H,CTR-PRO8,1,0*
VAR,5,9,I,CTR-PRO9,1,0*
VAR,5,10,J,CTR-PRO10,1,0*
PLO,6,TIM,13,10,0,1E5*
VAR,6,1,1,Q-LEN-P1,1,1,0,20*
VAR,6,2,2,Q-LEN-P2,1,1,0,20*
VAR,6,3,3,Q-LEN-P3,1,1,0,20*
VAR,6,4,4,Q-LEN-P4,1,1,0,20*
VAR,6,5,5,Q-LEN-P5,1,1,0,20*
VAR,6,6,6,Q-LEN-P6,1,1,0,20*
VAR,6,7,7,Q-LEN-P7,1,1,0,20*
VAR,6,8,8,Q-LEN-P8,1,1,0,20*
VAR,6,9,9,Q-LEN-P9,1,1,0,20*
VAR,6,10,T,Q-LEN-P10,1,1,0,20*
PRI,1,LVF,2*
PRI,2,FIFO*
PRI,3,LVF,17*
PRI,4,FIFO*
PRI,5,FIFO*
PRI,6,FIFO*
PAR,1,1E5,0,1.7E38,1*
PAR,2*
PAR,3*
PAR,4*
PAR,5*
PAR,6*
PAR,7*
PAR,8*
PAR,9*
PAR,10*
PAR,11,250,50,1000,50*
PAR,12*
PAR,13*

PAR,14*
PAR,15*
PAR,16*
PAR,17*
PAR,18*
PAR,19*
PAR,20*
PAR,21,10,24.8031,1000,1*
PAR,22,10,347.2434,1000,1*
INI,1,Y,Y,O,10E6,Y*
SEE,43183,19249,45212,15893,
67377,65297,34183,71249,
17212,27893,76377,56397*
FIN*
'PRO,',16,32,10,
'ARL,',2,2,1,8E3,
'SZE,',143,4,3,100,
'DES,',1,.FALSE.,2,
'QUE,',0,.FALSE.,25,1,
'LEN,',42,
'COM,',121,
'PRI,',10000,.TRUE.
'AB1,',1,3,1,
'AB2,',0,
'AB3,',16,16,1,1,
'AB4,',0.0,0.0,
'AB6,',0,0,
'TP1,',0,1.0,0,
'DBG,',.FALSE.,.FALSE.,
'ABB,',0,1,1,3,
'TP5,',65,64,
'TP6,',11,64,
'TP7,',64,64,
'TP9,',0,1000,
'AB9,',1,1,1,16,
'ER1,',0.0,100,0.,
'DL3,',0,0,0,0,
'DL2,',0,0,0,0,
'DL1,',0,0,0,0,
'UC2,',0.0,1.7E38,5.538,
'UC3,',0.0,
'ABC,',.FALSE.,.FALSE.,.FALSE.,

IR&D TEST #11
SIMULATION DATA

ARRIVAL RATE = 1.0E-5/MICRO-SECOND

MESSAGE SIZE = 100 BITS

MESSAGE OVERHEAD = 42 BITS

NUMBER OF PROCESSORS = 16

STATISTICS FOR VARIABLES BASED ON OBSERVATION

	MEAN	STD DEV	SD OF MEAN	CV	MINIMUM	MAXIMUM	OBS
T-PKS-SY	0.1491E+04	0.8038E+03	0.2039E+02	0.5393E+00	0.1705E+03	0.6050E+04	1554
PK-XFER	0.9575E+03	0.6009E+03	0.1524E+02	0.6275E+00	0.1660E+03	0.2492E+04	1554
PK-XMIT	0.9575E+03	0.6008E+03	0.1524E+02	0.6275E+00	0.1661E+03	0.2492E+04	1554
PK-WAIT	0.5330E+03	0.5305E+03	0.1346E+02	0.9952E+00	0.1000E+01	0.4778E+04	1554
PK-SZ-SY	0.1000E+03	0.0000E+00	0.0000E+00	0.0000E+00	0.1000E+03	0.1000E+03	1554
PK-OVERH	0.4200E+02	0.0000E+00	0.0000E+00	0.0000E+00	0.4200E+02	0.4200E+02	1554
TIM-M-SY	0.1491E+04	0.8038E+03	0.2039E+02	0.5393E+00	0.1705E+03	0.6050E+04	1554
MS-XFER	0.9575E+03	0.6009E+03	0.1524E+02	0.6275E+00	0.1660E+03	0.2492E+04	1554
MS-XMIT	0.9575E+03	0.6008E+03	0.1524E+02	0.6275E+00	0.1661E+03	0.2492E+04	1554
MS-WAIT	0.5330E+03	0.5305E+03	0.1346E+02	0.9952E+00	0.1000E+01	0.4778E+04	1554
MS-SZ-SY	0.1000E+03	0.0000E+00	0.0000E+00	0.0000E+00	0.1000E+03	0.1000E+03	1554
MS-OV(%)	0.4200E+02	0.0000E+00	0.0000E+00	0.0000E+00	0.4200E+02	0.4200E+02	1554
MS-LATE	0.1370E+04	0.8038E+03	0.2039E+02	0.5869E+00	0.4950E+02	0.5929E+04	1554
MS-SZ-P1	0.1000E+03	0.0000E+00	0.0000E+00	0.0000E+00	0.1000E+03	0.1000E+03	89
MS-SZ-P2	0.1000E+03	0.0000E+00	0.0000E+00	0.0000E+00	0.1000E+03	0.1000E+03	116
MS-SZ-P3	0.1000E+03	0.0000E+00	0.0000E+00	0.0000E+00	0.1000E+03	0.1000E+03	85
MS-SZ-P4	0.1000E+03	0.0000E+00	0.0000E+00	0.0000E+00	0.1000E+03	0.1000E+03	97
MS-SZ-P5	0.1000E+03	0.0000E+00	0.0000E+00	0.0000E+00	0.1000E+03	0.1000E+03	108
MS-SZ-P6	0.1000E+03	0.0000E+00	0.0000E+00	0.0000E+00	0.1000E+03	0.1000E+03	100
MS-SZ-P7	0.1000E+03	0.0000E+00	0.0000E+00	0.0000E+00	0.1000E+03	0.1000E+03	101
MS-SZ-P8	0.1000E+03	0.0000E+00	0.0000E+00	0.0000E+00	0.1000E+03	0.1000E+03	93
MS-SZ-P9	0.1000E+03	0.0000E+00	0.0000E+00	0.0000E+00	0.1000E+03	0.1000E+03	96
MS-SZ-PX	0.1000E+03	0.0000E+00	0.0000E+00	0.0000E+00	0.1000E+03	0.1000E+03	94
STEPS	0.0000E+00	0.0000E+00	0.0000E+00	0.1000E+06	0.0000E+00	0.0000E+00	1554
SCAN	0.8757E+03	0.4388E+03	0.4106E+01	0.5011E+00	0.3720E+03	0.5731E+04	11419

P1-Q-LEN	0.4760E-02	0.6883E-01	0.0000E+00	0.1000E+01	0.1000E+08	0.0000E+00
P2-Q-LEN	0.6015E-02	0.7732E-01	0.0000E+00	0.1000E+01	0.1000E+08	0.0000E+00
P3-Q-LEN	0.4116E-02	0.6553E-01	0.0000E+00	0.2000E+01	0.1000E+08	0.0000E+00
P4-Q-LEN	0.4898E-02	0.6981E-01	0.0000E+00	0.1000E+01	0.1000E+08	0.0000E+00
P5-Q-LEN	0.6115E-02	0.7840E-01	0.0000E+00	0.2000E+01	0.1000E+08	0.0000E+00
P6-Q-LEN	0.5967E-02	0.7701E-01	0.0000E+00	0.1000E+01	0.1000E+08	0.0000E+00
P7-Q-LEN	0.4936E-02	0.7214E-01	0.0000E+00	0.2000E+01	0.1000E+08	0.0000E+00
P8-Q-LEN	0.5069E-02	0.7153E-01	0.0000E+00	0.1000E+01	0.1000E+08	0.0000E+00
P9-Q-LEN	0.5163E-02	0.7167E-01	0.0000E+00	0.1000E+01	0.1000E+08	0.0000E+00
PX-Q-LEN	0.4298E-02	0.6542E-01	0.0000E+00	0.1000E+01	0.1000E+08	0.0000E+00
SY-Q-LEN	0.8283E-01	0.2941E+00	0.0000E+00	0.3000E+01	0.1000E+08	0.0000E+00
QS-BLOCK			NO VALUES RECORDED			
CONT-BLK			NO VALUES RECORDED			
MS-SY	0.2316E+00	0.4877E+00	0.0000E+00	0.4000E+01	0.1000E+08	0.0000E+00
PKS-SY	0.2316E+00	0.4877E+00	0.0000E+00	0.4000E+01	0.1000E+08	0.0000E+00
I-THROU	0.9993E+02	0.2610E+01	0.0000E+00	0.1000E+03	0.1000E+08	0.1000E+03
SY-THROU	0.1419E+03	0.3713E+01	0.0000E+00	0.1420E+03	0.1000E+08	0.1420E+03
CB1-BUSY	0.8506E+00	0.3565E+00	0.0000E+00	0.1000E+01	0.1000E+08	0.1000E+01
CR2-BUSY			NO VALUES RECORDED			
CB3-BUSY			NO VALUES RECORDED			
CB4-BUSY			NO VALUES RECORDED			
DB1-BUSY	0.1488E+00	0.3559E+00	0.0000E+00	0.1000E+01	0.1000E+08	0.0000E+00
DB2-BUSY			NO VALUES RECORDED			
DB3-BUSY			NO VALUES RECORDED			
DB4-BUSY			NO VALUES RECORDED			

These are used to drive the model for the simple run.

Using the same capability the user could run multiple instantiations of the model with varying paramater values to get a statistical view of how the network will run under the set range of initialization conditions.

The following is representative of the type of data output that is generated by this model. The user can get compacted statistics on a fine granular set of points on the model's run time activities via histograms, graphs, or traces of events as shown.

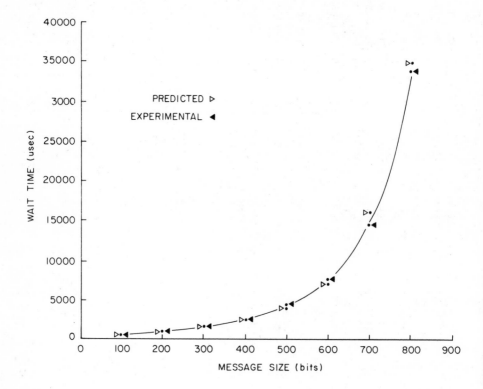

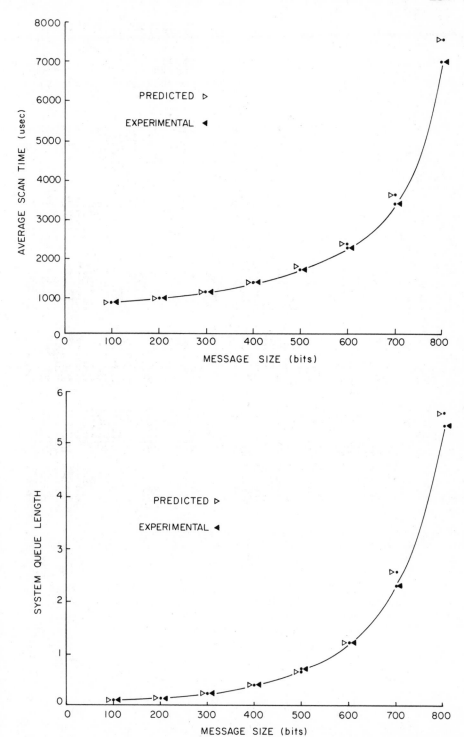

GASP SUMMARY REPORT

SIMULATION PROJECT NUMBER 1 BY FORTIER

DATE 1/ 15/ 1981   RUN NUMBER   1 OF   1

CURRENT TIME = 0.1000E+09

PARAMETER SET 1 =	0.5000E+06	0.0000E+00	0.1000E+11	0.1000E+01
PARAMETER SET 2 =	0.1500E+02	0.0000E+00	0.1000E+21	0.0000E+00
PARAMETER SET 3 =	0.1000E+02	0.0000E+00	0.1000E+21	0.0000E+00
PARAMETER SET 4 =	0.0000E+00	0.0000E+00	0.1000E+21	0.0000E+00
PARAMETER SET 5 =	0.0000E+00	0.0000E+00	0.1000E+21	0.0000E+00
PARAMETER SET 6 =	0.0000E+00	0.0000E+00	0.1000E+21	0.0000E+00
PARAMETER SET 7 =	0.0000E+00	0.0000E+00	0.1000E+21	0.0000E+00
PARAMETER SET 8 =	0.0000E+00	0.0000E+00	0.1000E+21	0.0000E+00
PARAMETER SET 9 =	0.0000E+00	0.0000E+00	0.1000E+21	0.0000E+00
PARAMETER SET 10 =	0.2500E+03	0.5000E+02	0.1000E+04	0.5000E+02
PARAMETER SET 11 =	0.2500E+03	0.0000E+00	0.1000E+21	0.0000E+00
PARAMETER SET 12 =	0.0000E+00	0.0000E+00	0.1000E+21	0.0000E+00
PARAMETER SET 13 =	0.0000E+00	0.0000E+00	0.1000E+21	0.0000E+00
PARAMETER SET 14 =	0.0000E+00	0.0000E+00	0.1000E+21	0.0000E+00
PARAMETER SET 15 =	0.0000E+00	0.0000E+00	0.1000E+21	0.0000E+00
PARAMETER SET 16 =	0.0000E+00	0.0000E+00	0.1000E+21	0.0000E+00
PARAMETER SET 17 =	0.0000E+00	0.0000E+00	0.1000E+21	0.0000E+00
PARAMETER SET 18 =	0.0000E+00	0.0000E+00	0.1000E+21	0.0000E+00
PARAMETER SET 19 =	0.0000E+00	0.0000E+00	0.1000E+21	0.0000E+00
PARAMETER SET 20 =	0.0000E+00	0.0000E+00	0.1000E+21	0.0000E+00
PARAMETER SET 21 =	0.1000E+02	0.1000E+03	0.1000E+04	0.1000E+01
PARAMETER SET 22 =	0.1000E+02	0.1000E+02	0.1000E+04	0.1000E+02

STATISTICS FOR VARIABLES BASED ON OBSERVATION

	MEAN	STD DEV	SD OF MEAN	CV	MINIMUM	MAXIMUM	OBS
T-PK8-SY	0.3822E+05	0.2588E+05	0.2292E+03	0.6771E+00	0.1600E+02	0.2471E+06	12748
PK-XFER	0.1500E+02	0.0000E+00	0.0000E+00	0.0000E+00	0.1500E+02	0.1500E+02	12748
PK-XMIT	0.1000E+02	0.0000E+00	0.0000E+00	0.0000E+00	0.1000E+02	0.1000E+02	12748
PK-WAIT-	0.3825E+05	0.2588E+05	0.2292E+03	0.6767E+00	0.4600E+00	0.2471E+06	12748
PK-8Z-SY	0.1165E+03	0.4569E+02	0.4047E+00	0.3920E+00	0.5920E+00	0.2100E+04	12748
PK-OVERH	0.4121E+02	0.1389E+02	0.1230E+01	0.3370E+01	0.1400E+02	0.2471E+06	5947
TIK-M-SY	0.5418E+05	0.2160E+05	0.2801E+03	0.3987E+00	0.3160E+03	0.2471E+06	5947
M8-XFER-	0.3214E+02	0.6122E+01	0.7939E-01	0.1905E+00	0.1500E+02	0.6000E+02	5947
M8-XMIT-	0.2143E+02	0.4081E+02	0.5293E+01	0.1905E+01	0.1000E+01	0.4000E+02	5947
M8-WAIT	0.8196E+05	0.4905E+05	0.6464E+03	0.6082E+00	0.3460E+02	0.6514E+06	5947
M8-8Z-SY	0.2497E+03	0.5080E+02	0.6587E+00	0.2034E+00	0.5500E+02	0.4630E+03	5947
M8-QV(X)	0.1832E+02	0.2891E+01	0.3749E-01	0.1578E+00	0.1400E+02	0.3618E+02	5947
M8-LATE	0.2990E+05	0.2106E+05	0.2754E+03	0.7043E+00	0.3520E+03	0.2221E+05	5847
M8-8Z-P1	0.2496E+03	0.5222E+02	0.3702E+01	0.2092E+00	0.5550E+02	0.3930E+03	199
M8-8Z-P2	0.2500E+03	0.4868E+02	0.3367E+01	0.1948E+00	0.1130E+03	0.3900E+03	209
M8-8Z-P3	0.2480E+03	0.5346E+02	0.4007E+01	0.2156E+00	0.1400E+02	0.4140E+03	178
M8-8Z-P4	0.2548E+03	0.4899E+02	0.3725E+01	0.1923E+00	0.1260E+03	0.3730E+03	173
M8-8Z-P5	0.2571E+03	0.5048E+02	0.3550E+01	0.1963E+00	0.1010E+03	0.3600E+03	202
M8-8Z-P6	0.2473E+03	0.5433E+02	0.3630E+01	0.2197E+00	0.8600E+02	0.4110E+03	224
M8-8Z-P7	0.2483E+03	0.4345E+02	0.3153E+01	0.1750E+00	0.1100E+03	0.3800E+03	190
M8-8Z-P8	0.2520E+03	0.4935E+02	0.3386E+01	0.1985E+00	0.1190E+03	0.4070E+03	214
M8-8Z-P9	0.2469E+03	0.5122E+02	0.3668E+01	0.2075E+00	0.1040E+03	0.4190E+03	195
M8-8Z-P1	0.2491E+03	0.5282E+02	0.3725E+01	0.2121E+00	0.1310E+03	0.3800E+03	201
STEPS-1	0.1000E+01	0.0000E+00	0.0000E+00	0.0000E+00	0.1000E+01	0.1000E+01	5947

NON-GASP INPUT VARIABLE INITILIZATION

```
PROCESSOR COMMON:       NPE    = 30        WS     = 32          MAXMUL = 10       ACSIZE = 1000.00
ARRIVAL COMMON:         ATYPE  = 2         ADIST  = 2           ASEED  = 1        CSIZE  = 400
SIZE COMMON:            MAXSIZ = 150       MSTYPE = 1           BSEED  = 3
DESTINATION COMMON:     IDESTN = 1         SELF   = F           DSEED  = 2
QUEUE COMMON:           QSIZE  = 100       QWARN  = 1           OVRFLO = 1

LENGTH COMMON:          LENGTH = 21.00
COMPLETION COMMON:      CTME   = 25000.00
COLLECT PERIOD:         PERIOD = 80000.00  DSPLAY = F           ITYPE  = 1        FIRST  = 1
ARBITOR 1 COMMON:       CORD   = 1         ISUBT  = 1
ARBITOR 2 COMMON:       NP     = 0
ARBITOR 3 COMMON:       MCNT   = 30        PMCNT  = 30          PP     = 30
ARBITOR 6 COMMON:       R      = 1.00      X      = 1           COLREC = 0        NIRN   = 1
TOPOLOGY 1 COMMON:      CLSN   = 1         COLTIM = 1000000.00  IND    = 2                 = 4
TOPOLOGY 3 COMMON:      VALD   = 1         CD     = 1           UTYP   = T               3.00
USE COMMON:             LIM    = 1         LIMAPP = F                                       2
DEBUG COMMON:           DEBUG  = F
```

```
THE TOTAL NUMBER OF MESSAGES PROCESSED =                            5947.00
THE TOTAL NUMBER OF PACKETS PROCESSED =                           12748.00
THE TOTAL NUMBER OF MESSAGES REMAINING IN THE SYSTEM =                4.00
THE TOTAL NUMBER OF PACKETS REMAINING IN THE SYSTEM =                5.00
THE TOTAL NUMBER OF MESSAGES LOST =                                  0.00
THE TOTAL NUMBER OF MESSAGES LOST DUE TO A FULL QUEUE =              0.00
THE TOTAL NUMBER OF MESSAGES LOST DUE TO BIT ERROR =                 0.00
THE TOTAL NUMBER OF MESSAGES LOST DUE TO A STATUS CHANGE =           0.00
THE PROBABILITY OF DATA LATE =                                      0.98
THE PROBABILITY OF RETRANSMISSION =                                 0.00
THE TOTAL NUMBER OF PACKETS LOST =                                  0.00
THE TOTAL NUMBER OF PACKETS LOST DUE TO A FULL QUEUE =              0.00
THE TOTAL NUMBER OF PACKETS LOST DUE TO BIT ERROR =                 0.00
THE TOTAL NUMBER OF PACKETS LOST DUE TO A STATUS CHANGE =           0.00
```

NON GASP INPUT VARIABLES @ TNOW =   0.10E+09

```
TPUT   =         0.00     RTRANS  =        0.00
TNMA   =      5951.00     TNML    =     5947.00
TNPA   =     12753.00     TML     =        0.00
TMLQ   =         0.00     TMLB    =        0.00
TMLS   =         0.00     THLATE  =     5847.00
TPL    =         0.00     TPLQ    =        0.00
TPLB   =         0.00     TPLS    =        0.00
TRANS  =         0.00     DARB    =        0.00
ACTIVE =            F
```

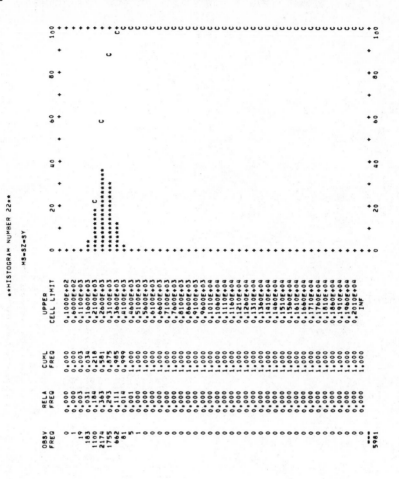

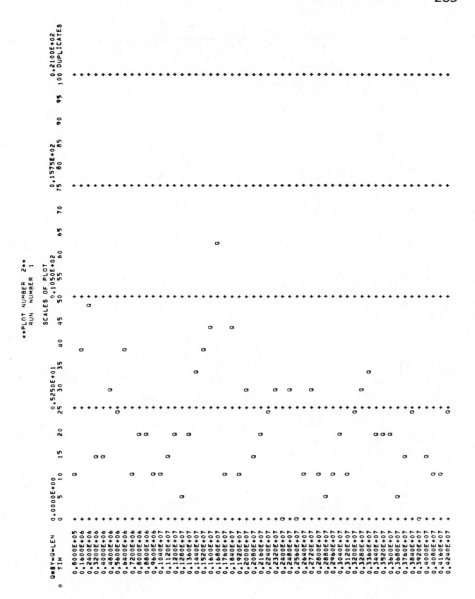

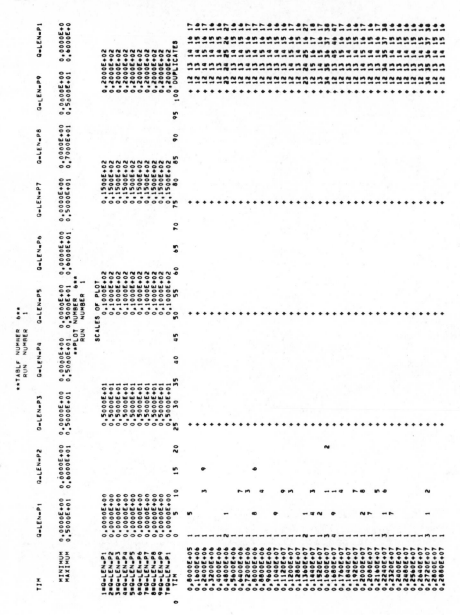

Data, such as that shown on the previous graphs, represents the composite of many data runs performed in relation to the three validation parameters defined below:

1. AVG-WAIT-TIME. This represents the average time a message must wait from generation time to start of transmission time for all messages.
2. AV-SCAN-TIME: This represents the average time required to perform one total control cycle from beginning to end and back to beginning.
3. AV-SYS-QUEUE-LENGTH: This represents the aggregate average total queue length for all active processors in a network.

This type of data can be generated using the post-processing packages that can reformat data based on user specification in an interactive form.

In Closing

The thrust for building and using simulation programs stems from the observation that a simulator is an artificial laboratory. Once a system is accurately modeled and programmed, experiments can be performed using the model. These experiments, or simulations, permit inferences to be drawn about a system without building the system, if it is only a proposed design; without disturbing it, if the operating system is costly or unsafe to experiment with; and without destroying it, if the object of an experiment is to determine limits of stress.

In this way, simulation programs can be used for design procedural analysis and performance assessments.

Once such a simulation of a modeled system is operational, it can be used as a tool to examine and test how the addition of new devices, technological improvements, and computing techniques will affect a given system(s) performance under varying conditions, for design changes to be quickly and cheaply tested before acceptance, for additional details to be included in testing as data becomes available, for use as a training tool by providing an insight into system operation which may not be otherwise available, and for testing and aiding in the design of distributed LCN hardware, operating systems, data base management systems, functional partitioning, and other system issues as they become relevant in a design. The above examples represent but a few of the possible uses of such a generic tool.

Summary

This chapter provided the reader with a more descriptive overview of tools for computer-aided design of the total system. The tools provided techniques to assist the designer/architect with a means to specify, design, and test systems in a methodical manner.

The tool described represents a current effort to create such tools and as such it is hoped that this presentation will stimulate others to research such tools and strive to perfect ideas presented in this text into fully functional design tools for hardware and software development of computer systems.

This text was geared to individuals who wish to view distributed computer systems from the total systems view and, as such, the reader was exposed to the full gamut of technologies which comprise such systems, as well as a variety of techniques for specifying, designing, and evaluating distributed systems.

The interested reader is directed to the numerous references and bibliographies to expand his knowledge in any area of interest.

Appendix

Formatted Problem Statement

Parameters: DB=-EXADB FILE=-PSANAME NOINDEX NOPUNCHED-NAMES PRINT
  NOPUNCH SMARG=5 NMARG=20 AMARG=21 BMARG=25 RNMARG=70 CMARG=1
  HMARG=40 ONE-PER-LINE COMMENT NONEW-PAGE NONEW-LINE
  NOALL-STATEMENTS COMPLEMENTARY-STATEMENTS LINE-NUMBERS PRINTEOF
  DLC-COMMENT NOSORT-NAME-LIST DBNBUF=200 WIDTH=84 LINES=60
  INDENT=8 HEADING PARAMETERS PAGE-CC=ON EXPLANATION PN-REPETITION

```
 1 DEFINE INPUT                          employee-information;
 2      /*   DATE OF LAST CHANGE - Jun 17, 1981, 08:57:38 */
 3      GENERATED:       BY departments-and-employees;
 4      RECEIVED:        BY payroll-processing;
 5
 6 DEFINE INTERFACE                      departments-and-employees;
 7      /*   DATE OF LAST CHANGE - Jun 17, 1981, 08:57:38 */
 8      GENERATES:     employee-information;
 9      RECEIVES:      paysystem-outputs;
10
11 DEFINE OUTPUT                         paysystem-outputs;
12      /*   DATE OF LAST CHANGE - Jun 17, 1981, 08:57:38 */
13      GENERATED:      BY payroll-processing;
14      RECEIVED:       BY departments-and-employees;
15
16 DEFINE PROCESS                        payroll-processing;
17      /*   DATE OF LAST CHANGE - Jun 17, 1981, 08:57:38 */
18      GENERATES:     paysystem-outputs;
19      RECEIVES:      employee-information;
20      UPDATES:       payroll-master-information;
21
22 DEFINE SET                            payroll-master-information;
23      /*   DATE OF LAST CHANGE - Jun 17, 1981, 08:57:38 */
24      UPDATED BY:    payroll-processing;
25
26 EOF EOF EOF EOF EOF
```

```
PSA Version A5.2RO              Jun 16, 1981  15:20:29     Page     5
                        Payroll-Example-PSL/PSA-A5.1

                            Structure Report


   1    1 payroll-processing                    PROCESS
   2    2   new-employee-processing             PROCESS     (SUBPARTS ARE)
   3    3     salaried-information-creation     PROCESS     (SUBPARTS ARE)
   4       4     salaried-information-addition
                                                PROCESS     (SUBPARTS ARE)
   5    3     hourly-information-creation       PROCESS     (SUBPARTS ARE)
   6       4     hourly-information-addition    PROCESS     (SUBPARTS ARE)
   7    3     hire-report-entry-generation      PROCESS     (SUBPARTS ARE)
   8    3     department-file-addition          PROCESS     (SUBPARTS ARE)
   9    2   terminating-emp-processing          PROCESS     (SUBPARTS ARE)
  10    3     destroy-salaried-information      PROCESS     (SUBPARTS ARE)
  11       4     salaried-information-deletion
                                                PROCESS     (SUBPARTS ARE)
  12    3     destroy-hourly-information        PROCESS     (SUBPARTS ARE)
  13       4     hourly-information-deletion    PROCESS     (SUBPARTS ARE)
  14    3     term-report-entry-generation      PROCESS     (SUBPARTS ARE)
  15    3     department-file-removal           PROCESS     (SUBPARTS ARE)
  16    2   employee-processing                 PROCESS     (SUBPARTS ARE)
  17    3     hourly-employee-processing        PROCESS     (SUBPARTS ARE)
  18       4     hourly-paycheck-validation     PROCESS     (SUBPARTS ARE)
  19         5     time-card-validation         PROCESS     (SUBPARTS ARE)
  20       4     hourly-emp-update              PROCESS     (SUBPARTS ARE)
  21         5     hours-update                 PROCESS     (SUBPARTS ARE)
  22       4     h-report-entry-generation      PROCESS     (SUBPARTS ARE)
  23       4     hourly-paycheck-production     PROCESS     (SUBPARTS ARE)
  24         5     h-gross-pay-computation      PROCESS     (SUBPARTS ARE)
  25         5     total-hours-computation      PROCESS     (SUBPARTS ARE)
  26    3     salaried-employee-processing      PROCESS     (SUBPARTS ARE)
  27       4     salaried-paycheck-validation PROCESS       (SUBPARTS ARE)
  28       4     salaried-emp-update            PROCESS     (SUBPARTS ARE)
  29       4     s-report-entry-generation      PROCESS     (SUBPARTS ARE)
  30       4     salaried-paycheck-production PROCESS        (SUBPARTS ARE)
  31         5     s-gross-pay-computation      PROCESS     (SUBPARTS ARE)
  32    2   process-library                     PROCESS     (SUBPARTS ARE)
  33    3     pay-computation-validation        PROCESS     (SUBPARTS ARE)
  34    3     tax-computation                   PROCESS     (SUBPARTS ARE)
  35    3     net-pay-computation               PROCESS     (SUBPARTS ARE)
  36    3     total-deductions-computation      PROCESS     (SUBPARTS ARE)
  37    3     gross-pay-update                  PROCESS     (SUBPARTS ARE)
  38    3     federal-deductions-update         PROCESS     (SUBPARTS ARE)
  39    3     state-deductions-update           PROCESS     (SUBPARTS ARE)
  40    3     fica-deductions-update            PROCESS     (SUBPARTS ARE)
  41    3     funds-update                      PROCESS     (SUBPARTS ARE)
```

Level	Count	Level	Count	Level	Count	Level	Count	Level	Count
1	1	2	4	3	19	4	12	5	5

Extended Picture

```
NAME=tax-comp                                              PAGE 1 OF 2
 +                                                                      +
              *                        ***PROCESS***    /--ELEMENT--    T
                                       *total-dedu-*    |  total-     | O
                                  ....* ctions-  *......|deductions   |
                 /--ELEMENT--     .   *computation*     |             | P
                 |          |     .   *USES TO DRV*      --DERIVED--/  A
            ....|federal-tax|...  .                                   G
            .    |          |     .                                   E
            .     --DERIVED--/    ***PROCESS***    /--ELEMENT--
            .                  .   * federal- *    |cumulative-|      2
            .                  ....*deductions-*......| federal-  |
            .                     *  update   *    |deductions |      0
            .                     *USES TO UPD*      --UPDATED--/     F
            .
            .                                                          2
            .                     ***PROCESS***
 ***PROCESS*** .                  *total-dedu-*    Name occurs
 *   tax-   *  .                  ....* ctions- *    elsewhere.
 *computation*...  /--ELEMENT--   .   *computation*
 *          *  .   |         |    .   *USES TO DRV*
 ************  ....| fica-tax |   .
            .      |         |    .
            .       --DERIVED--/  .   ***PROCESS***    /--ELEMENT--
            .                  .   *  fica-   *    |cumulative-|
            .                  ....*deductions-*......|  fica-    |
            .                     *  update   *    |deductions |
            .                     *USES TO UPD*      --UPDATED--/
            .
            .
            .  /--ELEMENT--        ***PROCESS***
            .  |          |        *total-dedu-*    Name occurs
            ....| state-tax|......* ctions-  *    elsewhere.
               |          |        .   *computation*
                --DERIVED--/   .   *USES TO DRV*
                               .
                               .
                               .   ***PROCESS***    /--ELEMENT--
                               .   *  state-  *    |cumulative-|
                               ....*deductions-*......|  state-   |
                                   *  update   *    |deductions |
                                   *USES TO UPD*      --UPDATED--/


              *                                                  *


 +                                                                      +
```

```
PSA Version A5.2R0                    Jun 16, 1981  15:20:29      Page     6
                            Payroll-Example-PSL/PSA-A5.1

                            Contents Comparison Report

        Basic Contents Matrix


                                        45 gross-pay -------------------- /
                                        44 error-code ------------------- / |
                                       43 hours-per-day ---------------- / | |
                                      42 overtime-hours-worked -------- / | | |
                                      41 regular-hours-worked --------- / | | | |

                                  40 pay-date -------------------- / | | | | |
                                 39 current-date ----------------- / | | | | | |
                                38 pay-rate -------------------- / | | | | | | |
                                37 birth-date ------------------- / | | | | | | |
                               36 termination-date ------------ / | | | | | | | |

                           35 skill-classification --------- / | | | | | | | | |
                          34 skill-description ------------ / | | | | | | | | | |
                         33 skill-code ------------------ / | | | | | | | | | | |
                        32 job-title -------------------- / | | | | | | | | | | |
                        31 job-number ------------------ / | | | | | | | | | | | |
                                                         | | | | | | | | | | | | |
        ---------------------------------------------+-|-|-|-+-|-|-|-+-|-|-+-----+
         1 department-information -------              |       |       |       |
         2 hourly-employee-information --              |       |       |       |
         3 job-classification -----------   * * *      |       |       |       |
         4 salaried-employee-information               |       |       |       |
         5 skill-category --------------       * * *   |       |       |       |
                                            +----------+---------+---------+---------+
         6 employment-termination-form --              | *     |       |       |
         7 hourly-employment-form -------   * *        |   * * *       |       |
         8 salaried-employment-form -----   *          |   *   *       |       |
         9 tax-withholding-certificate --              |       *       |       |
        10 time-card --------------------              |       |   *   | * * * |
                                            +----------+---------+---------+---------+
        11 error-listing ---------------              |       |       |     *   |
        12 hired-employee-report --------             |       |       |       *  |
        13 hourly-employee-report -------             |       |       |       *  |
        14 pay-statement ---------------              |       |   *   |       *  |
        15 salaried-employee-report -----             |       |       |       *  |
                                            +----------+---------+---------+---------+
        16 terminated-employee-report --- |           |   *   |       |       |
        ---------------------------------------------+----------+---------+---------+---------+
```

Data Base Summary

Parameters: DB=SKBX:WP176.DB PERCENT SYNONYM DESCRIPTION
NORESPONSIBLE-PROBLEM-DEFINER NOSOURCE NOSECURITY NOKEYWORD
NOATTRIBUTE NOMEMO NOTRACE-KEY NOASSERT NOASSERTED DBNBUF=200
WIDTH=84 LINES=60 INDENT=8 HEADING PARAMETERS PAGE-CC=ON
EXPLANATION

Object Type	Count	Number with SYNONYM	Percent with SYNONYM	Number with DESC	Percent with DESC
*** Undefined ***	2	0		0	
ATTRIBUTE	18	0		5	27.78
CONDITION	8	0		0	
ELEMENT	54	1	1.85	13	24.07
ENTITY	6	5	83.33	3	50.00
EVENT	13	0		4	30.77
GROUP	24	1	4.17	5	20.83
INPUT	8	7	87.50	7	87.50
INTERFACE	5	5	100.00	5	100.00
MEMO	7	0		4	57.14
OUTPUT	8	8	100.00	7	87.50
PROCESS	42	4	9.52	7	16.67
PROCESSOR	3	1	33.33	1	33.33
RELATION	9	0		4	44.44
RESOURCE	2	1	50.00	1	50.00
SET	9	5	55.56	5	55.56
SYSTEM-PARAMETER	20	0		5	25.00
UNIT	6	1	16.67	1	16.67
** Total **	244	39	15.98	77	31.56

Activity Flow Diagram

```
        Data-In                payroll-processing          Data-Out
+------------------+     +------------------+     +------------------+
| hourly-          |-->| new-employee-    |-->| hired-employee-  |
| employment-form  |     | processing       |     | report           |
| salaried-        |     |                  |     |                  |
| employment-form  |     |                  |     |                  |
| tax-withholding- |     |                  |     |                  |
| certificate      |     |                  |     |                  |
+------------------+     +------------------+     +------------------+
| employment-      |-->| terminating-emp- |-->| terminated-      |
| termination-     |     | processing       |     | employee-report  |
| form             |     |                  |     |                  |
+------------------+     +------------------+     +------------------+
|                  |-->| employee-        |-->|                  |
|                  |     | processing       |     |                  |
+------------------+     +------------------+     +------------------+
|                  |-->| process-library  |-->|                  |
+------------------+     +==================+     +------------------+
                         | complexity-      |
                         | level=           |
                         | very substantial |
                         +------------------+
```

PSA Version A5.2RO   Jun 17, 1981 09:53:58   Page   1
                        Payroll-Example-PSL/PSA-A5.1

                             Query System

Parameters: DB=SKBX:WP176.DB INPUT=*MSOURCE* FILE=-PSANAME NOPUNCH
   EMPTY NOPUNCHED-NAMES DBNBUF=200 WIDTH=84 LINES=60 INDENT=8
   HEADING PARAMETERS PAGE-CC=ON EXPLANATION

        Set Name: ** not defined **
        Query: INTERFACES AND NOT (? GENERATES INPUT OR ? RECEIVES
                   OUTPUT OR ? RESPONSIBLE FOR SET)
        The Number of Objects is: 2
        The Objects are:

        Object Name   Object Type
        -----------   -----------

        departments   INTERFACE
        other-departments   INTERFACE

        Set Name: ** not defined **
        Query: PROCESSOR AND NOT (? PART OF !)
        The Number of Objects is: 1
        The Objects are:

        Object Name   Object Type
        -----------   -----------

        payroll-processor   PROCESSOR

        Set Name: ** not defined **
        Query: RELATION AND NOT (? COMPONENT IN !)
        The Number of Objects is: 9
        The Objects are:

        Object Name   Object Type
        -----------   -----------

        department-employee-relation   RELATION
        dept-hourly-emp-relation   RELATION
        dept-salaried-emp-relation   RELATION
        hourly-emp-job-code-relation   RELATION
        hourly-emp-skills-relation   RELATION
        inter-departmental-assignments   RELATION
        job-code-skills-relation   RELATION
        salar-emp-job-code-relation   RELATION
        salaried-emp-skills-relation   RELATION

References

1. Abrams, M. D., and I. W. Cotton, "Introduction to Computer Networks: A Tutorial," Computer Network Association, 1978.
2. Agrawala, A. K., J. R. Agre, K. D. Gordon, "The Slotted Ring vs. the Token-Controlled Ring: A Comparative Evaluation," Proceedings of Computer Software and Applications Conference, Chicago, Nov. 13-16, 1978.
3. Agarwal, R., M. Carey, D. DeWitt, "Deadlock Detection is Cheap," Sigmod Record, Vol. 13, No. 2, Jan. 1983.
4. Akin, T. Allen, Perry B. Flinn, Daniel H. Forsyth, "A Prototype for an Advanced Command Language," Proceedings of the 16th Annual South-Eastern Regional ACM Conference, April 1978, pp 96-102.
5. Akkoyunlu, E., A. Bernstein, R. Schantz, "Interprocess Communication Facilities for Network Operating Systems," Computer, June 1974, pp 36-55.
6. Akoka, J., "Optimization of Distributed Database Systems and Computer Networks," MEIT, March 1977, pp 916-977.
7. Albrecht, H. R., L. C. Thomason, "I/O Facilities of the Distributed Processing Programming Executive (DPPX)," IBM System Journal, Vol. 18, No. 4, 1979, pp 526-546.
8. Alsberg, P., "A Principle for Resilient Sharing of Distributed Resources," Proceedings of 2nd International Conference on Software Engineering, Oct. 1976.
9. Anderson, George A., and E. Douglas Jensen, "Computer Interconnection Structures: Taxonomy, Characteristics, and Examples," Computing Surveys 4, Dec. 1975, pp 197-213.
10. Anderson, R. R., J. F. Hayes, D. N. Sherman, "Simulated Performance of a Ring-Switched Data Network," IEEE Transactions on Communications, Vol. COM-20, No. 3, June 1972, pp 576-591.
11. Aoki, M., "Control of Large-Scale Dynamic Systems by Aggregation," Tutorial: Distributed Control, IEEE cat. No. EHO 153-7, 1979.
12. Arora, S. K., "WCRL: A Data Model Independent Language for Database Systems," University of Hamilton, Ontario, Canada, 1980.
13. Ayling and Moore, "Main Monolithic Memory," IEEE Journal of Solid State Circuits, 1971, SC-6: pp 276-279.

14. Bachman, Charles, and Mike Canepa, "The Session Control Layer of an Open System Interconnection," *Compcon*, Sept., 1978, pp 150-156.

15. Bachman, C., "Data Structure Diagrams," ACM Conference on Data Bases, Summer 1969.

16. Balzer, R. R., "PORTS—A Method for Dynamic Interprogram Communication and Job Control," AFIPS Conference Proceedings 38, 1971 Spring Joint Computer Conference, pp 485-489.

17. Bannerjee, J., D. K. Hsiao, D. D. Kerr, "DBC Software Requirements for Supporting Network Databases," Ohio State University, Columbus, Ohio, 1977 (M).

18. Baskett, F., and A. Smith, "Interference in Multiprocessor Computer Systems with Interleaved Memory," Communications of the ACM No. 19, June 1976, pp 327-334.

19. Baskin, H. R., et al, "PRIME—A Modular Architecture for Terminal-Oriented Systems," AFIPS Conference Proceedings, Vol. 40, 1972 Spring Joint Computer Conference, May 1972, pp 431-437.

20. Bedford, G., E. Grapa, "Setting Clocks 'Back' in a Distributed Computing System," 1st International Conference on Distributed Computing Systems, Oct. 1979, pp 612-616.

21. Bernard, D., "Intercomputer Networks: An Overview and a Bibliography," Master's Thesis, University of Pennsylvania, May 1973 (M).

22. Bernstein, P. A., N. Goodman, J. B. Rothnie, C. A. Papadimitriou, "Analysis of Serializability in SDD-1: A System for Distributed Databases (The Fully Redundant Case)," Computer Corporation of America, Technical Report CCA-77-05, Cambridge, Massachusetts, June 15, 1977.

23. Bernstein, P. A., D. W. Shipman, J. B. Rothnie, N. Goodman, "The Concurrency Control Mechanism of SDD-1: A System of Distributed Databases (The General Case)," Computer Corporation of America, Technical Report CCA-77-09, Cambridge, Massachusetts, Dec. 15, 1977.

24. Bhandarkar, D., "Analysis of Memory Interference in Multiprocessors," IEEE Transactions on Computers, No. 24, Sept. 1975, pp 897-908.

25. Bieber, J., S. Florek, "A Performance Tool for Design and Installation Support of Distributed Database Systems," 1st International Conference on Distributed Computing Systems, Oct. 1979, pp 440-447.

26. Biochot, P., "Score IV, Distributed Checkpointing in a Distributed Data Management System," Aug. 1981.

27. Boebert, W. E., W. R. Franta, E. D. Jensen, R. Y. Kain, "Kernel Primitives of the HXDP Executive," Proceedings of Computer Software and Applications Conference, Chicago, Nov. 13-16, 1978.

28. Ibid, "Decentralized Executive Control in Distributed Computer Systems," Proceedings of Computer Software and Applications Conference, Chicago, Nov. 13-16, 1978.

29. Bonczek, R. H., C. W. Holsapple, A. B. Whinston, "Information

Transferral Within a Distributed Data Base via a Generalized Mapping Language," Krannert Graduate School of Management, Purdue University, West Lafayette, Indiana, Paper No. 577, Nov. 1876 (M).

30. Bosc, P., "An Overview of Freres: A System to Interrogate Distributed Data," Irisa-Rennes, Jan. 1980.

31. Boudenant, J., "A Reliable Distributed Data Management Algorithm, A Case Study: Sirius-Delta," Santa Monica, June 1982.

32. Ibid, "Score III, The Consistency and Concurrency Control in Sirius-Delta," 1981.

33. Brinch, Hansen P., "Distributed Processes: A Concurrent Programming Concept," Communications of the ACM, Nov. 21, 1978, pp 934-941.

34. Bray, Olin H., Distributed Data Base Management Systems, Lexington Books, Lexington, Massachusetts, 1982.

35. Burkhard, W. A., "Partial-Match Hash Coding: Benefits of Redundancy," ACM Transaction on Database Systems, 1979.

36. Cabanel, J. P., M. N. Marouane, R. Besbes, R. D. A. Sazbon, and A. K. Diarra, "A Decentralized OS for ARAMIS Distributed Computer System," Proceedings of the 1st International Conference on Distributed Computing Systems, Oct. 1979, pp 529-535.

37. Cabanel, J. P., R. D. Sazbon, A. K. Diarra, M. N. Marouane, and R. Besbes, "A Decentralized Control Method in a Distributed System," Proceedings of the 1st International Conference on Distributed Computing Systems, Oct. 1979, pp 651-659.

38. Cady, G. M., G. Luther, "Trade-Off Studies in Computer Networks," IEEE Computer Conference 1973, pp 147-150.

39. Case, P. W., et al, "Solid Logic Design Automation," IBM Technical Journal of Research and Development, Vol. 8, No. 2, April 1964, pp. 127-140.

40. Casey, R. G., "Allocation of Copies of a File in an Information Network," Proceedings Spring Joint Computer Conference, AFIPS Press Vol. 40, 1972, pp 61-625.

41. Cardenas, A. F., "Evaluation and Selection of File Organizations—A Model and System," Committee of the ACM, Sept. 1973.

42. Canaday, R. H., R. D. Harrison, E. L. Ryder, L. A. Wehr, "A Backend Computer for Data Base Management," Communications of the ACM, Vol. 17, No. 10, Oct. 1974, pp 575-582.

43. Champine, G. A., "Six Approaches to Distributed Data Bases," Datamation, May 1977, pp 69-72.

44. Chandy, K. M., J. Misra, "A Distributed Algorithm for Detecting Resource Deadlocks in Distributed Systems," Proceedings ACM SIGACT-SIGOPS Symposium on Principles of Distributed Computing, Aug. 1982.

45. Chandy, K. M., L. M. Haas, J. Misra, "Distributed Deadlock Detection," ACM Transactions on Computer Systems, Vol 1, No. 2, May 1983.

46. Chappelli, S. G., C. H. Elmendorf, and L. D. Schmidt, " LAMP: Logic Circuit Simulators," Bell System Technical Journal, Vol. 53, Oct. 1974, pp 1451-1476.

47. Chandy, K. M., "File Allocation in Distributed Systems." Proceedings of International Symposium on Computer Performance Modeling, Measurement and Evaluation, 1976.

48. Ciampi, P. L., A. D. Donovan, and J. D. Nash, "Control and Integration of a CAD Data Base," Proceedings 13th Design Automation Conference, 1976, pp 285-289.

49. Chin, W. N., "Some Comments on Deadlock Detection is Cheap" Sigmod Record, Vol. 14, No. 1, March 1984.

50. Chow, T. S., "Analysis of Software Design Modeled by Multiple Finite State Machines," Proceedings of Computer Software and Applications Conference, Chicago, Nov. 13-16, 1978.

51. Chu, W., "Optimal File Allocation in a Multiple-Computer System," IEEE Transaction on Computers, Vol. C-18, No. 10, Oct. 1969.

52. Clark, David D., and Liba Svobodova, "Design of Distributed Systems Supporting Local Autonomy," Compcon, Feb. 1980, pp 438-444.

53. Clark, Jon, Data Base Selection, Design, and Administration, Praeger, New York, 1980.

54. Clark, D. D., et al, "An Introduction to Local Area Networks," Proceedings of the IEEE, Vol. 66, No. 11, Nov. 1978, pp 1497-1517.

55. Codd, E. F., "A Relational Model for Large Shared Data Banks," Committee ACM, Vol. 13, No. 6, June 1970, pp 377-387.

56. Cook, Robert P., "The STARMOD Distributed Programming System," Compcon, Sept. 1980, pp 729-735.

57. Cellery, W., and O. Meyers, "A Multi-Query Approach to Distributed Processing in a Relational Data Base System," 1980.

58. Chen, K. A., et al, "The Chip Layout Problem: An Automatic Wiring Procedure for LSI," Proceedings 14th Design Automation Conference, 1977, pp 289-302.

59. Case, P., H. Graff, and M. Kloomok, "The Recording, Checking, and Printing of Logic Diagrams," IBM Corp. Technical Report No. TR 00.01110.672, Nov. 1958.

60. Date, C. J., An Introduction to Data Base Systems, 3rd edition, Addison-Wesley, Reading, Massachusetts, 1981.

61. Ibid, "Locking and Recovery in a Shared Data Base System: An Application Programming Tutorial," Very Large Data Base Conference, Oct. 1979.

62. Davies, D. W., D. L. A. Barber, W. L. Price, and C. M. Solomonides, Computer Networks and Their Protocols, Wiley, New York, 1979.

63. Denning, Peter J., "Operating Systems Principles for Data Flow Networks," Computer, July 1978, pp 86-96.

64. Denoia, L., "Performance and Timeliness in a Distributed Data Base," Ph.D. Thesis, Brown University, 1980.

65. Derning, P. J., and J. L. Peterson, "The Impact of Operating Systems Research on Software Technology," in *Research Directions in Software Technology*, edited by Peter Wegner, MIT Press, Cambridge, 1975, pp 490-513.

66. DesJardins, Richard, and George White "ANSI Reference Model for Distributed Systems," *Compcon*, Sept. 1978, pp 144-149.

67. Doll, D. R., "Telecommunications Turbulence and the Computer Network Evolution," *Computer*, Feb. 1974, pp 13-22.

68. Draffan, I. W., and F. Poole, *Distributed Data Bases*, Cambridge University Press, Cambridge, England, 1980.

69. Deitel, H. M., *An Introduction to Operating Systems*, Addison-Wesley, Reading, Massachusetts, 1984.

70. Dijkstra, E. W., "Cooperating Sequential Process," Technological University, Eindhoven, Netherlands, 1965.

71. Duerr, J., "Data Communications Testing Overview-Protocol Analysis," *Computer Design*, Feb. 1979, pp 10-22.

72. Eckhouse, R. J., Jr., J. A. Stankovic, A. VanDam, "Issues in Distributed Processing—An Overview of Two Workshops," *IEEE Computer*, pp 22-26, Jan. 1978.

73. Elam, J., J. Stutz, "Some Considerations and Models for the Distribution of a Data Base," University of Texas at Austin, Center for Cybernetic Studies, Research Report CSS 279, May 1976 (M).

74. Elson, M., "Concepts of Programming Languages," Science Research Association, 1973.

75. Enslow, Philip H., Jr., ed., *Multiprocessors and Parallel Processing*, Wiley, New York, 1974.

76. Enslow, Philip H., Jr., "What is a 'Distributed' Data Processing System?" *Computer*, Jan. 1978, pp 13-21.

77. Enslow, P. H., Jr., "What Does 'Distributed Processing' Mean?" School of Information and Computer Science, Georgia Institute of Technology, Atlanta, 1976.

78. Elam, J. J., "A Model for Distributing a Database Working Paper," Department of Decision Sciences, University of Pennsylvania, Philadelphia, 1978.

79. Farber, D. J., "Distributed Data Bases—An Exploration," University of California at Irvine.

80. Ibid, "Software Considerations in Distributed Architectures," *Computer*, March 1974, pp 31-35.

81. Ibid, "The Design of the Distributed Computer System," University of California at Irvine.

82. Farber, D. J., J. Feldman, F. R. Heinrich, M. D. Hopwood, K. C. Larson, D. C. Loomis, L. A. Rowe, "The Distributed Computer System," Proceedings of the 7th Annual IEEE Computer Society International Conference, Feb.—March 1973, pp 31-34.

83. Farber, D. J., F. R. Heinrich, "The Structure of a Distributed Com-

puter System—The Distributed File System," Proceedings of the International Conference on Computer Communications, Oct. 1972, pp 364-370.

84. Farber, D. J., J. Feldman, F. R. Heinrich, M. D. Hopwood, K. C. Larson, D. C. Loomis, and L. A. Rowe, "The Distributed Computing System," Compcon, Feb. 1973, pp 31-34.

85. Feldman, J. A., "High-Level Programming for Distributed Computing," Communications of the ACM 22, June 1979, pp 353-368.

86. Ferran, G., "Distributed Checkpointing in a Distributed Data Management System," Real-Time Systems Symposium, Miami, Dec. 1981.

87. Ferrier, A., "Heterogeneity in a Distributed Database Management System," VLDB 82, Mexico, Sept. 1982.

88. Fischer, Michael, et al, "Optimal Placement of Identical Resources in a Distributed Network," IEEE, 1981.

89. Finkel, R. A., M. H. Solomon, "Processor Interconnection Strategies," IEEE Transactions on Computers, Vol. C-29, No. 5, May 1980.

90. Fitzgerald, A. K., B. F. Goodrich, "Data Management for the Distributed Processing Programming Executive (DPPX)," IBM System Journal, Vol. 18, No. 4, pp 547-564, 1979.

91. Fletcher, J. G., "Several Communication Protocol Simplifies Data Transmission and Verification," Computer Design, July 1978, pp 77-86.

92. Flowers, J., "Digital Type Manufacture: An Interactive Approach," IEEE Computer, Vol.17, No. 5, May 1984.

93. Fortier, P., "A General Simulation Model for the Evaluation of Distributed Processing Systems," 14th Annual Simulation Symposium, March 1981.

94. Ibid, "Generalized Simulation Model for the Evaluation of Local Computer Networks," Proceedings of HICSS, Jan. 16, 1983.

95. Ibid, "A Communications Environment for Real-Time Distributed Control Systems," Proceedings of ACM Northeast Regional Conference, March 1984.

96. Ibid, "A Reliable Distributed Processing Environment for Real-Time Process Control," Proceedings of HICSS, Jan. 18, 1985.

97. Franta, W., "Hyperchannel Local Network Interconnection Through Satellite Links," IEEE Computer, Vol. 17, No. 5, May 1984.

98. Foster, D., "File Assignment in Memory Hierarchies," Proceedings 2nd International Symposium on Measurement, Modeling and Analysis of Computer Systems, Stresa, Italy, Oct. 1976, pp 119-128.

99. Franck, A., et al, "Some Architectural and System Implications of Local Computer Networks," Compcon, Feb. 1979, pp 272-276D.

100. Fraser, A. G., "On the Interface Between Computers and Data Communictions Systems," Communications of the ACM, Vol. 15, No. 7, July 1972, pp 566-573.

101. Farber, D. J., "A Ring Network," Datamation, Feb. 1975, pp 44-46.

102. Gardarin, G., W. W. Chu, "A Distributed Control Algorithm for Reliably and Consistently Updating Replicated Databases," IEEE Transactions on Computers, Vol. C-29, No. 12, Dec. 1980, pp 1060-1068.

103. Garcia-Molina, H., "Performance Comparison of Update Algorithms for Distributed Databases, Crash Recovery in the Centralized Locking Algorithm," Progress Report No. 7, Stanford University, 1979.

104. Gligor, V. D., S. H. Shartuck, "On Deadlock Detection in Distributed Systems," IEEE Transactions on Software Engineering, Vol. SE-6, No. 5, Sept. 1980, pp 435-440.

105. Gonzalez, M. J., B. W. Jordan, "A Framework for the Quantitative Evaluation of Distributed Computer Systems," 1st International Conference on Distributed Computing Systems, Oct. 1975, pp 156-165.

106. "Deadlock Problem in Computer Networks," Technical Report MIT/TR-185, Laboratory of Computer Science, MIT Cambridge, Massachusetts, Sept. 1977.

107. Gordon, G., "System Simulation," Prentice-Hall, 1969.

108. Gray, J. N., *Notes on Database Operating Systems: An Advanced Course*, Springer-Verlag, Berlin, 1978.

109. Gretton, W. P., "Distributed Database Network Architecture," 1981.

110. Gligor, V., S. H. Shattuck, "On Deadlock Detection in Distributed Systems," IEEE Transactions on Software Engineering, Vol. SE-6, No. 5, Sept. 1980.

111. Haas, L. M., C. Mohan, "A Distributed Deadlock Detection Algorithm for Resource-Based System," IBM Research Report RJ3765(43392), Jan. 25, 1983.

112. Hamacher, V. C., G. S. Shedler, "Performance of a Collision-Free Local Bus Network Having Asynchronous Distributed Control," IEEE, 1980, pp 80-87.

113. Hannan, J., L. Fried, "Should You Decentralize?" *Computer Decisions*, Feb. 1977, pp 40-42.

114. Harris, M. J., "A Prototype Ring Interface for the NPS Data Communications Ring," Master's Thesis, Naval Postgraduate School, Monterey, California, June 1974 (M).

115. Hays, G. G., "Computer-Aided Design: Simulation of Digital Design Logic," IEEE Transactions on Computers, Vol. C-18, Jan. 1969, pp 1-10.

116. Heart, F. E., *The ARPA Network*, Bolt, Beranek, and Newman Inc., Cambridge, Massachusetts.

117. Herman, D., J. P. Verjus, "An Algorithm for Maintaining the Consistency of Multiple Copies," 1st International Conference on Distributed Computing Systems, Oct. 1979, pp 625-631.

118. Hert, K. A., "A Prototype Ring-Structured Computer Network Using Micro-Computers," Naval Postgraduate School, Monterey, California, Dec. 1973 (M).

119. Hightower, D. W., "The Interconnection Problem—A Tutorial," Pro-

ceedings of 10th Design Automation Workshop, 1973, pp 1-12.

120. Ibid, "A Solution to Line-Routing Problems on a Continuous Plane," Proceedings ACM-IEEE Design Aids Workshop, 1969, pp 1-24.

121. Hoare, C. A. R., "Communicating Sequential Processes," Communications of the ACM 21, Aug. 1978, pp 666-677.

122. Hoffman, M. G., "Hardware Implementation of Communication Protocols: A Formal Approach," IEEE 1980, pp 253-263.

123. Hopper, K., H. J. Kugler, and C. Unger, "Abstract Machines Modeling Network Control Systems," Operating Systems Review 13, Jan. 1979, pp 10-24.

124. Hevner, A., "The Optimization of Query Processing on Distributed Data Base Systems," Ph.D. Dissertation, Purdue, Dec. 1979.

125. Ho, Gary S., C. V. Ramamoorthy, "Protocols for Deadlock Detection in Distributed Database Systems," IEEE Transactions on Software Engineering, Vol. SE-8, No. 6, Nov. 1982.

126. Hsiao, D. C., D. S. Kerr, S. E. Madnick, "Operating System Security: A Tutorial of Current Research," Proceedings of Computer Software and Applications Conference, Chicago, Nov. 13-16, 1978.

127. Iran, "A Model for Combined Communications Network Design and File Allocation for Distributed Data Base," 1st International Conference on Distributed Data Base Systems, Huntsville, Alabama, 1979.

128. Isloor, S. S., T. A. Marsland, "System Recovery in Distributed Data Bases," IEEE CompSac, Chicago, Nov. 6-8, 1979, pp 421-426.

129. Ibid, "The Deadlock Problem: An Overview," IEEE Computer, Sept. 1980, pp 58-70.

130. Jafari, H., T. G. Lewis, J. D. Spragins, "Simulation of a Class of Ring-Structured Networks," IEEE Transactions on Computers, Vol. C-29, No. 5, May 1980, pp 385-392.

131. Jagannathan, J. R., R. Vasudevan, "A Distributed Deadlock Detection and Resolution Scheme Performance Study," IEEE, 3rd International Conference on Distributed Systems, 1982.

132. Jensen. E. P., G. A. Anderson, "Computer Interconnection Structures: Taxonomy, Characteristics, and Examples," ACM Computing Surveys, Vol. 7, No. 4, Dec. 1975, pp 197-212.

133. Jensen, E. D., "The Honeywell Experimental Distributed—An Overview," IEEE Computer, Jan. 1978, pp 28-38.

134. Ibid, "The Influence of Microprocessors on Computer Architecture: Distributed Processing," ACM 1975 Proceedings of the Annual Conference, Minneapolis, Oct. 20-22, 1975.

135. Jensen, E. D., W. E. Boebert, "Slides on Partitioning and Assignment of Distributed Processing Software," Honeywell Systems & Research Center, Minneapolis.

136. Jensen, E. D., G. D. Marshall, J. A. White, W. F. Helmbrecht, "The Impact of Wideband Multiplex Concepts on Microprocessor-Based Aeronic System Architecture," Honeywell Systems & Research Center,

Minneapolis, Feb. 1978.

137. Jensen, E. D., K. J. Thurber, G. M. Schneider, "A Review of Systematic Methods in Distributed Processor Inter-Connection," IEEE International Conference on Communications, Philadelphia, June 14, 1976.

138. Johnson, D. E., "FAST: A Second Generation Program Analysis System," Proceedings of 3rd International Conference on Software Engineering, Atlanta, May 1978, pp 142-148.

139. Jagannathan, J. R., R. Vasudevan, Comments on "Protocols for Deadlock Detection in Distributed Database Systems," IEEE Transactions on Software Engineering, Vol. SE-9, No. 3, May 1983.

140. Kaneoko, A., Y. Nishihara, K. Tsuruoka, M. Hattori, "Logical Clock Synchronization Method for Duplicated Data Base Control," 1st International Conference on Distributed Computing Systems, Oct. 1979, pp 601-611.

141. Keller, T. W., D. F. Towsley, K. M. Chandy, J. C. Brown, "A Tool for Network Design: The Automatic Analysis of Stochastic Models of Computer Networks," Texas A & M.

142. Kiely, S. C., "An Operating System for Distributed Processing— DPPX," IBM System Journal, Vol. 18, No. 4, 1979, pp 507-525.

143. Kim, K. H., "Strategies for Structured and Fault-Tolerant Design of Recovery Programs," Proceedings of Computer Software and Applications Conference, Chicago, Nov. 13-16, 1978.

144. Kimbleton, Stephen R., and Richard L. Mandell, "A Perspective on Network Operating Systems," AFIPS Conference Proceedings 45, National Computer Conference, 1976, pp 551-559.

145. Kimbleton, S. R., "Data-Sharing Protocols: Structure, Requirements, and Interrelationships," Compsac, 1978, pp 270-276.

146. Kleinrock, L., "On Communications and Networks," IEEE Transactions on Software Engineering, Vol. C-25, No. 12, Dec. 1976, pp 1326-1335.

147. Kleinrock, L., W. E. Naylor, H. Opderbeck, "A Study of Line Overhead in the ARPANET," Communications of the ACM, Vol. 19, No. 1, Jan. 1976, pp 3-13.

148. Korenjak, A. J., and A. H. Teger, "An Integrated CAD Data Base System," Proceedings 12th Design Automation Conference, 1975, pp. 399-406.

149. Khokhani, K. H., and A. M. Patcl, "The Chip Layout Problem: A Placement Procedure for LSI," Proceedings 14th Design Automation Conference, 1977, pp 291-297.

150. Kuhns, R. C., M. C. Shoquest, "A Serial Data Bus System for Local Processing Networks," IEEE Compcon, Spring 1979, pp 266-271.

151. Kumar, B., "Performance Evaluation of Highly Concurrent Computers by Deterministic Simulation," Committee of the ACM, Nov. 1978.

152. Kurii, T. L., and K. M. Kurii, "An Architecture for Evolutionary Database System Design," Proceedings of Compsac, Chicago, 1978, pp 382-

386.

153. Lam, S. S., "Packet Switching in a Multi-Access Broadcast Channel with Application to Satellite Communication in a Computer Network," University of California at Los Angeles, School of Engineering and Applied Science, April 1974 (M).

154. Lam, S. S., and L. Kleinrock, "Dynamic Control Schemes for a Packet Switched Multi-Access Broadcast Channel," National Computer Conference, Anaheim, California, May 1975, AFIPS Conference Proceedings, Vol. 44, 1975.

155. Ibid, "Packet Switching in a Multi-Access Broadcast Channel; Dynamic Control Procedures," IEEE Transaction on Communications, Vol. Com-23, Sept. 1975.

156. Lam, S. S., "Store-and-Forward Buffer Requirements in a Packet Switching Network," IEEE Transaction on Communications, Vol. Com-24, April 1976.

157. Ibid, "Queuing Networks with Population Size Constraints," IBM Journal of Research and Development, Vol. 21, July 1977.

158. Lam, S. S., and M. Reiser, "Congestion Control of Store-and-Forward Networks by Input Buffer Limits," National Telecommunications Conference, Vol. 1, Dec. 1977; reprinted in *Advances in Computer Communications and Networks*, edited by W. W. Chu, Artech House, 1979.

159. Lam, S. S., "On Protocols for Satellite Packet Switching," Independent Conference on Communications, Boston, June 1979.

160. Ibid, "A Study of the CSMA Protocol in Local Networks," Proceedings 4th Berkeley Conference on Distributed Data Management and Computer Networks, San Francisco, Aug. 1979.

161. Ibid, "Congestion Control Techniques for Packet Networks," 2nd International Conference on Information Sciences and Systems, Patras, Greece, July 1979; reprinted in *Advances in Communications*, D. Lainiotis and N. Tzannes (editors), D. Reidel, Holland, 1980.

162. Ibid, "Multiple-Access Protocols," book chapter in *Computer Communications*, Vol. 1: *Principles*, edited by W. Chou, Prentice-Hall, Englewood Cliffs, New Jersey, 1981.

163. Ibid, "Data Link Control Procedures," book chapter in *Computer Communications*, Vol. 1: *Principles*, edited by W. Chou, Prentice-Hall, Englewood Cliffs, New Jersey, 1981.

164. Larson, James A., "Data Base Management System Anatomy," Lexington Books, Lexington, Massachusetts, 1982.

165. Kobayashi, Hisashi, "Modeling and Analysis: An Introduction to Systems Performance Evaluation Methodology," IBM Corp., Addison-Wesley, Reading, Massachusetts, 1978.

166. Lann, G., "Consistency Issues in Distributed Data Bases," Proceedings of On-Line Conference on Distributed Data Bases, London, March 1981.

167. Li, Victor, "Performance Models of Distributed Data Base Systems,"

MIT, Cambridge, Massachusetts, 1981.
168. Litwin, W., "Sirius Systems for Distributed Data Management," 2nd International Symposium on Distributed Data Bases, Berlin, Sept. 1982.
169. Levin, K., "Optimal Program and Data Locations in Computer Networks," CACM Vol. 20, 1977, pp 315-321.
170. L'Archeveque, J. V. R., G. Yan, "On the Selection of Architectures for Distributed Computer Systems in Real-Time Applications," Vol. NS-24, No. 1, Feb. 1977.
171. LaVoie, P., "Distributed Computing Systematically," *Computer Decisions*, March 1977, pp 44-45.
172. Lawson, J. T., M. P. Mariani, "Distributed Data Processing System Design—A Look at the Partitioning Problem," Proceedings of Computer Software and Applications Conference, Chicago, Nov. 13-16, 1978.
173. Lee, C., "Queuing Analysis of Global Locking Synchronization Schemes for Multicopy Databases," IEEE Transactions on Computers, Vol. C-29, No. 5, May 1980, pp 371-384.
174. LeLann, G., "An Analysis of Different Approaches to Distributed Computing," IEEE, 1979, pp 222-232.
175. Levin, K., "Organizing Distributed Data Bases In Computer Networks," Wharton School of Finance and Commerce, University of Pennsylvania, Sept. 1974(M).
176. Levin, K. D., H. L. Moran, "Optimizing Distributed Data Bases—A Framework for Research," Wharton School, University of Pennsylvania, Jan. 1975 (M).
177. Leham, L. S., "Computer Simulation and Modeling," Lawrence Erlbaum Association, 1977.
178. Liebowitz, B. H., "Multiple Processor Minicomputer Systems—Part 1: Design Concepts," *Computer Design*, Oct. 1978, pp 87-95.
179. Ibid, B. H., "Multiple Processor Minicomputer Systems—Part 2: Implementation," *Computer Design*, Nov. 1978, pp 121-131.
180. Lien, Y. E., J. H. Ying, "Design of Distributed Entity—Relationship Database System," Procdings of Computer Software and Applications Conference, Chicago, Nov. 13-16, 1978.
181. Lientz, B. P., J. W. Schenck, I. R. Weiss, "A Model for Performing Trade-Offs in Computer Communication Networks," University of California at Los Angeles, Graduate School of Management, Dec. 1975 (M).
182. Liesey, J., "Interprocess Communication and Naming in the Mininet System," IEEE *Compcon*, Spring 1979, pp 222-229.
183. Lorin, H., "Distributed Processing: An Assessment," IBM System Journal, Vol. 18, No. 4, 1979, pp 582-603.
184. Mariani, M. P., "Distributed Data Processing (DDP) Technology Program," Vol. 1, Final Report, TRW and Burroughs Corp., Dec. 31, 1977 (M).
185. Ibid, "Distributed Data Processing (DDP) Technology Program," Vol.

2, Research Appendices, TRW and Burroughs Corp., Dec. 31, 1977 (M).

186. Mariana, M. P., and D. F. Palmer, "Tutorial: Distributed System Design," IEEE Catalog No. EHO151-1, Oct. 1979.

187. Maryanski, F. J., "A Survey of Developments in Distributed Data Base Management Systems," IEEE *Computer*, Feb. 1978, pp 28-37.

188. Maccabe, Arthur B., and Richard J. Leblanc, "A Language Model for Fully Distributed Systems," *Compcon*, Sept. 1980, pp 723-728.

189. Mahmoud, S., "Optimal Allocation of Resources in Distributed Information Networks," ACM Transaction in Data Base System, Vol. 1, 1976, pp 66-68.

190. Maryanski, F., P. Fisher, V. Wallentine, "Usability and Feasibility of Back-End Minicomputers," Department of Computer Science, Kansas State University, Manhattan, Kansas, June 1975 (M).

191. Martin, James, *Computer Data Base Organization*, Prentice-Hall, Englewood Cliffs, New Jersey, 1975.

192. Ibid, *Principles of Data Base Management*, Prentice-Hall, Englewood Cliffs, New Jersey, 1976.

193. Metcalfe, R. D., D. Boggs, "Ethernet: Distributed Packet Switching for Local Computer Networks," Communications of the ACM, Vol. 19, No. 7, July 1976, pp 395-404.

194. Meadow, C., "The Analysis of Information Systems," Wiley, New York, 1967.

195. "Menasce, D. A., and R. R. Muntz, "Locking and Deadlock Detection in Distributed Databases," IEEE Transactions on Software Engineering, Vol. SE-5, No. 3, May 1979.

196. Metcalfe, R. M., and D. R. Boggs, "Ethernet—Distributed Packet Switching for Local Computer Networks," Communications of the ACM, July 19, 1976, pp 395-404.

197. Mills, D. L., "Dynamic File Access in a Distributed Computer Network," University of Maryland, Department of Computer Science, Technical Report TR-415, Feb. 1976 (M).

198. Mockapetris, P. V., M. R. Lyle, D. J. Faber, "On the Design of Local Network Interfaces," University of California at Irvine, Department of Information and Computer Science; also IFIP, 1977.

199. Miranda, S., "Specification and Verification of a Decentralized Controlled Locking Protocol (DPL) for Distributed Data Bases," i.e., R.I.S.S., University des Sciences de Toulouse, France, Feb. 1979.

200. Morgan, Howard L., and Levin K. Dan, "Optimal Program and Data Locations in Computer Networks," Communications of the ACM, May 20, 1977, pp 315-322.

201. Morgan, D. E., W. Banks, D. P. Goodspeed, R. Kolanko, "A Computer Network Monitoring System," IEEE Transactions on Software Engineering, Vol. SE-1, No. 3, Sept., pp 299-311.

202. Moulton, P. D., R. C. Sancier, "Another Look at SNA," *Datamation*,

March 1977.

203. Mitchell D., "Distributed Algorithms for Deadlock Detection and Resolution," ACM 3rd Proceedings on Distributed Computing, Aug. 1984.

204. Mullery, A. P., "The Distributed Control of Multiple Copies of Data," IBM Thomas J. Watson Research Center, Yorktown Heights, New York, Aug. 1975.

205. Palmer, D. F., W. M. Denny, "Distributed Data Processing Requirements of Engineering: High-Level DDP Design," Proceedings of Computer Software and Applications Conference, Chicago, Nov. 13-16, 1978.

206. Mohan, C., "Distributed Database Management, Some Thoughts and Analyses," TR-129, University of Texas at Austin, May 1979.

207. Sinha, M. K., and N. Natarajan, "A Distributed Deadlock Detection Algorithm Based on T Timestamps," IEEE, 4th Conference on Distributed Systems, May 1984.

208. Larson, R. E., "Tutorial: Distributed Control," IEEE catalog, No. EHO153-7, Oct. 1979.

209. Obermarck, R., ·"Deadlock Detection for all Resource Classes," IBM Research Report RJ2955.

210. Obermarck, R., and C. Mohan, "R* A Distributed Database-Manager," Transactions on Computer Systems, Feb. 1984.

211. Moto-Oka, T., T. Kurachi, T. Shiino, and M. Sugimoito, "Logic Design System In Japan," Proceedings of 12th Design Automation Conference, 1975, pp 241-250.

212. Mills, D. L., "An Overview of the Distributed Computer Network," AFIPS Conference Proceedings, VVl. 45, National Computer Conference, 1976, pp 523-531.

213. Moulinoux, C., "Messidor: A Distributed Information Retrieval System," ACM & BCS, Berlin (RFA), May 1982.

214. Metcalf, R. M., and D. R. Boggs, "Ethernet: Distributed Packet Switching for Local Computer Networks," Communications of the ACM, Vol. 19, No. 7, July 1976, pp 395-404.

215. Nelson, David L., and Gordon Robert L., "Computer Cells—A Network Architecture for Data Flow Computing," Compcon, Sept. 1978, pp 296-301.

216. Nize, J. H., and J. G. Cox, Essentials of Simulation, Prentice-Hall, Englewood Cliffs, New Jersey, 1968.

217. Nguyen, G. T., "Distributed Architecture and Decentralized Control for a Local Network Database System," ACM International Computing Symposium, London, March 1982.

218. Ousterhout, John K., "Partitioning and Cooperation in a Distributed Multiprocessor Operating System: Medusa," Ph.D. Thesis, Carnegie-Mellon University, April 1980.

219. Ousterhout, John K., Donald A. Scelza, and Pradeep S. Sindhu, "Medusa: An Experiment in Distributed Operating System Structure,"

Communications of the ACM, Feb. 23, 1980, pp 92-105.

220. Peebles, Richard, and Thomas Dopirak, "ADAPT: A Guest System," *Compcon*, Feb. 1980, pp 445-454.

221. Peebles, R., E. Manning, "System Architecture for Distributed/Data Management," IEEE *Computer*, Jan. 1978, pp 40-47.

222. Piatowski, T. F., D. C. Hull, R. J. Sunderstrom, "Inside IBM's System Network Architecture," *Data Communications*, Feb. 1977, pp 33-48.

223. Peterson and Wesloychu, Tutorial, "Centralized and Distributed Data Base Systems," IEEE Computer Society, 1979.

224. Popek, G., and S. Miranda, "Specification and Verification of a Decentralized-Controlled Locking Protocol (DLP) for Distributed Data Bases," C.E.R.I.S.S., Toulouse, France, 1979.

225. Postel, J. B., "A Graph Model Analysis of Computer Communications Protocols," University of California at Los Angeles, School of Engineering and Applied Sciences, Jan. 1974 (M).

226. Postel, J. B., E. J. Feinler, "ARPA Network—Current Network Protocols," Stanford Research Institute, Dec. 1974 (M).

227. Pouzin, L., "Critical Evaluation of New Data Networks."

228. Pritsker, A. B., "The GASP IV Simulation Language," School of Industrial Engineering, Purdue University, Wiley, 1974.

229. Ibid, *Introduction to Simulation and SlamII*, Systems Publishing Corp., 1984.

230. Rahimi, S. K., W. R. Franta, "A Postal Update Approach to Concurrency Control in Distributed Data Base Systems," 1st International Conference on Distributed Computing Systems, Oct. 1979, pp 632-641.

231. Ramsey, "The Placement of Relations on a Distributed Relational DB," International Conference on Distributed Data Base, Huntsville, Alabama, 1979.

232. Reitman, J., *Computer Simulation Applications*, Wiley, New York, 1971.

233. Ritchie, D. M., and K. Thompson, "The UNIX Time-Sharing System," The Bell System Technical Journal 57, July-Aug. 1978, pp 1905-1929.

234. Rosko, J. S., "Digital Simulation of Physical Systems," Addison-Wesley, Reading, Massachusetts, 1972.

235. Roch, C., "An Implementation of Capabilities on the PDP 11/45," Operating Systems Review 14, 1980, pp 22-32.

236. Ross, Ronald G., "Data Base Systems: Design Implementation and Management," *Amacon*, 1978.

237. Rothnie, J. B., "Distributed DBMS No Longer Just a Concept," *Data Communications*, Jan. 1980, pp 61-67.

238. Rothnie, J. B., N. Goodman, "An Overview for the Preliminary Design of SDD-1: A System for Distributed Data Bases," Computer Corporation of America, Technical Report CCA-77-04, Cambridge, Massachusetts, March 31, 1977.

239. Rothnie, J. B., N. Goodman, P. A. Bernstein, "The Redundant Update Methodology of SDD-1: A System for Distributed Databases (The Fully Redundant Case)," Computer Corporation of America, a Technical Report CAA-77-02, Cambridge, Massachusetts, June 15, 1977.

240. Samari, N. K., G. M. Schneider, "The Analysis of Distributed Computer Networks Using M/D/R and M/M/1 Queues," 1st International Conference on Distributed Computing Systems, Oct. 1979, pp 143-155.

241. Sarfati, J., "Measures on the SIRIUS-DELTA Distributed Data Prototype," Feb., 1981.

242. Scheuermann, P., "Assimulation Model for Data Base Systems," Ph.D. Dissertation, State University of New York at Stony Brook, 1976.

243. Seguin, J., G. Sergeant, P. Wilms, "A Majority Consensus Algorithm for the Consistency of Duplicated and Distributed Information," 1st International Conference on Distributed Computing Systems, Oct. 1979, pp 617-624.

244. Senko, M. E., "Details of a Scientific Approach to Information Systems," Data Base System, Courant Computer Science Symposium, 1971.

245. Severino, E. F., "Databases and Distributed Processing," *Computer Decisions*, March 1977, pp 40-42.

246. Ibid, "Using Distributed Processing," *Computer Decisions*, May 1977, pp 46-50.

247. Shirey, R. W., "Management and Distributed Computing," *Computer World*.

248. Siler, K. F., "A Stochastic Evaluation Model for Data Base Organizations in Data Retrieval Systems," Committee of the ACM, Feb. 1976.

249. Samll, D. L., W. W. Chu, "A Distributed Data Base Architecture for Data Processing in a Dynamic Environment," IEEE *Compcon* Spring 1979, pp 123-127.

250. "Performance Analysis and Evaluation: The Connection to Reality," in Research Directions in Software Technology, edited by Peter Wegner, MIT Press, Cambridge, Massachusetts, 1979, pp 557-583.

251. Smith, C., "Performance Specifications and Analysis of Software Designers," Proceedings of ACM/SIGNMETRICS Conference on Simulation, Measurement and Modeling of Computers Systems, Boulder, Colorado, 1979, pp 173-182.

252. Ibid, "Modeling Software Systems for Performance Predictions," Proceedings Computer Measurement Group X, Dallas, Dec. 1979, pp 175-196.

253. Ibid, "Aspects of Software Design Analysis: Concurrency and Blocking," Proceedings of Performance 80, Toronto, May 1980, pp 175-186.

254. Saponas, Timothy G., and Phillip L. Crews, "A Model for Decentralized Control in a Fully Distributed Processing System," *Compcon*, Sept. 1980, pp 307-312.

255. Smith, Reid G., "The Contract Net Protocol: High-Level Communication and Control in a Distributed Problem Solver," Proceedings of the 1st International Conference on Distributed Computing, Oct. 1979, pp 185-192.
256. Ibid, "The Contract Net Protocol: High-Level Communication and Control in a Distributed Problem Solver," IEEE Transactions on Computers C-29, Dec. 1980, pp 1104-1113.
257. Smoliar, S. W., J. E. Scalf, "A Framework for Distributed Data Processing Requirements," IEEE ComoSac, Chicago, Nov. 6-8, 1979, pp 535-541.
258. Sadt, T., D. Ross, and K. E. Schoman, Jr., "Structured Analysis for Requirements Definition," Proceedings of 2nd International Conference on Software Engineering, San Francisco, Oct. 13-15, 1976.
259. Senko, M. E., "Details of a Scientific Approach to Information Systems, Data Base Systems," Courant Computer Science Symposium, 1971.
260. Shupe, C. F., "Automatic Component Placement in the NOMAD System," Proceedings 12th Design Automation Conference, 1975, pp 162-172.
261. Sorenson, P. G., "Distributed Data Base Query System Based on a Forms Interface," Information Processing Society of Canada, 1979.
262. Stepczyk, F., "A Case Study in Real-Time Distributed Processing Design," Proceedings of Computer Software and Applications Conference, Chicago, Nov. 13-16, 1979.
263. Strom, C. A., R. K. Walker, "Distributed Computer Communications Networks," Symposium on Computer Communications Networks and Teletraffic, Polytechnic Institute of Brooklyn, New York, April 4-6, 1972.
264. Stone, H., Introduction to Computer Organization and Data Structures, McGraw-Hill, New York, 1972.
265. Ibid, Microcomputer Interfacing, Addison-Wesley, Reading, Massachusetts, 1982.
266. Swan, R. J., et al, "CM*—A modular, Multi-Microprocessor," AFIPS Conference Proceedings, Vol. 46, 1977, pp 637-644.
267. Tajibnapis, W. D., "A Correctness Proof of a Topology Information Maintenance Protocol for a Distributed Computer Network," Communications of the ACM, Vol. 220, No. 7, July 1977, pp 447-485.
268. Teng, A. Y., M. T. Liu, "A Formal Approach to the Design and Implementation of Network Communication Protocol," Proceedings of Computer Software and Applications Conference, Chicago, Nov. 13-16, 1978.
269. Thurber, K. J., and H. A. Freeman, "Local Computer Network Architectures," Compcon, Feb. 1979, pp 258-261.
270. Ibid, "Distributed Processing Communication Architecture: A Tutorial," IEEE Catalog No. EH0152-9, Oct. 1979.
271. Thurber, K. J., and H. A. Freeman, "A Bibliography of Local Com-

puter Network Architectures," *Computer Architecture News*, Vol. 7, No. 5, Feb. 1979, pp 22-27, and *Computer Communication Review*, Vol. 9, No. 2, April 1979, pp 1-6.

272. Thurber, K. J., "Tutorial: Distributed Processor Communications Architecture," IEEE Catalog No. EHO152-9, Oct. 1979.

273. Thurber, K. J., and H. A. Freeman, "Architecture Considerations for Local Computer Networks," Sperry Univac, St. Paul, Minnesota.

274. Teichroew, D., and H. Sayani, "Automation of System Building," *Datamation*, Aug. 15, 1971, p 2503.

275. Ibid, "A Survey of Languages for Stating Requirements for Computer-Based Information Systems," Proceedings FJCC, 1972, pp 1203-1224.

276. Tsichrotzis, D. C., "Data Management Systems," Academic Press, 1977.

277. Thomas, Robert H., Richard E. Schantz, and Harry C. Forsdick, "Network Operating Systems," Bolt Beranek and Newman Report No. 3796, March 1978.

278. Thorton, J. E., et al, "A New Approach to Network Storage Management," *Computer Design*, Vol. 14, No. 11, Nov. 1975, pp 81-85.

279. Schwartz, M., "Computer Communication Network Design and Analysis," Prentice-Hall, Englewood Cliffs, New Jersey, 1977.

280. Towsley, D. F., and K. M. Chandy, "Models for Parallel Processing Within Programs: Application to CPU:I/O and I/O:I/C," Committee ACM, 21, 10, pp 821-831.

281. Ullman, Jeffery D., *Principles of Data Base System*, Computer Science Press, Potomac, Maryland, 1980.

282. Unger, E. A., et al, "Design for the Integration of a Data Base Management System into a Network Environment," IEEE, 1979.

283. Van Cleemput, W. M., "An Hierarchical Language for the Structural Description of Digital Systems," Proceedings 14th Design Automation Conference, 1977, pp 377-385.

284. Van Duyn, Julia, *Developing a Data Dictionary System*, Prentice-Hall, Englewood Cliffs, New Jersey, 1982.

285. Viemont, Y. H., "A Distributed Concurrency Control Algorithm Based on Transaction Commit Ordering," Fault Tolerant Computing Symposium, Los Angeles, June 1982.

286. Von Issendorff, H., W. Grunewald, "An Adaptable Network for Functional Distributed Systems," IEEE, 1980, pp 196-201.

287. Wiederhold, G., "Knowledge and Database Management," IEEE *Software*, Vol. 1, No. 1, Jan. 1984.

288. Ward, Stephen A., "TRIX: A Network-Oriented Operating System," *Compcon*, Feb. 1980, pp 344-349.

289. Walden, D. C., "A System for Interprocess Communication in a Resource-Sharing Computer Network," Communications of the ACM, Vol. 15, No. 4, April 1972, pp 221-230.

290. Watson, R. W., "Network Architecture Design for Back-End Storage Networks," IEEE *Computer*, Feb. 1980, pp 32-48.

291. Wilms, P., "Qualitative and Quantative Comparison of Update Algorithms in Distributed Data Bases," Images Grenoble, France, March 1980.

292. Weidermold, George, "Data Base Design." McGraw-Hill, New York, 1977.

293. Wong, Patrick K. M., *Performance Evaluation of Data Base Systems*, Ann Arbor, Michigan, UMI Research Press, 1981.

294. Yajima, S., et al, "Labolink: An Optically Linked Laboratory Computer Network," *Computer*, Nov. 1977, pp 52-59.

295. Weinstock, C. B., M. W. Green, "Reconfiguration Strategies for the Sift Fault-Tolerant Computer," Proceedings of Computer Software and Applications Conference, Chicago, Nov. 13-16, 1978.

296. Whitley-Strevens, C., "Towards the Performance Evaluation of Distributed Computing Systems," Proceedings of Computer Software and Applications Conference, Chicago, Nov. 13-16, 1978.

297. White, G. W., "Message Format and Data Communication Link Control Principles," IEEE Transactions on Communications, Vol. Com-20, No. 4, June 1972, pp 678-684.

298. Wong, E., "Retrieving Dispersed Data from SDD-1: A System for Distributed Databases," Computer Corporation of America, Technical Report CCA-77-03, Cambridge, Massachusetts, March 15, 1977.

299. Wood, L., "A Cable Bus Protocol Architecture," Proceedings of Datacom, Nov. 1979.

300. Yee, J. G., S. Y. H. Su, "A Scheme for Tolerating Faulty Data in Real-Time Systems," Proceedings of Computer Software and Applications Conference, Chicago, Nov. 13-16, 1978.

301. Yuen, M. L. T., B. A. Black, E. E. Newhall, A. N. Venetsanopoulas, "Traffic Flow in a Distributed Loop Switching System," Symposium on Computer-Communications Networks and Teletraffic, Polytechnic Institute of Brooklyn, New York, April 4-6, 1972.

302. *Computer* Magazine, Feb. 1980, "Backend Storage Network."

303. *Computer* Magazine, June 1979, "Circuit Switching."

304. *Computer* Magazine, Sept. 1979, "Network Protocol."

305. *Computer* Magazine, March 1980, "Fault Tolerant Computing."

306. *Computer* Magazine, Oct. 1979, "Learning with Simulation."

307. *Computer* Magazine, Jan. 1978, "Distributed Processing."

308. *Computer* Magazine, Nov. 1977, "Computer Networks."

309. *Computer* Magazine, April 1977, "The Many Faces of Simulation."

310. Freeman, P., "Software Systems Principles," Science Research Association, 1975.

311. Proceedings, "Trends and Applications," May 1979, IEEE Catalog No. 79 CH1402-7C.

312. Trends and Applications, "Computer Networks," Nov. 1976, IEEE Catalog No. 76 CH1143-7C.

313. Proceedings, "Computer Networking Symposium," December 13,

     1973, IEEE Catalog No. 78 CH1400-1C.

314. "Computer Networks: A Tutorial," 1978, IEEE Catalog No. EH0127-1.

315. Distributed Processing Seminar, IBM Federal Systems Division, March 23, 1979.

316. Distributed Processing, 2nd edition, IEEE Catalog No. EH0127-1.

317. Proceedings, "1st International Conference on Distributed Computing Systems," Huntsville, Alabama, Oct. 1-5, 1979, IEEE Catalog No. 79 CH1445-6C.

318. *Computer* Magazine, April 1980, "Analytical Queuing Models."

319. "Local Area Networking," Report of a Workshop Held at the National Bureau of Standards, Aug. 22-23, 1977, Ira W. Cotten, editor, U.S. Dept. of Commerce, National Bureau of Standards, April 1978.

320. Proceedings University of Minnesota Workshop on Local Computer Networks, Sept. 16-17, 1976, Oct. 13-14, 1977, and Oct. 23-24, 1978, P. C. Patton and A. Franck, editors, University of Minnesota.

321. Proceedings of the 3rd Berkeley Workshop on Distributed Data Management and Computer Networks, Aug. 29-31, 1978.

322. *Compcon*, Feb. 27-Mar. 2, 1979.

323. Kuhns, R. C., and M. C. Shoquist, "A Serial Data Bus System for Local Processing Networks," *Compcon* Digest of Papers, Feb. 1979, pp 266-271.

324. Jensen, E. D., "The Honeywell Experimental Distributed Process—and Overview," *Computer*, Vol. 11, No. 1, Jan. 1978, pp 28-38.

325. "Data Management in Engineering," Proceedings of Society of Engineering Science, Hampton, Virginia, Oct. 1976, pp 775-790.

326. "A Critical Overview of Computer Performance Evaluation," Proceedings of 2nd International Conference on Software Engineering, San Francisco, California, Nov. 1976.

327. Computer Corporation of America, "A Distributed Data Management System for Command and Control Systems," Jan. 1979.

328. Gardarvin, George, and Wesley Chu, "A Reliable Distributed Control Algorithm for Updating Replicated Data Bases," IEEE, 1979.

329. International Conference on Very Large Data Bases, IEEE Computer Society: 1st, Framingham, Massachusetts, 1975; 2nd, Brussels, Belgium, 1971; 4th, Berlin, Germany, 1978; 5th, Rio de Janeiro, Brazil, 1979; 6th, Montreal, Canada, 1980; 7th, Cannegi, France, 1981.

330. Proceedings of the 5th Berkeley Conference on Distributed Data Management and Computer Networks, University of California, Berkeley, California.

331. INFOTECH, "Distributed Data Bases," Vol. 1 and 2, INFOTECH International, Lt., Maidenhead, Berkshire, England, 1977.

332. Thurber, Kenneth J., *Data Structures and Computer Arch. Design Issues at the NW/SW Interface*, Lexington Books, 1979.

333. Calculon Corp., "Distributed Data Base Technology, State of the Art Review," Rome Air Development Center, New York, 1980.

334. LeLann, G., "A Distributed System for Real-Time Transaction Processing," IEEE *Computer*, Vol. 14, No. 2, Feb. 1981.

335. Takizawa, M., "Query Translation in Distributed Databases," Information Proceedings, Tokyo, Japan, 1980.

336. Pactel, "Distributed Data Base Technology," NCC Publications, Manchester, England, 1979.

337. "System R: A Relational Data Base Management System," *Computer*, May 1979.

338. Jones, M. N., "HIPO for Developing Specifications," *Datamation*, March 1976, pp 112-125.

339. Zucker, Steven, "Interprocess Communication Extensions for the UNIX Operating System: II. Implementation," Rand Technical Report R-2064/2-AF, June 1977.

340. "Proceedings of the Second Berkeley Workshop on Distributed Data Management and Computer Networks," Berkeley Laboratory, University of California, Berkeley, May 1977 (M).

341. "Berkeley Workshop on Distributed Data Management and Computer Networks," Berkeley, California, May 25-26, 1976 (M).

342. "Tutorial on Distributed Processing," second edition, The Institute of Electrical Electronics Engineers, New York, New York.

343. Brooks, F. P., Jr., "The Mythical Man-Month," *Datamation*, Dec. 1974.

344. Wasserman, A. I., "Information System Design Methodology" Journal of the American Society for Information Science, Jan. 1980.

345. Freeman, P., "Software Reliability and Design: A Survey," Proceedings of 13th Design Automation Conference, June 1976.

346. Ross, D. T., and K. E. Schoman, Jr., "Structured Analysis for Requirements Definition," IEEE Transactions on Software Engineering, Jan. 1977.

347. Davis, C. G., and C. R. Vick., "The Software Development System," IEEE Transactions on Software Engineering, Jan. 1977.

348. Wasserman, S., "A Specification Method for Interactive Information Systems," Proceedings of Specifications of Reliable Software, April 1979.

349. Teichroew, D., and E. A. Hershey, III, "PSL/PSA: A Computer-Aided Technique for Structured Documentation and Analysis of Information Processing Systems," IEEE Transactions on Software Engineering, Jan. 1977.

350. Parnas, D. L., "On the Criteria to be Used in Decomposing Systems into Modules," Communications of the ACM, Dec. 1972.

351. Stevens, W. P., G. J. Myers, L. L. Constantine, "Structured Design," IBM Systems Journal, 1974.

352. Riddle, W. E., "An Event-Based Design Methodology Support by DREAM," Formal Models and Practical Tools for Information Systems Design, 1979.

353. Caine, S. H., and E. K. Gordon, "PDL-A Tool for Software Design,"

Proceedings of National Computer Conference, 1975.

354. Wirth, N., "Program Development by Stepwise Refinement," Communications of the ACM, April 1971.

355. Wasserman, A. I., and P. Freeman, "Software Engineering Education: Status and Prospects," Proceedings of the IEEE, Aug. 1978.

356. Stonebraker, M., "A Formal Model of Crash Recovery in a Distributed System," IEEE Transactions on Software Engineering, Vol. 1, SG-9, No. 3, May 1983.

357. Lindsey, B., et al, "Notes on Distributed Data Bases," IBM Research Division, San Jose, California, Rj2571, July 14, 1979.

358. Kleinrock, L., *Queuing Systems: Volume I; Theory, 1975, Volume II: Computer Applications, 1976*, Wiley, New York.

359. Lavenburg, S., *Computer Performance Modeling Handbook*, Academic Press, New York, 1983.

360. Trivedi, K., *Probability and Statistics with Reliability, Queuing and Computer Science Applications*, Prentice-Hall, Englewood Cliffs, New Jersey, 1982.

361. Sauer, C., and K. Chandy, *Computer Systems Performance Modeling*, Prentice-Hall, Englewood Cliffs, New Jersey, 1981.

362. Kobagashi, A., *Modeling and Analysis: An Introduction to Systems Performance Evaluation Methodology*, Addison-Wesley, Reading, Massachusetts, 1980.

363. Enslow, P., "Multiprocessors Organization," *Computing Surveys*, No. 9, March 1977, pp 103-129.

364. Swan, R., "The Implementation of the CM* Multimicroprocessor," Proceedings of AFIPS 1977 National Computer Conference, pp 645-655.

365. Tang, C., "Cache System Design in the Tightly Coupled Multiprocessor System," Proceedings of AFIPS 1977 National Computer Conference, pp 749-753.

366. Wulf, W., "C.MMP—A multiminiprocessor," Proceedings of AFIPS 1972 Fall Joint Computer Conference.

367. IEEE *Computer*, Special Issue on Computer Architectures for Image Processing, Jan. 1983.

368. Rosenfield, A., and A. Kak, *Digital Picture Processing*, Academic Press, New York, 1982.

369. IEEE *Computer*, Special Issue on Architectures for Array Processors, Sept. 1981.

370. Bell and Newell, *Computer Structures: Readings and Examples*, McGraw-Hill, New York 1971.

371. Taylor, R., and R. Frank, "Data Base Management Systems," *Computing Surveys*, Vol. 8, No.1, March 1976.

372. Peterson, J., *Operating Systems Concepts*, Addison-Wesley, Reading, Massachusetts, 1983.

373. Hanson, B., *Operating Systems Principles*, Prentice-Hall, Englewood

Cliffs, New Jersey, 1973.

374. Proceedings of the 7th ACM Symposium on Operating Systems Principles, 1979.

375. Stone, H., "Introduction to Computer Architecture," SRA Inc., 1980.

376. Eckhouse, R., *Minicomputer Systems Organization and Programming (PDP-11)*, Prentice-Hall, Englewood Cliffs, New Jersey, 1975.

377. Baer, J., *Computer Systems Architecture*, Computer Science Press, Rockville, Maryland, 1980.

378. Tannenbaum, A., *Structured Computer Organization*, Prentice-Hall, Englewood Cliffs, New Jersey, 1976.

379. Von Neumann, in *Computer Structures Readings and Examples*, McGraw-Hill, New York, 1971.

380. Aho, Hopcroft, and Ullmann, *The Design and Analysis of Computer Algorithms*, Addison-Wesley, Reading, Massachusetts, 1974.

381. Ibid, "Data Structures and Algorithms," Addison-Wesley, Reading, Massachusetts, 1984.

382. Clark, D., "An Introduction to Local Area Networks," Proceedings of the IEEE, Vol. 66, Nov. 1978, pp 1497-1517.

383. Pierce, R., "Network Operating Systems Functions and Microprocessor Front End," IEEE *CompCon*, Spring 1977.

384. Liu, M., "The Design of the Distributed Loop Computer Network," Proceedings of International Computer Conference, 1975.

385. Yajima S., "Labolink: An Optically Linked Laboratory Computer Network," IEEE *Computer*, Nov. 1977, pp 52-59.

386. Sincoskie, W., "The Series 1 Distributed Operating System," IEEE *CompCon*, 1980.

387. Guillemont, M., "The Chorus Distributed Operating System, Design and Implementation," Proceedings of IFIP TC 6, April 1982.

388. Liskov, B., "Primitives for Distributed Computing," 7th ACM Symposium on Operating Systems Principles, 1979.

389. Knuth, *The Art of Computer Programing*, Vol. 1, 1968, Vol. 2, 1969, Vol. 3, 1973.

390. Shipman, D., "The Functional Data Model and the Data Language Daplex," ACM Transactions on Data Base Systems, Vol. 6, No. 1, March 1981.

391. Wong, E., "Decomposition—A Strategy for Query Processing," ACM Transactions on Data Base Systems, Vol. 1, No. 3, Sept. 1976.

392. Seguin, J., "A Majority Consensus Algorithm for the Consistency of Duplicated and Distributed Information," 1st International Conference on Distributed Computing Systems, Oct. 1979.

393. Thomas, R., "A Majority Consensus Approach to Concurrency Control for Multiple-Copy Data Base," BBN Inc., Report 3733, Dec. 1977.

394. Whitney, V., "A Study of Optimal File Assignment and Communication Network Configuration," Ph.D. Dissertation, University of Michigan, 1970.

395. Bernstein, P., "Concurrency Control in Distributed Data Bases," *Computing Surveys*, Vol. 13, No. 2, June 1981.
396. Lee, C., "An Algorithm for Path Connections and Its Applications," IRE Transactions on Electronic Computers, Vol. Ec-10, No. 3, Sept. 1961, pp 346-365.
397. Anderson, T., and P. Lee, "Fault Tolerance Principles and Practice," Prentice-Hall, Englewood Cliffs, New Jersey, 1981.
398. Tannenbaumn, A., "Computer Networks," Prentice-Hall, Englewood Cliffs, New Jersey, 1981.
399. Chen, P., "The Entity-Relationship Model—Toward a Unified View of Data," ACM Transaction on Data Base Systems, Vol. 1, No. 1, March 1976.
400. Chu, W., and P. Hurley, "Optimal Query Processing for Distributed Data Base Systems," IEEE Transactions on Computers, Vol. c-31, No. 9, Sept. 1982.

INDEX

User Control Data File, 232
user-oriented metrics, 165
user-to-system primitive, 106
update synchronization, 146-149
   majority read update, 148-149
   majority vote update, 148
   moving primary updates,
     147-148
   primary copy update, 147
   unanimous agreement, 146-147

vector processor, 33-34
very large scale integration, 5

video display terminal/teletype,
   24-25
von Neumann machine, 1-3, 13,
   29, 32-33, 37, 39, 41, 44
   ALU, 4
   control unit, 4
   input unit, 3
   memory unit, 4
   output unit, 4
   read/execute cycle, 4

Wilkes, 3

ABOUT THE AUTHOR

Paul J. Fortier is a Senior Systems Engineer at the U.S. Naval Underwater Systems Center where he specializes in the research and development of various aspects of distributed real-time computer systems architectures. He has published numerous professional journal articles on performance evaluation and design of distributed computer systems and their related technologies. Mr. Fortier is a member of I.E.E.E. technical committees on computer communications, data base engineering, simulation, fault tolerant computing, and distributed processing.